FLIGHT OF THE TITANS

About the Author

Kenny Kemp is an award-winning journalist and writer. The founding business editor of the *Sunday Herald*, Kenny Kemp was Scotland's Business Writer of the Year in both 2001 and 2003. He is the co-author, with Barbara Cassani of *Go: An Airline Adventure*, which won the 2004 Business Book of the Year in the WH Smith Awards.
He lives in Edinburgh.

FLIGHT OF THE TITANS

Kenny Kemp

This revised and updated edition first published
in Great Britain in 2007 by
Virgin Books Ltd
Thames Wharf Studios
Rainville Road
London
W6 9HA

First published in hardback in Great Britain in 2006 by
Virgin Books Ltd

A catalogue record for this book is available from the
British Library.

ISBN 978 0 7535 1345 3

Typeset by TW Typesetting, Plymouth, Devon
Printed and bound in Great Britain by
CPI Bookmarque, Croydon, CR0 4TD

1 3 5 7 9 10 8 6 4 2

CONTENTS

Conversion factors:
1 nautical mile = 1.852 kilometres
1 nautical mile = 1.151 statute mile
1 kilometre = 0.6214 statute mile
1 tonne = 0.9842 ton
1 tonne-km = 0.6116 ton-mile
1 billion = 1,000 million
1 gallon = 4.546 litres
1 litre = 0.220 gallons

ACKNOWLEDGEMENTS

This book has been a stimulating commission. I am not an aviation anorak but I have come to understand the appeal of this global industry. The pilots, engineers and the marketing people enjoy long careers working in a business that they love. The good folks of Airbus and Boeing that I was fortunate to meet were deeply proud of the parts they played in this terrific story. So many people have been gracious with their time and knowledge. Any mistakes, errors or omissions are entirely of my own making.

Firstly, I would like to thank Roger Beteille for allowing me to interview him extensively. He is a remarkable and inspirational human being. Thanks also to Mike Turner at BAE Systems and Iain Gray at Airbus UK. And, at Boeing, special thanks to Randy Baseler, who carved out time from his schedule when he was incredibly busy.

I would like to thank Sir Richard Branson, Will Whitehorn and Sir Rod Eddington, former head of British Airways, for their input.

At Airbus in Toulouse, I'd like to thank Jürgen Thomas, Adam Brown, Gerrit Van Dijk, Corrin Higgs, and Yves Mary. And a grateful thanks to their press team including Emma Boya, David Velupillai and Barbara Kracht.

At Boeing, Richard Dalton, Theodore Austell and Amanda Landers, in Washington; and Russ Young, Sandy Angers, Samir Belyamani, Anita Polt, Amy Wisch, Leslie Nichols, Joseph Sutter, and the wonderful Mary Jean Olsen, in Seattle. Happy retirement, Mary Jean.

Other helpers have been Rob Stokes in Spain, Thorsten Langenbahn in Germany, Dick Kennedy in Chicago and Yashraj

Tonga in India. I'd also like to thank the hard-working team at Virgin Books and KT Forster, managing director at Virgin Books.

And, finally, a special thank-you to my wife, Gail, who has been deprived of my company during the hours I've spent in the library and on the laptop and who missed out on the exotic foreign travel. She remained at home in Edinburgh attending to the needs of Florrie, Katie and Sam. My ambition now is for both of us to sample the delights of the A380 and the Boeing 787 Dreamliner.

Kenny Kemp, August 2007

1. AN OASIS OF OPTIMISM

The desert sun beat down unrelentingly on the baking expanse of concrete highway while, in the manicured central reservation, a sprinkler whipped around, soaking the row of palm trees that separated the opposite sides of the road. The morning traffic was light on Dubai's Al-Shindagha Road, but still it was halted by three policemen as the electric gates of a whitewashed palace sprung open. Seconds later, a white Mercedes, followed by a bullet-proof, sky-blue Bentley, closely tailed by an identical white Mercedes, glided out from the gates and turned into the temporarily held-up traffic.

The leading car carried four security men wearing Oakleys, while ensconced on the Bentley's ample leather backseat was one of the most important men in Dubai. Sheikh Ahmed bin Saeed Al Maktoum, rich beyond the imagination of most mortals, was leafing through a racing paper as the limo headed on and through the Al-Shindagha tunnels towards Deira, the old heart of the city.

After a few moments, he put the paper down and turned to his friend and business colleague, Maurice Flanagan, an elderly Englishman in a blazer and striped tie, and said, 'You know, I haven't felt butterflies like this since Frankie Dettori won the Oaks in 1994. Of course, I love thoroughbred race horses. I love buying great horses. But today, well, today, this is something extra special.'

'Yes, your Highness,' replied the dapper gent. 'We have a truly memorable day ahead of us.' The two men smiled and resumed their private thoughts, their mutual excitement palpable.

Sheikh Ahmed bin Saeed Al Maktoum is a man used to spending vast sums of money. Indeed, he and his family have totally rebuilt the United Arab Emirates, making the desert state, and its capital Dubai, one of the most stunning places in the world. As the Bentley purred on through the traffic, the evidence was laid out before the occupants. Abras and dhows crisscrossed the Dubai Creek, while the miles of glass that comprised an avenue of the world's most amazing skyscrapers shimmered and reflected the November morning sun. The motorcade, however, didn't stop, their destination was further along at the luxurious Hilton Dubai Creek on Baniyas Road, where they would meet a bespectacled Frenchman who knew his luck had changed dramatically.

Six weeks earlier, Noel Forgeard, the then Chief Executive of Airbus, had all but given up on his plans for a brand-new aircraft. The airborne terrorist attacks on the World Trade Center in New York City seemed to have scuppered any chance of his major European airline project taking off in style. Sure, there had been other airlines signing up for the plane, including Air France, Singapore Airlines, Qantas and Virgin Atlantic. But this meeting with the Middle Eastern outfit would spark a new-found confidence in the Airbus A380. Forgeard was about to have his faith in humanity fully restored – and in spades.

Sheikh Al Maktoum and Flanagan stepped out of the car and were greeted with a broad smile by Tim Clark, the President of Emirates Airlines. The entourage swept through the lobby, into the lift and were whisked up to a private executive suite on the 28th floor. As they – and Forgeard – sipped thick chicory coffee, they ironed out a few formalities before a major public announcement. The Sheikh was given a final briefing about the historic deal he would later sign at the Dubai International Air Show.

The Sheikh's airline, Emirates, had made one of the boldest decisions in aviation history, by choosing to commit to a massive order of 45 of the all-new double-decker Airbus A380. The airline believed it had stolen a march on its rivals. Emirates was ambitious and wanted nothing more than to become the biggest and best in the world. Dubai was emerging as a natural global hub, a stepping stone between Europe and the Far East, on the doorstep of south Asia and Africa, and an attractive stopover point for passengers flying between Europe and Australia. The A380 would give the airline the capacity it needed.

With Emirates celebrating twenty years of rapid growth, Maurice Flanagan – Vice-Chairman and Group President of Emirates – realised that the greatest impediment to the airline's next phase of development was not customer demand but the number of seats the airline could offer. The deal that the Sheikh was about to sign would make Emirates the world's largest operator of the four-engine A380 for at least its first decade in service.

The news was delivered two hours later at a packed press conference in the main chalet at Dubai International Airport. Sheikh Ahmed Al Maktoum, the Emirates Chairman, and his elder brother General Sheikh Mohammed bin Rashid Al Maktoum, the Crown Prince of Dubai and United Arab Emirates' Defence Minister, sat alongside Forgeard at the opening of the international event – now as prestigious as the more established shows at Paris and Farnborough in the UK. An official called for quiet and the general opened the press conference.

'Our country today stands four-square at the crossroads of the world, and has transformed itself into a major player on the global stage. Our goal now is to expand its dynamic growth into every area of commerce, tourism and transport,' he said. 'Our unwavering aim is to make this the best place to do business, the top tourist destination and transport hub of the region and the undisputed commercial and communications capital of the Middle East. This record-breaking aircraft order is a key component in this charismatic strategy . . . We are not content simply to wait for the future – we are building it.'

At this point, Sheikh Ahmed Al Maktoum took his turn. 'The timing of this order – hard on the heels of recent events – is no coincidence. We are determined not to allow present difficulties to deflect our resolve.'

It was a brave decision for the UAE considering the mounting global tension after the atrocities in the United States. The American invasion of Afghanistan was under way and soon a US Navy aircraft carrier would be steaming through the nearby Straits of Hormuz towards Iraq. But the Sheikh was undeterred.

'The A380 is an ambitious aircraft that meets our ambitious growth strategy. Every single one of the A380s we have ordered has been carefully planned for and supports present and future network needs,' he continued. 'It will play a significant part in our expansion in a way that no other aircraft could ... We will be able to offer more seats, in ever greater comfort, without depending so much on frequency increases.'

A perspiring journalist from an aircraft trade magazine raised his hand. 'May I ask, your Highness, why did you decide to go for the Airbus rather than Boeing?'

The Sheikh's advisers fidgeted nervously, but he leaned forward and spoke clearly and decisively. 'The A380 will give us some of the lowest seat costs in the industry. It is an essential solution at slot-constrained airports. It will be an impressive people carrier, while offering more, not less, passenger comfort and amenities. We are striving to make the flying experience enjoyable again, and the A380 will be a great tool in support of this goal.'

It was the ringing endorsement that the designers, the engineers, the planners and the sales people back at Airbus's headquarters in Toulouse had been working for many years and months to secure. At last, here was someone willing to give them the substantial financial backing that was essential if their daring project was to progress to the next level. It was a day that changed the dynamics of international commercial aviation for ever.

Airbus's coup was nothing short of remarkable. That a European business had been able to take on – and temporarily overtake – the power and influence of a major American organisation was practically unthinkable. The growth of Emirates Airlines, helped by an open-skies policy allowing anyone to fly to and from Dubai, mirrored the success of Airbus. Indeed, the airline's first planes were Airbus's original jet, the A300, which flew twice a day between Dubai and Pakistan. The Sheikhs' aspirations were infectious; and an inspiration to nearby Gulf states, such as Qatar and Etihad in Abu Dhabi, to spend their petro-dollar billions on new Airbus planes too.

The only rivals were the smooth-talking Americans. The Boeing Corporation, now headquartered in Chicago but with its main assembly plants in Seattle, has been a top-bracket enterprise for decades. World class in the spheres of both commercial and defence, a company 'Built To Last', it has designed and produced a range of reliable products renowned for their excellence. Starting with its first jetliner, the Boeing 707, through to the world's most identifiable aircraft, the iconic Boeing 747 jumbo jet, the company has commanded the skies. Airbus, by contrast, had been a going concern for just over two and a half decades, and was considered little more than a pretender to the throne; the A380's arrival was expected to change all that.

When Airbus Industrie was set up in 1970, Boeing was one of three mighty commercial aircraft producers in the world. Along with McDonnell Douglas and Lockheed, it made and sold most of the world's passenger aircrafts. So the Europeans even having the audacity to challenge such market supremacy is an incredible tale. The cost of entering the mass aircraft market is so prohibitive that no single business can afford the start-up costs to become a plane-maker, and, therefore, it has required consistent multi-government support.

This is unique too. There is no single industrial endeavour that has married the skills of the German, the French, the Spanish, the British and other European nations. Some could point to the joint Eurofighter Typhoon involving five nations, but the French didn't stick with this. When the post-war founders of Europe created a common market to protect the continent's iron, steel and coal industry, and support the French and German farmers, they could not have conceived of an industrial complex such as Airbus.

But it has cost a great deal of money. Taxpayers' money, at that. Over the years, the governments of Europe have ploughed billions of pounds into a project fraught with squabbling, acrimony and petty nationalistic feuds – particularly in the UK where special ties with America have often threatened to rip the accord apart. Yet still Airbus was able to overtake Boeing.

While there is no single reason for this state of affairs, Boeing allowed its own crown to slip and has had several setbacks over recent years. Two Chief Executive Officers – Phil Condit and Harry Stonecipher – have been forced out in less than two years, while its Chief Financial Officer, Mike Sears, was sent to prison for his role in illegally recruiting a former US Air Force procurement official. And, as if to further undermine the business, these messy corporate incidents have been exacerbated by strikes and stoppages at the plants in Seattle.

Boeing, however, points an accusing finger at Airbus and its funding. It objects to the way European governments have consistently provided 35 years of subsidy and soft loans to design and build new planes. Boeing has cried foul and has taken its boxing gloves off for a fist fight. The Europeans have countered the allegations by arguing that Boeing has made billions of dollars from decades of lucrative US defence and aerospace contracts. If this is a free market, they say, why are European companies denied access?

While this debate rumbles on, the flight of the titans is far from over – in fact, it has barely begun. The Airbus A380 is now flying and delighting travellers around the world. There are firm orders for over 170 planes from 14 airline customers and leasing companies. Its first paying passengers, aboard a Singapore Airlines flight, have just taken to the skies from Singapore to Sydney, and it has been hailed as a 'gentle giant' and a wonderfully smooth and quiet experience.

But Airbus conceded several desperate own goals just as the ball game kicked off. Huge delays in the A380 programme, caused by electrical wiring problems and bitter political feuding by its executives – including allegations of insider trader dealings – almost destroyed the entire adventure.

The implosion within the European business in late 2005 was seismic and spilled into 2006 and beyond. It became increasingly bitter and acrimonious as senior heads rolled including Noel Forgeard's. Airbus plunged $750 million into the red and more than $6 billion in projected profits through to 2010 were wiped out in a flash – money that was vital for new research and developments. It all had political implications at the highest levels of government, straining relations in Britain, France, Germany and Spain. And, like a pack of rabid wolves, aviation analysts and financiers rounded on Airbus's whole strategy of pitching a massive new commercial aircraft against Boeing's smaller, more direct aircraft. In this battle, no quarter has been given.

Boeing took the time to regain its composure. After all, the American business has always been resilient, never used to losing, and Airbus's woes allowed the Americans to emerge stronger and more lithesome – refusing to take second place. Boeing's ringmaster James McNerney, who understands commercial airplanes, is a ruthless competitor who first had to sort out his own company's mess. But Boeing has been able to snipe at the A380 in a classic pincer movement. Firstly, it has brought the 787 Dreamliner to market, a smaller two-engine plane that will fly further and more directly to more destinations. It has proven to be an outstanding success, notching up nearly 600 orders – making it the most successful aircraft launch in aviation history. It goes into service in 2008. Boeing also brought out a new longer-range version of its popular Boeing 777 – the 777-200LR – and it now has an advanced version of the jumbo jet, the 747-8 Intercontinental with new composite technologies and fuel-efficient engines.

But it is the 787 Dreamliner which has dealt Airbus the deepest blow. While the massive A380 was held up by two-year delays – angering its loyal and bemused launch customers – the Boeing plane touched a sweet spot with its environmentally friendly credentials. Just as the world was increasingly concerned about global warming and the greenhouse gas emissions caused by flying, here was Boeing marketing an advanced product that would allow guilt-ridden passengers to take to the air more easily. McNerney is no mug though: 'We have to assume that Airbus is going to be back in all their glory – which they will – and we have to assume that every dogfight will be a dogfight to the death,' he told the *Financial Times*, prior to the Paris Air Show in 2007.

While Airbus was humiliated and forced to go back to the drawing board, it has shown nerves of steel and resolve. Its new president and chief executive Louis Gallois has emerged with pressing assignments for his leadership – to soothe the shareholders, stabilise a mammoth operation on the verge of collapse and compete again head-on with Boeing. Airbus had originally planned to launch its own twin-engined A350 to take on the 787. But no one was interested – or even believed Airbus was able to deliver a better product. So the plane's original concept was scrapped and, after several false starts, Airbus announced a newer, more innovative wide-bodied version, the A350 XWB (Extra Wide Body).

Once again it was the cash-rich Middle Eastern backers who came to Airbus's rescue. In May 2007, Airbus won a $16 billion pledge from Qatar Airlines for 80 A350 XWBs. It was such a significant deal that Chief Executive Akbar Al-Baker and Louis Gallois signed the deal in the Elysee presidential palace in Paris. A few weeks later, he added an order for three more A380s, bringing its total to five. Deliveries will start in 2013 – if there are no delays.

Prior to this face-saving announcement, Airbus had sealed only 13 firm orders for the A350 compared to Boeing's 567 orders for the Dreamliner. So this announcement – and others at the Paris Air Show in 2007 – gave Gallois a breathing space with over 150 firm orders and it stopped the rot, temporarily. But the fight of the titans will go on. It is a struggle requiring abnormal strength, visionary leadership and technological prowess that will be playing itself out over the next 25 years. It has also brought a more honest debate about the true cost of flying – and the impact it has on our fragile environment – into the public arena. It remains a clash of two visions of the way we will be flying in the middle of the twenty-first century. It's impossible to predict who will be right. Expect plenty of turbulence.

2. COME ON, LET'S FLY!

Why fly? And what is the attraction of boarding a plane with 554 other passengers? Just over a century ago, it was a fundamental scientific challenge, a technological breakthrough instigated by the Wright brothers; fifty years later, it was a magical and inexplicable experience for the rich. Now, well into the twenty-first century, how does the average passenger see it? Too often, as a chore that has long since lost its sparkle.

The modern airport offers its passengers the pleasures and social reassurances of the boarding lounge, but for most of us it's a glorified shopping mall, with its endless stairs, bland corridors and uncomfortable plastic chairs. Your eyes are never far from a television monitor awaiting the announcement of a boarding gate. Then there's a scramble before reaching the threshold of the plane. Eventually on board, you push past other passengers to find your seat, stow your hand luggage, squeeze into your place, and fasten your belt.

Regular air travellers are blasé about what happens next. Why else does the captain, cooing to you over the public address system, insist that you put down your newspaper or book and pay attention to the safety instructions for a few moments? Yet, by the time the demonstrator's life jacket, oxygen mask and the whistle are packed away in a locker, a cabin-crew member has slammed the pressurised cabin door shut. What happens next is beyond your control.

As a willing passenger on an airborne Boeing, Airbus or any other plane, you enter the equivalent of an intensive care ward in a major hospital. You are as helpless as a patient on the operating table. The oxygen you breathe is filtered through a HEPA (High-efficiency Particulate Air Filtration) system that strains 99.97 per cent of all pollen and dust particles and filters out all dangerous microscopic bugs. Your life is now in the hands of a professional you are unlikely to have met or will ever meet. You've selected an airline you believe is safe and reliable. But you're never completely sure. The mind of a nervous traveller flicks momentarily to the hazy television images of an Airbus attempting to land with front wheels stuck on their side, or to a Boeing that has skidded off a rain-lashed runway. But the brain quickly switches to something more pleasing.

Nevertheless, you have voluntarily given up control of your own destiny. Until you step off the plane at your destination, you are embarking on a supreme act of trust and faith. Once the plane has surged along the runway at 200 mph and lifted off, it takes a few minutes for the plane to reach the equivalent of Mount Everest – 29,035 ft. Outside, the temperature will be −34° Fahrenheit (minus 37°C). Inside, you're sitting comfortably in a sweatshirt or jacket, while the cabin crew begin to push a trolley up the aisle dispensing drinks and snacks. But your plane has far higher to go. As it bursts through to 35,000 ft, the outside temperature is now −76° Fahrenheit (minus 60°C). You have still to reach the cruising altitude of around 40,000 ft. Outside this giant pressurised cigar-tube, with the window-seat passenger separated from the atmosphere by an aluminium skin of 4 cm, the environment is unforgiving. It is a place where no human has any right to be.

Flying five miles high, the temperature outside is −77° Fahrenheit (minus 61°C), colder than the South Pole on a winter's night. The air is so thin you would be gasping for just three seconds before falling unconscious. And as you plummeted, accelerating at 120 ft per second, you would last four more seconds before falling into a coma. You would be dead several minutes before your body hit the ground.

If you ponder all this, it is rather alarming. Yet at any one time there are over one million people in the air. And each year this number increases. Air travel has tripled since 1980, and Boeing forecasts that world air traffic will grow at 4.8 per cent every year over the next twenty years. Since the arrival of Airbus as a plane-making consortium in 1970, world air traffic has grown almost sevenfold, on average increasing by 5.7 per cent per year. This is despite some major global shocks: including several harsh recessions, the 1991 Gulf War, the Asia financial crisis of 1997, the collapse of US airlines following the 9/11 attacks on America in 2001 and the SARS epidemic in 2003. Most humans love to travel, no matter what is going on around them. And it has become safer and safer.

But it isn't just the pilots and cabin crews we have to trust, it is the airplanes themselves and this is where the story really begins. Walt Gillette, as Head of Development for the Boeing 787 Dreamliner, is someone who should know. Revered in airline circles, he has worked on every major commercial plane project within Boeing since 1967. A thin and wiry academic type, he is feted as an elder statesman, someone who embodies all the traditional virtues of the company's engineering legacy.

'You know the statistics that I am most proud of?' Gillette asks. 'We have built one and a half thousand 737 new generation planes and they are all flying today. Without a loss. We've built five hundred Boeing 777 planes. All flying today without a loss. And, you know, our rivals Airbus have built a similar number of A330 and A340, also without a loss. There are over two and a half thousand new generation planes out there, which are flying eighteen hours a day, seven days a week and they are safer than anything ever devised by human endeavour. That is something to think about.'

Gillette believes that the detail and dedication to safety and precision in aircraft building is unmatched in our modern society, yet he understands the flying public's reticence. 'We routinely manufacture a plane that is hugely complicated and defies the knowledge of a single person. It has millions of individual parts, many placed under extreme stress for thousands of hours. The plane then flies at 550 mph up to five miles in the sky,' he explains. 'Our fear of flying comes from a human being's surrender of control. If you are driving a car, you can avoid an accident. You can stop and pull over. Flying is one of those human activities where you have to trust others.'

What do we want as passengers? 'Number one is a safe and reliable service. We all want to arrive at our destinations safely and on time. We all want the shortest trip times and, if possible, non-stop point-to-point flights,' says Gillette.

Airbus and Boeing, the two biggest suppliers of airplanes in the world, are going head-to-head in a battle for supremacy in the skies. Both claim to have their own answers but their solutions are radically different. For both, 2007 has been a bumper year for orders. And with predictions that over 25,700 new airplanes will be needed over the next twenty years, there is scope for further growth. In these new planes, both Airbus and Boeing will be using more new technologies than ever before.

Yet we all know air travel is messing up our planet. Environmental pressure groups and concerned government agencies are increasingly pointing at air travel as a major cause of global pollution. Consumers are now aware that their two weeks in the sunshine on a foreign holiday causes a significant carbon footprint. Each tonne of Jet-A aviation fuel, which is combusted in an airplane's jet engine, produces three and a half tonnes of carbon dioxide. A modern jumbo jet, such as the Boeing 747-400ERF, fills up with 53,985 US gallons of aviation fuel. That's about 204,000 litres. The average motor car holds about 40 litres.

The aircraft industry attracts the finest engineering brains and knows it has to create planes with engines that are substantially more fuel efficient, less noisy and far more economical. It means designing and building a new generation of planes. And both Airbus and Boeing are chasing this market. The sales people from Toulouse and Seattle say their Airbuses and Boeings will be far more fuel efficient and have greatly reduced CO_2 emissions. That's imperative; our planet depends on this.

Gillette believes the future lies with smaller, more economical planes that are finely attuned to the modern passenger. 'We need to have planes that are more comfortable. There is less altitude tolerance today. Thirty years ago, the average air passenger was fitter and healthier and could cope with a pressurised cabin atmosphere. We now have more people with sedentary lifestyles and poorer diets. There is a far wider socio-economic group flying worldwide today. Our cardiovascular state is poorer, so we're more susceptible to pressurised cabins.'

Boeing's viewpoint is that the discerning traveller of the twenty-first century wants to step on a plane and fly directly to more destinations. It says the Dreamliner will be 'a new sensation for passengers'. There will be huge improvements in cabin humidity, temperature and air quality, larger windows and bigger seats. There will be more headroom, liquid-crystal mood lighting that changes throughout the flight and a much smoother ride.

Airbus would argue that these standards of comfort will be matched, if not exceeded, by the A380, yet its approach to the economy and environmental impact of its planes differs from that of Boeing. The A380 is a whale of a beast, with the capacity to seat 850 passengers on its two decks, though many airlines are expected to configure their A380s for between 313 and 555 seats, using the remaining room for upper-class luxuries such as casinos, shops, fitness rooms, spas and bars. John Leahy, Airbus's swash-buckling Chief Operating Officer and a key player in this story, claims it is 50 per cent quieter than a Boeing 747-400 and that the costs of a seat-mile (used to measure profitability) are 15 to 20 per cent less than a Boeing jumbo. 'The A380 will cost the airlines 20 per cent less to operate.' Leahy also says the larger plane will mean fewer aircraft movements at airports – that's fewer take-offs and landings, when the worst damage is done.

Both are aiming to restore the magic and sparkle. Boeing and Airbus are pulling out all the stops to ensure that boarding a 787 or A380 will be a comfortable, reliable, exciting and environment-ally friendly experience. And both are vying with their competi-tors to prove their vision is the correct one.

3. SIR ROD MAPS OUT THE BATTLEFIELD

The spectacular take-off of the double-decker A380 – costing $285m per plane – from Changi airport in Singapore will change the experience of international flying for millions of passengers. Amid all the clamour and public relations hype, Huang Cheng Eng, of Singapore Airlines, wasn't exaggerating when he talked proudly about his company's first A380 passenger flight as one of the most significant events in the history of commercial aviation. It is a landmark event well worth celebrating. The arrival of the double-decker A380 is certain to change the experience of international flying for millions. But why will it make such an impact? To answer this, it was necessary to find a neutral airline sage immersed in the intricacies of both Airbus and Boeing. On a sparkling May morning, I took an eight-quid mini-cab trip from Heathrow Airport to meet British Airways' former supremo Sir Rod Eddington.

BA's Riverside headquarters, designed by Norwegian architect Niels Torp and completed in 1997, is an incongruous, modern masterpiece of glass and stone. It was intended to be a catalyst for change for the airline once dubbed 'the world's favourite airline'. Pushing through the glass-plated front door, you can hear the high-pitched whining of jets as they land near by. In the spacious foyer, beyond the security turnstile, there is an actual-size set of landing gear complete with Firestone tyres used as a backdrop for countless photo shoots. Nearing lunchtime, there is a flurry of activity in the cobbled high street, with its babbling brook, a bank, coffee shops, a hairdresser and a few convenience stores. The street is a modern meeting place, alive with gossip, impromptu meetings and bustling with activity. This thoroughfare connects the six office complexes that house nearly 3,000 BA employees and the constant stream of suppliers, airline company reps and sundry visitors.

A glass-capsule lift whisks you upstairs to the executive suite and Sir Rod's office suite. Here it is quieter. There are more refined huddles, with secretaries typing memos and answering phones in a suite of open-plan offices and conference rooms. Vibrant house plants flourish in the temperate climate and the display cases are lined with British Airways' memorabilia. When I visited, the Chairman's office was neat and empty, awaiting some fresh cigarette fumes, while the Group Finance Director was spied straining over some hefty-looking sheets of figures.

The Chief Executive of British Airways was in fine fettle. Sir Rod Eddington – 'Just call me, Rod' – had delivered the airline's best ever set of results, his swansong after five years at the helm. He was passing over the controls to Willie Walsh, the former pilot who joined from Ireland's national carrier Aer Lingus. Walsh built his reputation after turning around the Dublin-based airline with some drastic cost-cutting, the kind of desperate measures needed to compete with Ireland's low-cost meteor Michael O'Leary, of Ryanair. A damaging dispute and strike over Gate Gourmet, the airline-food supplier, that ruined thousands of summer holidays and marred Eddington's final days was a few weeks in the future.

Rod Eddington is a sporty chap – he's an Australian after all. He loves a gamble and a pugnacious game of rugby or cricket. A non-executive on the board of directors of Rupert Murdoch's News Corporation, he is an influencer and decision-maker with global business tentacles; he has an insight into the airline business at a senior level that is second to none. And British Airways has had a central starring role in the whole Airbus versus Boeing saga. Though he's chummy, Eddington is no pushover.

When we met, sales and marketing teams were wooing British Airways because they had been holding off from making a decision about whether to buy the A380. At an analysts' briefing, Chairman Martin Broughton, also the chair of British American Tobacco, was consistently asked when the British carrier would make its decision. Yet British Airways had more in common with some of the troubled American carriers. In the City of London, investors joked about the 'pension fund with wings', a reference to the airline's massive pension liability. In 2005, as Walsh took over, it faced a £2bn pension deficit, 40 per cent of its market value. This was part of a burden of debt which was painfully being brought under control. New planes would have to wait.

'Are you an anorak?' he asked quizzically. (An anorak is a British expression for someone who follows the minutiae of aviation with a compulsion bordering on sadness.)

'No, I'm not.'

'Good. Neither am I.'

As a prelude, Eddington wandered around the conference room, bedecked with historical references to BA's history, stretching back to its days before the merger of BEA and BOAC. While Rod is an airline man through and through, he has an erudition that is able to place the business in a wider context. He was part of an exclusive joint study at Cathay Pacific that was invited by Boeing to create the plane that became the Boeing 777. Cathay Pacific was a launch customer for the Boeing 777 – as was British Airways.

British Airways is still a Boeing customer. But in 1998 it made a significant decision that paved the way for the Airbus A380. When Noel Forgeard took over at the helm of Airbus at the beginning of 1998, he had the British operator in his sights. Within weeks of his taking over, British Airways announced it would buy 220 new aircraft, including up to 188 Airbus regional jets. It was an order for Airbus worth £3bn – the largest number of aircraft ever chosen by British Airways in a single deal and the largest single commitment yet made to the European consortium by any airline outside of the United States.

On Thursday, 26 November 1998, the UK Prime Minister Tony Blair made the announcement in Toulouse and, with one giant leap, Britain's major airline was back in bed with Europe. BA placed orders for 59 Airbus aircraft in the A320 family, including the A319, with options on another 129. BA had inherited a handful of Airbuses after its merger with British Caledonian, but this was the first time it had bought them brand new. The same morning, BA also announced an order for another sixteen Boeing 777s, with options on a further sixteen. This was a sweetener for Boeing, their long-running partner and old friend. But the damage was done. There was shock and dismay in Seattle, home of Boeing, and delight in Paris and Berlin. Some of these new 777 orders were substitutes for existing orders for five 401-seat Boeing 747-400s. Was BA thinking ahead about the un-numbered A3XX? asked the journalists at the time. By the summer of 2007, Willie Walsh and his team still hadn't made that decision, although he expressed more interest in the advanced Boeing 747-8 than in the A380, which, he said, 'had a big question mark beside it'. He also appeared to prefer Boeing's 787 to an A350 that was still on the drawing board.

Back in 1998, the then BA Chief Executive Bob Ayling said, 'We have ordered the right aircraft at the right time at the right price. This is a great investment in our future, made possible by the commercial success of British Airways. The regional jet orders have been placed after one of the most exhaustive and competitive tendering processes in the history of British Airways. Airbus won by offering the better terms. We are delighted to be in a position to order Airbus aircraft for the first time – while remaining Boeing's biggest customer outside the United States and ensuring we obtain the best deal for investors in our company.'

Some jaundiced commentators said it was a gift. A giveaway even. It appeared as a *volte-face* for an airline that had been disparaging about Airbus for decades. Boeing said BA's decision to buy Airbus was patently unfair. But Mike Turner, the Chief Executive of BAE Systems, which had a 20 per cent stake in Airbus, disagrees. 'We had to work very hard at Airbus, with the support of British Aerospace, in convincing Colin Marshall [the Chairman at the time] and his team that it was the right route to go down. It was a very competitive offer that we made to them on the single aisle. In spite of the rumours at the time, we did make a bit of money on it. It wasn't a loss leader as the market suggested but it was the big strategic breakthrough,' he says.

But this all happened before Rod's reign. He inherited the situation when he arrived in 2000, but the breakthrough order from BA gave Forgeard and Airbus the impetus and confidence to push ahead with the A380. The Australian boss proceeded to draw up the battle picture of where the fight is now between Airbus and Boeing. Sir Rod talked about the vast costs involved in launching a new aircraft. It requires mammoth investment and government support up front, with no guarantees of sales. This kind of risk-taking by the manufacturers has been dubbed 'the sporty game'. It is about betting the whole future of the business on a single, next aircraft design. It is like playing a roulette table in a casino and placing your entire stake on either black or red. This, more or less, is what Airbus has done by building the A380 super jumbo.

In 1985, John Newhouse, the author of *The Sporty Game*, summed it up: 'The business of making and selling commercial airliners is not for the diffident or faint of heart. It is remarkably difficult and, by anyone's standard, intensely competitive. There are few industries that consume as much or more capital; certain others rely as heavily on quantities of highly skilled personnel; probably no other is involved with as many advanced technologies.

'But what really sets the commercial airplane business apart is the enormity of the risks as well as the cost that must be accepted; they create an array of obstacles to profitability, hence viability, which discourages all but the bold and the committed.'

He might have added the incredibly stubborn and foolhardy. So why does this matter to the traveller? Because cutthroat competition has forced the plane-makers and the engine-builders to make more economical planes. This in turn has brought down airline fares encouraging more people to fly. But the irony is that, while more people than ever before are flying, most of the world's airlines have struggled to simply break even.

The deregulation of airlines in the United States in the 1970s, and the subsequent European deregulation in the 1990s, has led to the low-cost boom and the spectacular success of no-frills players such as Southwest and JetBlue in the US and Ryanair and easyJet in Europe, but the truth is that there are still too many airlines fighting off bankruptcy. Consolidation led to the merger of Air France and KLM, the Dutch carrier, while Delta Air Lines and Northwest were the latest US carriers with large networks to tumble into Chapter 11 bankruptcy protection. They joined United Airlines and troubled US Airways, which merged with America West to form a new carrier. Delta lost $2bn in 2005, while Northwest's losses mushroomed from $46m in the third quarter of 2004 to $475m in the same period in 2005.

The no-frills interlopers have none of the legacies of the older carriers. The new economic reality is that anyone who can raise enough capital can lease some planes, train a flight crew in three weeks, hire some sacked or retired pilots and start a business. If they hire young guys, they have no pension issues and low health premiums, with the added bonus that they might drive older companies – saddled with such issues – out of business. While there is almost no barrier to entry, every seat on every plane is highly perishable. It only has a value if someone actually sits in it and pays. It's worse than selling fresh tomatoes. At least with fruit and vegetables you can drop the prices until it ends up in the pigswill bin.

The type of planes an airline chooses depends on the routes it wants to fly. No two airlines have an identical set of destinations, so different types of planes do different kinds of jobs.

Rod Eddington picked up his pen and drew a line on a white sheet of A4. Then he marked 'B737' with the figure 100 underneath at the left-hand side, and then 'B747', with the figure 400 underneath, three inches from the right-hand edge. Then he drew the 'B767' and 'B777' in the middle of the top line and directly underneath he penned in 'A330' and the 'A340'. The numbers below refer to the number of seats. Underneath the 'B737', he placed the 'A319/A320'. He betrayed no single preference to either company. Even-handed and scrupulous like an Aussie Rules referee.

'Let me say, first and foremost, both Airbus and Boeing make really good planes. Very good planes indeed,' he emphasised. 'The question is: if Airbus hadn't overtaken Boeing as the market leader, and pushed all the way by Airbus, would Boeing still be forced to find a replacement for the jumbo jet? Because there comes a point when your trusty retainer is no longer up to it.'

Eddington made a string of assessments about Boeing and Airbus. Then he looked up over his rounded glasses and said, 'There's no room for sentiment in this business. The American commercial aerospace companies involved in production of large civil aircraft have lost significant global market share to their European competitors over the last twenty-five years. Boeing is the only remaining US manufacturer of large civil aircraft – down from Boeing, McDonnell Douglas, Lockheed in the 1970s. It hasn't been easy. Boeing has laid off nearly a quarter of its workforce since September 11, 2001.

'Then in 2003, for the first time in history, Airbus delivered more new commercial aircraft than Boeing, and it did it again in 2004. In 2005, it is nip and tuck again.' (Boeing surged ahead in 2006 and 2007, outselling Airbus by three to one.)

He leaned over and looked me straight in the eye. 'Boeing and Airbus are pursuing diverging strategies for commercial airplanes in the international air services market. Airbus has been focusing in recent years on the high-capacity, long-range A380 that is geared towards large-capacity flights between major international hub airports.

'On the other hand, Boeing appears to be focused on building aircraft for increasingly liberalised markets by introducing the long-range but smaller-capacity 787 Dreamliner that is well suited for long routes with comparatively fewer passengers.'

Eddington picked up his pen again and added 'A380' to the extreme right of his diagram, with the figure 555.

Who is right? The flight of the titans is between the Airbus A380 and the smaller Boeing 787 Dreamliner. And Boeing's new 747-8 jumbo jet will join the fray. 'Will it be Airbus or Boeing who triumph? Because most airline analysts and aviation commentators believe both cannot be right,' pondered the Australian. 'I think Boeing is placing a ten bob each way bet with the 747-8.'

Then he added the final flourish to his impromptu diagram. He marked 'A350' and then 'B787', just to the left of the '747' and then he circled them several times for emphasis. He tapped his pen in the circle. 'Now the waters have been muddied further. Airbus appears to be hedging its bets with the introduction of another new plane, the A350, which has similar operating characteristics to the Boeing 787. This has been a declaration of open war for Boeing. They don't like the fact that the A350 is being subsidised by European governments. This, say the Americans, isn't fair. It isn't competitive. And it has to stop. Now.'

Rod Eddington didn't betray any preference for either option. He simply set out the facts. But now it is worth looking at the present order of battle and the key planes made by Airbus and Boeing. Here three main factors determine what kind of plane an airline should buy or lease: the number of seats, the range of the aircraft's flight and its engine type. But airlines don't just buy a plane's airframe, they also choose an engine and the three global players have been Rolls-Royce, General Electric and Pratt & Whitney.

Boeing makes a clear statement in that it builds airplanes to serve every passenger market from 100 seats to more than 500 seats. From the Boeing 717 to the 747 jumbo, it manufactures a range of planes with incremental increases of about 20 per cent.

Airbus has four families of aircraft ranging from 107 to 555 seats. The Toulouse marketing team likes to talk about 'families'. The single-aisle A320 family covers the A318, A319, A320, A321; the wide-body A300 and A310 family; and the long-range A330, A340 and A380 family. The A350 is the new baby waiting to join its bigger brothers and sisters.

The smallest plane is the Boeing 717, a tough twin-jet used for the short-haul, high-frequency 100-seater passenger market. Boeing, facing stiff competition from the Airbus A318 and other regional jet makers, halted the 717 production at Long Beach in California, where the Douglas Aircraft Corporation once employed 16,000 aircraft workers, in 2006 when the last orders were delivered. Boeing had inherited the business after its merger with McDonnell Douglas in August 1997.

Next up on Boeing's roster is one of the greatest flying machines of all time: the Boeing 737. The original version was first flown in April 1967 yet it is still one of the most popular single-aisle airplanes on the market today. Ask Europe's low-cost operators. It has become a money-spinner for RyanAir, easyJet and most of the other fifty no-frills operators now operating in Europe. The low-cost players love it because on busy routes it can make profits. It is safe, reliable and easy to fly. The pilots love it because they have the controls to fly it like a traditional plane. The plane comes in four sizes: the 737-600 can carry 110 to 132 passengers; the 737-700, 126 to 149 passengers; the 737-800, 162 to 189 passengers; and the largest model, the 737-900, 177 to 189 passengers.

'It is a wonderful plane but it is still the Boeing 737,' said Eddington. 'Boeing had the classic problem of what to do with it. Do they just junk everything and start again? Or do they keep making updated derivatives of their existing planes?'

Boeing argues that the 737 has evolved to become a modern next-generation airplane. 'While these new versions retain some characteristics from the earlier 737 models, the whole plane has undergone dramatic revisions including a brand-new wing design, improved fuel capacity and increased aerodynamic efficiency, leading to increased range and speed,' says Randy Baseler, Boeing's Head of Marketing.

And it has been highly profitable for Boeing too. In February 2006, Boeing celebrated the 5,000th 737 to come off the production line at Renton with the *Guinness Book of Records* acknowledging the plane as the most successful large commercial jet in aviation history. So, if it sells well, why change the formula? Partly because it faces tough challenges from the newer A319 and the A320.

The 737 family's range is approximately 3,200 nm (5,926 km), an increase of up to 900 nm (1,667 km) over earlier 737 models. This is a huge bonus because it has allowed low-cost transcontinental flying across America.

A Boeing 737 Next-Generation plane cruises at a maximum altitude of 41,000 ft compared to 37,000 ft for earlier models. It has two engines, powered by the bestselling CFM56-7 engine produced by CFMI, a joint venture of General Electric Company and Snecma of France. It has plenty of advantages but it is up against newer planes from Airbus.

The A318 entered service in July 2003 and can take 107 passengers in two classes or up to 132 passengers in a single-class layout. It is 2.5 m shorter than the A319, first delivered in April 1996, with a standard 124 seats and a range of up to 3,700 nm (6,800 km). Airbus offers an A319 option, as ordered by easyJet, allowing increased seating up to 156 seats.

What has given Airbus an edge over the Boeing 737 has been its single-aisle A320 family, which is more environmentally sound, with a lower fuel burn, less emissions and noise. Launched in March 1984, the A320 entered airline service in April 1988 and became the industry standard on short- and medium-haul routes. The A320 is now a key to Airbus's ambitious survival plans and the Europeans are planning to crank up the production to forty a month by the end of 2009 – a tall order and the highest output for a jet in commercial aviation history. Typically seating 150 passengers in two classes or up to 180 for low-cost operations, the A320 has a range of up to 3,000 nm (5,700 km). The largest member of the A320 family, the A321, which began flying paying passengers in 1994, has a range of up to 3,000 nm (5,700 km). It can carry 185 passengers in two classes, though it can seat up to 220 passengers for charter and low-cost operators.

But Airbus has consistently extolled the virtues of the A320's 'operational commonality' and the arrival of the A318 gave airlines improved overall reliability and reduced maintenance costs. This has given Boeing a hill to climb. Airbus has also scored over Boeing on another issue. All of the planes have similar flight decks and need only minimal additional training for pilots, one of the most expensive assets in an airline. This means a senior pilot, earning £130,000 a year, can switch from a single-aisle type to larger twin-aisle aircraft very easily, even flying a different type the next day.

The A310 and A300-600 from Airbus's wide-body, twin-aisle family have provided many airlines with the versatility, economy and reliability they needed. The A300 and A310 feature wider fuselage cross sections, which has given more room for the passengers. The A310, which entered service in 1983, carries 220 passengers up to 5,200 nm (9,600 km), while the A300-600, which entered airline service in March 1984, transports 266 passengers up to 4,150 nm (7,700 km). An A300-600 freighter version, capable of carrying up to 54.5 tonnes (120,000 lbs) of cargo, entered service in 1994 and has become a bestselling cargo freighter.

The twin-engine A300 and A310 have a choice of engines: General Electric's CF6-80C2 or Pratt & Whitney's PW4000. Again, with the same cockpit, the A310 and A300-600 have the same rating, so pilots qualified on one can fly the other without additional training. It also means the same teams of mechanics can maintain either aircraft.

Airbus's long-range market-leading wide-body jet is the A340. The A340-300 carries 295 passengers up to 7,400 nm (13,700 km) and is operated by dozens of airlines around the world. The four-engine A340-600, which entered service in July 2002, has four CFM56-5C/P engines. It accommodates 380 passengers with a range of up to 7,900 nm (14,640 km) while the ultra-long-range 313-seat A340-500 can fly passengers up to 9,000 nm (16,600 km). Singapore Airlines operates this plane on the longest scheduled air route between Singapore and New York, flying 16,600 km non-stop, although the flights can last up to eighteen hours depending on the winds. The A330 is a twin-engine sister to the A340 and was launched in 1987.

Boeing's mightiest long-range weapon has seen its power diminish because of this Airbus challenge. But the Boeing 747 jumbo jet remains one of the true icons of aviation. It is a plane everyone can instantly recognise. From its first flight in February 1969, the jumbo, powered by a Pratt & Whitney JT9D engine, transformed the way the world took to the air.

'The jumbo jet created a revolution in commercial airplanes. It's a great testimony that it's only now that the A380 has come along to challenge its undoubted supremacy. It has been a fantastic aircraft for British Airways – and a host of other major airlines,' said Eddington. British Airways has 57 747-400s.

Before the A380 arrived on the scene, it was still the biggest, fastest commercial airplane in operation, carrying more people and more cargo than any other commercial airplane. The 747-400 flies 416 passengers in three classes about 7,260 nm (13,450 km) and is available in five models. The latest, the 747-400ER (extended range), offers customers 410 nm (760 km) more range, or 35,000 lbs (15,876 kg) more payload. The 747-400ER, also available as a freighter, increases the 747-400's take-off weight from 875,000 lbs (396,900 kg) to 910,000 lbs (412,770 kg). Both 747-400ER models entered service in October 2002.

One of the future battlegrounds for the A380 is likely to be in the booming cargo market. Airbus's problems and poor sales have forced it to put the freighter on hold for now. World trade depends increasingly on air freight and Boeing was not going to relinquish this easily. The 747 Freighter fleet still provides about half the total worldwide cargo lift capability. And the 747-400 Freighter was carrying twice as much cargo double the distance of its nearest competitor.

Randy Baseler says, 'Today's 747-400F provides low tonne-kilometre costs, offers significantly lower trip costs than the proposed A380F and accommodates high-revenue outsized loads with its nose door. With its huge capacity, extended range and improved fuel efficiency, the 747-400 offers the lowest operating costs per seat of any commercial jetliner and the lowest tonne-mile cost of any commercial freighter.

'We are working with customers to develop the next-generation versions of the 747, called the 747-8 Intercontinental and 747-8 Freighter. These airplanes would offer increased capacity, some 787 technologies and superior economics.'

British Airways was the launch customer for the Boeing 757. It was an inauspicious start as Boeing struggled to sell the plane before it gradually picked up. There are two passenger models – the 757-200 and the larger 757-300 – and a freighter, which is based on the 757-200 fuselage. Boeing delivered its last 757 in April 2005, ending 23 years of production. More than 1,000 of the twinjets have been delivered to customers around the world, making it one of only seven commercial airplane programmes to hit this milestone.

The 767 is a larger two-aisle twinjet. The airplane, which is now the most widely used airplane across the Atlantic, comes as the 767-200ER (ER stands for extended range), with seating for 224 passengers in two classes or 181 passengers in a three-class configuration, with a range of up to 6,600 nm (12,220 km); the 767-300ER, with seating for 269 in two classes and 218 in three classes with a range of 6,105 nm (11,305 km); and the 767-400ER that provides seating for 304 passengers in two classes and 245 in three classes with a range of 5,645 nm (10,450 km).

The Boeing 777 was designed as the 'twenty-first century jet'. It was intended to combat Airbus's family concept, its fly-by-wire advance technology and the commonality that was now appealing to airlines. After some barren years, the 777, designed to fill the gap between the 767 and 747, is now trouncing the Airbus A340 in terms of sales. The 777-200 twinjet seats 305 passengers in a three-class configuration. The 777-200, which was first delivered in May 1995, has a range of up to 5,210 nm (9,649 km). The 777-200ER (extended range) was first delivered in February 1997. This model is capable of flying the same number of passengers up to 7,730 nm (14,316 km). The 777-300, in service since May 1998, is a stretched version that provides seating for 368 passengers in a three-class configuration. It has a range of 5,955 nm (11,029 km). BA has 43 Boeing 777 and ten 767s in its long-haul fleet.

In February 2000, Boeing announced the launch of two longer-range 777s. The 777-300ER, which entered service in May 2004, has a range of 7,880 nm (14,594 km) and carries 365 passengers in a three-class configuration. Then there is the 777-200LR Worldliner (Longer Range), now the world's longest-range commercial airplane, capable of flying 9,420 nm (17,446 km) and carrying 301 passengers in a typical three-class configuration.

The first 777-200LR Worldliner, with two powerful engines, GE90-115B was delivered to Pakistan International Airlines on 27 January 2006. An aircraft's long range has become a critical factor, especially so that airlines can fly non-stop from London to Australia, or Asia to America. Boeing is now bidding to extend this to the magic number of 10,000 nm (18,500 km) by adding auxiliary fuel tanks and lighter interiors.

A new world record for a non-stop commercial airplane flight was set on 10 November 2005 when a Boeing 777-200LR

Worldliner landed at Heathrow Airport. The 777-200LR flew 11,664 nm (21,601 km) during its 22-hour-42-minute flight after leaving Hong Kong flying eastwards. The plane took off at 10.30 p.m. local time and landed at Heathrow at approximately 1.30 p.m. GMT the next day. The airplane travelled eastbound, flying over the North Pacific Ocean, across North America, and then over the Atlantic Ocean en route to London. It was a marketing coup, and 2005 became the 777's most successful year with 118 orders to the A340's fourteen.

But the Holy Grail of commercial flying has still to become a reality: London to Sydney, non-stop, both ways. While the 17,000 nm trip south is now within touching distance, the return trip, against strong headwinds, is still an enticing target for both Boeing and Airbus – now pitching in with the A350-800.

So, with Rod Eddington's help, the order of battlefield was drawn up. With a courteous thank you, I left him to his final weeks in charge. He has now moved on from BA, handing over to a younger chief executive who faces some interesting decisions.

Despite uncertainty over global terrorism and serious international confrontation, most economic analysts are working on projections for the twenty-year period until 2027. The consensus predicts that the average growth for the world economy will be 2.9 per cent per year, and passenger traffic will grow on average by 4.8 per cent per year – with cargo traffic to grow by 6.2 per cent per year. And, while most Americans and Europeans have experienced a plane trip, even if just twice a year on holiday, it will be the Indians, the Chinese, the Asians and the Africans who will start to make it a habit too. This will be the battlefield for the new sales – but the two giants shouldn't expect to get it all their own way. In April 2007, China revealed more details of its own plans to build a passenger aircraft with more than 150 seats and a freighter to carry more than 100 tonnes. The project, still in its planning phases, hopes to start assembling the planes within ten years in Shanghai and Xi'an. China's aim is crystal clear – to compete head-to-head with Boeing and Airbus in the international market. Another player would mean less of the cream cake in the future.

Meanwhile, it is worth looking at the history of how Airbus and Boeing came to do battle. It is an intriguing tale that involves some intrepid characters and unlikely heroes.

4. THE COMET LEADS THE JET AGE

Those of the ageing, grey-tinged generation, weaned on Meccano, the *Hotspur* comic and the exploits of chip-eating runner Alf Tupper, would recall his baby-faced good looks. John Cunningham, at 82, remained a *Boys' Own* hero. Even in the midsummer of 1999, you could still identify the blond, record-breaking test pilot and RAF Mosquito ace whose antics graced countless Pathé News bulletins in the 1940s and 1950s. Group Captain Cunningham was the inspiration for a million schoolboys who wanted to reach for the sky and, more importantly, was the flight test pilot on the DH-106 Comet, the world's first commercial jet airliner which had its maiden flight on Friday, 27 July 1949. Typically modest, Cunningham, who started flying Tiger Moth biplanes in 1935 at just seventeen years old, described the experience as 'just another day at work'.

On that auspicious day, the plane, registered as G-ALVG, was rolled out of the hangar at the De Havilland Aircraft Company at Hatfield, Hertfordshire, and lifted off on a 31-minute flight, flying to 8,000 ft. It was at that moment that the jet age for the passenger had begun. The then *Glasgow Herald* newspaper reported the following morning that Cunningham told his boss, the legendary plane-maker Geoffrey De Havilland, that 'the aircraft was very nice to handle'.

The story went on to report: 'More conventional in appearance than expected, the Comet is a beautifully streamlined monoplane

... drag is reduced by the four Ghost engines being nearly buried in the comparatively thin wings ... to ensure the economic results from the jet engines, the Comet will fly at high altitudes, probably about 40,000 ft. On this account, the fuselage has been pressurised to about twice the pressure employed in most airliners now in service.'

It was the pinnacle of British aviation technology. On demonstration flights, the smoothness of the aircraft and its engines was shown by balancing coins on the edge of the meal tables and observing the absence of ripples in the Champagne glasses.

Nearly fifty years later, on a sweltering English summer's day, Cunningham made a pilgrimage to the De Havilland Heritage Centre, a ramshackle museum run by amateurs where slithers of fuselage, wing and propeller lie around waiting for some attention and large doses of cash. Across a field comes the constant rumble of the M25 near the South Minns junction, and here the relics of a once-proud British institution are scattered. De Havilland in the UK is no more, at first absorbed by Hawker Siddeley and now no more than a historical footnote for BAE Systems.

Cunningham, who died on 21 July 2002, was a brave man – the remnant of a dying breed of English gentlemen. In 1947, he had taken a De Havilland Vampire jet fighter to a then world record height of 59,492 ft, without a pressure suit, but it was the Mosquito for which he was most well known. And it was inside this old hangar at Salisbury Hall that the Mosquito – the wooden fighter-bomber which helped the Allies win the Second World War – was created in secrecy. Cunningham, dubbed 'Cats' Eyes' by the popular press, was by far its most famous pilot.

On his return to the scene of some of his triumphs, the yellow Mosquito prototype greeted him as it languished in the shed. But the Mosquito, despite all the memories it held, was not the object of his interest on this occasion.

As an ageing man, Cunningham had returned to the museum to visit a mocked-up cockpit of the original Comet. Inside the claustrophobic, fetid space, he sat in the battered leather pilot's chair pointing at dusty levers, gauges and broken switches. His eyes glinted with a strange familiarity and he recalled with affection the trial test flight. 'It's amazing how the memories flood back after so many years. This plane was a fantastic creation, designed by RE Bishop of Mosquito fame, and a dream to fly. In terms of design it was outstanding; it still looks so graceful.'

There was little fanfare when Cunningham and his crew of John Wilson, Frank Reynolds, Tony Fairbrother and Harry Waters landed back in 1949, just a ripple of applause from a brace of reporters and the Comet technical team.

'After the flight, I just drove back to my home at Kinsbourne Green, a few miles from Hatfield. Next day I had a call from Captain De Havilland. He asked me about the technical performance of the flight and said he was delighted I'd such a nice flight. He said it was a great birthday present for him. He was sixty-five. I said to him it had been my birthday too. It was an extraordinary coincidence. I was fortunate because Captain De Havilland treated me in many ways like a son,' he said.

It was with a sense of national pride that Britain moved into the jet airline age. Perhaps some British engineers seemed infuriatingly complacent to the French, Russian and Americans also chasing the same goals. Indeed, RE Bishop proclaimed, 'We feel we have a lead on the Americans of between four and five years on jet transport aircraft.'

The Americans were definitely flustered. Delos Rentzel, the American Civil Aeronautics Administrator, had warned the US Senate Commerce Committee in August 1947 that he feared American aviation would lose its leadership in the field of civil transport. 'When the Comet is put into regular operation – probably in 1952 – it is believed that flight schedules will be cut approximately in half. Unless other nations develop aircraft to compete, the De Havilland Comet will be the world's fastest air transport.'

While it would not last for ever, at that time Britain was able to build up a substantial lead over the rest of the world, with Boeing's prototype Dash Seven still only on the drawing board. But how was this possible?

Back in December 1942, Lord Brabazon of Tara set up a British government committee to make recommendations about the post-war development of airliners. It was a tall order, as British transport aircraft manufacturers had fallen far behind, as they concentrated on the life-or-death business of designing and building combat aircraft. There was a gaping lack of self-belief. In the closing stage of the Second World War, Lord Beaverbrook, the Canadian-born press magnet who owned the *Daily Express*, summed it up: 'The British aircraft industry is a hotbed of cold feet.'

While the Super-Marine Spitfire, the Hawker Hurricane and the Avro Lancaster bomber emerged in British minds as the icons of victory, it was America's immense air supremacy that eventually won the day against the Nazis and the Japanese. And it was Boeing products that brought the war to its cataclysmic conclusion. The B-29 Superfortress – 3,970 of which were rolled out of the aircraft plants in Renton, Seattle and Wichita, Kansas, from September 1942 – dropped the A-bombs on Hiroshima and Nagasaki.

Britain's wartime aviation industry, which employed 1.7 million workers at its peak, had to be turned into a national asset. Britain had made numerous technological breakthroughs – the radar and the jet engine to name just two – but a post-war lack of entrepreneurial zeal, a dearth of investment and venture capital, and woeful government understanding, decision-making and inconsistent financial support dogged the industry.

Brabazon's committee, reporting in November 1945, drew up a list of five recommendations. Some mirrored the aspirations of Howard Hughes's Spruce Goose – the world's largest transport plane, which flew briefly in 1947 – particularly the ill-inspired Bristol Brabazon and Saro Princess flying boats which were designed for non-stop flight between London and New York. Neither made it past the prototype stage.

However, the Committee's fourth recommendation was more compelling – and successful. It suggested the manufacture of a relatively small-powered jet to take letters and parcels across the North Atlantic. This idea, sandwiched neatly in the proposal, would be the beginning of the commercial jet boom. At that moment, the De Havilland Comet was conceived.

The De Havilland Aircraft Company, headed by the autocratic Sir Geoffrey De Havilland, had the dynamism and élan to take on the task, and began work on the project as soon as the war ended. As a business, De Havilland was run almost as a family affair, though this was tinged with tragedy. Two of Sir Geoffrey's sons died while testing his airplanes, the second of which, Geoffrey Jr, while piloting an experimental DH-108 jet over the Thames estuary in 1946. John Cunningham was charged with the task of discovering exactly why the DH-108 had crashed.

Cunningham made more than 160 flights in pursuit of the answers and became almost a surrogate son to De Havilland. The applied research, and endless hours of testing that Cunningham conducted on the DH-108's aerodynamics, ultimately paid off –

and with hugely successful results. The proposed revised wing design was adopted and has been applied to a succession of European aircrafts, including the Airbus of today.

During those three years, Cunningham, from his neat and tidy office in the corner of a hangar in Hatfield, lived with the Comet as it took shape. He knew everybody who worked on the project, even the apprentices who laboured in a workshop which was more reminiscent of a bicycle shed than a hi-tech test bed. Slowly, the aircraft began to take shape around him. New engines were tested aboard converted Lancaster bombers, Vampires and DH-108s, while Cunningham himself designed the flight deck, which was very much influenced by the Lockheed Constellations that he flew for the British Overseas Aircraft Corporation (BOAC) to try to acclimatise to the controls of bigger airliners.

After the war, passenger air travel boomed. In 1946, the introduction of the four-engine Douglas DC-4 and the Constellation enabled the major carriers to operate transcontinentally with only one intermediate stop. Scores of former RAF aces joined BOAC as pilots, so Cunningham felt at home as a temporary member of Britain's glamorous flying elite. Constellations flew at 18,000 ft, and at a speed of around 250 miles an hour. BOAC's arch Atlantic rivals were Pan American and TWA, owned by the entrepreneur Howard Hughes. The 2,500-mile hop across the pond took fourteen hours in a DC-4 and eleven hours in a Constellation, depending on the prevailing winds.

The American airline fares were fixed by regulators – New York to London was $720 return, or $522 in (coach) tourist class, which was introduced towards the end of 1948. Los Angeles and San Francisco to London was $1,011 or $720 for a tourist. The effect of the lower fares was dramatic. The new affluent middle classes of America wanted to travel and these reduced fares fuelled a surge in passengers. More capable turbo-prop planes were continually introduced to the transatlantic routes, including the Boeing Stratocruiser, the next-generation Super Constellations and the Bristol Britannia. But it was clear that commercial jets were the future – though not everyone agreed.

The Americans and the Soviet Union were spending fortunes on creating jet bombers, but didn't see the financial viability of passenger jets – for them, the economics still didn't stack up. The Russians eventually changed their minds and later developed the Tupolev Tu-104, which in 1955 became the second commercial jet-powered airliner after the Comet. However, the US Defense Department's priority remained speed for the military and there was little interest from the airlines.

Fortune magazine adopted a wonderfully patronising American tone in its 7 August edition. 'Jets' high fuel consumption,' it wrote, 'make them intrinsically more uncompetitive than propeller aircraft.'

But flying was here to stay. In the *Aircraft Year Book* for 1949, DC Ramsay, President of the US Aircraft Industries Association of America, wrote excitedly, 'The average citizen now is affected to an important degree by commercial aviation. During some summer months of the past year passenger miles on our commercial airlines exceeded those for Pullman travel. A conservative estimate is that one-half of our first-class travel in the entire country next year will be in the air ... there are 93,000 civil aircraft now flying and private and executive transport aircraft are being used by at least 100 different types of business enterprise. With its wartime, all-time-high production peak half a decade behind, the US aircraft manufacturing industry during 1949 had the best peace-time year in its history.'

While Britain held a flimsy lead, aviation was becoming a vital industry across the pond. In 1949, more than 249,000 Americans were employed in the aircraft, engine, propeller and service industry and sales volume for airframe, engine and propeller industries were worth $1,700m to the US economy.

Boeing, consumed by its military virility, broke two records in 1949. Six days after the new year, the first of the 71-ton, 340-miles-per-hour Boeing Stratocruisers were delivered to the US Air Force and, later in the same month, the first of the 56 Stratocruisers delivered that year for commercial airlines was sent out to Pan American World Airways. Then the Boeing XB-47 Stratojet bomber swept into the headlines early in February when, with Air Force majors RE Schleeh and Joseph Howell at the controls, it shattered all coast-to-coast speed records in a ferrying flight from Moses Lake Air Force base in Washington State to Andrews Air Force base, just outside Washington DC, at an average speed of 607 mph. It was futuristic in design, its engines, dangling from four pods underneath the wings, were so slender and fragile that they flapped during flight.

America was surging ahead in jet development for bombers and Air Secretary W Stuart Symington described the flights as 'an epochal step in the development of air power. What it actually does is turn our medium bombers into intercontinental bombers.' With such words, the precarious era of *Dr Strangelove* was born.

On 22 December 1951, the Baxter Report, a confidential stock-market newsletter, described the coming 'jet revolution'. Airline stocks were vulnerable and holders were advised to sell. It was going to cost around $40m to build a single experimental jet transport and not a single airline had this much money. Ironically, more than fifty years later, in 2005, most of the New York stock-market pundits were still saying the same thing about traditional airline stocks, with many of the US's major airlines facing bankruptcy.

But the De Havilland Comet was ahead of the game – and the stockbrokers. She was a beautiful bird, with a pressurised fuselage to carry passengers to 40,000 ft and four Goblin 50 turbojet engines buried in wings that were moderately swept back. It had a sci-fi appeal and it was a wake-up call.

Two DH-106 prototypes were ordered by the UK's Ministry of Supply in May 1946 and in the following year BOAC made a bold move by placing a preliminary order for eight aircraft at £450,000 each. The British airline proudly announced it was the first in the world to order commercial jet planes, but they were lone riders. The orders didn't flood in, principally because the all-metal jet only had room for 36 passengers which made it expensive to operate.

However, several spectacular trial record flights – with average speeds of 420 mph – whetted appetites. Before the first 36-seater was delivered to BOAC on 2 April 1951, ten more orders were received from Canadian Pacific Airlines, while a triumphant display at the Farnborough Air Show in September 1952 yielded orders from Air France and Union Aeromaritime de Transport, who took three each, and two were snapped up by the Royal Canadian Air Force. They did not rest on their laurels; the engines were upgraded and cabin modifications increased the capacity to 44 passengers. Things were looking good for the British upstarts.

On 2 May 1952, Comet Yoke Peter G-ALYP, in the sky-blue livery of BOAC, was the first commercial jet in service, stealing a full two years on the development of Boeing's 707, based on the B52 bomber. Put into service on the London to Johannesburg route, the Comet made five stops along the way, and landed next day after covering 6,724 miles in 23 hours and 34 minutes.

There was a definite spring in the step of British aviation. The next-generation Comet 2, with Avon-powered engines and a longer range, was proving to be an attractive option for prospective customers. Eddie Rickenbacker, the Chairman of Eastern Airlines, said he would take fifty Comets if they could be delivered on time, which was something of a tall order, and American Airlines and National Airlines were also queuing up to place orders.

This interest came from being the first jet aircraft on to the market, but the Comet paid a dear price for this competitive advantage. In October, the second Comet aircraft, G-ALYZ, was damaged beyond repair on take-off from Rome. Canadian Pacific's CF-CUN crashed in March 1953 at Karachi en route to Sydney, killing all eleven crew and technicians, and another was damaged at Dakar. The investigators blamed the aircraft's nose – if it was too high at take-off, they found that the plane could not reach flying speed. But this discovery did not stop the string of disasters.

On 2 May 1953, the BOAC Comet G-ALYV was taking off from Calcutta en route to Delhi and crashed, killing 43 people on board. Then Yoke Peter took off from Rome and juddered in the air before crashing into the Mediterranean with the loss of 35 passengers and crew. BOAC and Air France grounded the planes to carry out checks but these proved inconclusive and the planes went back into service. They were in service for just one more year before Comet G-ALYY took off from Rome on 8 April 1954 and crashed into Stromboli, killing 21 people on board. The fleet was permanently grounded later that week. The wreck was recovered and rebuilt at the Royal Aircraft Establishment, Farnborough, and was subjected to rigorous tests and analysis.

Sir Geoffrey De Havilland, in his autobiography *Sky Fever*, in a chapter entitled 'The Comet and After', wrote, 'One day Bishop and I flew over to Farnborough to see how the tests were progressing. Sir Arnold Hall was then Superintendent of the Royal Aircraft Establishment and had organised with his staff the vast job of testing out the wreckage, building the [water] tank and doing much work in a miraculously short time. We were talking in the office when he was rung up and told me that the pressure cabin in the tank had failed after a period of nine thousand hours' normal flying. We went at once to examine the failure, and found a rent in the side of the cabin which appeared to start from a rivet at the corner of the window-frame.'

A repair was made and the water-tank test was repeated and a similar failure started at the corner of the window frame. It was proof of a weakness in the cabin structure, caused by metal fatigue. Before those tests, metal fatigue had been understood, but only to a certain level. The effect of subtle variations of cabin pressure on metal, which was the catalyst for the disasters, was only discovered in this water-tank test.

A Court of Inquiry, ordered by Winston Churchill, was held in Church House, Westminster, between 19 October and 24 November 1954. The Right Honourable Lord Cohen was appointed Commissioner with Sir William Farren, Professor WJ Duncan and Air Commodore AH Wheeler as the assessors. Arnold Hall and his Farnborough crew were commended for the painstaking forensic reconstruction which made them world leaders in air-crash assessment. Their evidence was startling and gave Boeing's technical representatives at the inquiry plenty to think about.

The findings dealt with the construction and testing of the Comet at considerable length. The report said, 'Throughout the design, De Havilland relied on well-established methods essentially the same as those in general use by aircraft designers. But they were going outside the range of previous experience and they decided to make thorough tests of every part of the cabin structure.'

A dejected De Havilland admitted, 'In spite of the findings of the Court of Inquiry and the admittedly insufficient knowledge of fatigue problems, we realised that our technical reputation had suffered a reverse, and we also realised that it would take several years of hard work to regain our position.'

De Havilland never did, but the company was a pioneer. Without the extensive tests and research on the Comet, the next generation of planes – Boeing's V-winged 367-80 and Douglas's DC8 jetliner – would still have had the problems of metal fatigue and pressurised cabins. But the stiff-upper-lipped British believed they had been the pioneers.

Returning home on that sunny afternoon in 1999, Cunningham lamented, 'It's sad to believe that we lost the lead in the aviation race. We had brilliant designers, engineers and manufacturers but we were unlucky. The Comet design was completely changed and round windows added, but it was really too late for De Havilland. The airline buyers now saw the emerging Boeing 707 carrying one hundred and eleven passengers, while the new Comet could only manage seventy. Boeing admitted the disasters which befell the Comet taught them lessons about high-altitude flying and helped give them the competitive edge which made them world leaders.'

Cunningham went on to become a director of Hawker Siddeley Aviation, which swallowed up De Havilland in 1959, and then British Aerospace. He was involved in many other British aviation achievements such as the Harrier vertical take-off jump jet and Concorde. But the commercial failure of the Comet always rankled with him.

Nonetheless, the Comet was strengthened and lived on in its modified state as the Comet 2 and was given a clean bill of health by the RAF who had ten on order. After the Farnborough inquiry, BOAC ordered nineteen Comet 4s, which were more powerful. There was modest commercial success when British European Airways (BEA) ordered fourteen, which stayed in scheduled service until October 1971.

With the long-range market increasingly saturated, De Havilland began to look at twinjets, and then it proposed the three-engine DH-121 in May 1957. On Tuesday, 9 January 1962, John Cunningham, Peter Bugge and crew took off on the maiden flight of the first De Havilland 121 Trident dressed in BEA livery. *Flight International* reported, 'To those accustomed to watching Comets taking off, the quietness of the Rolls-Royce Speys was most noticeable.' The publicity clearly went to De Havilland's head.

Later, HG Sturgeon, managing director of De Havilland, was asked to comment on the Boeing's new competitor to the Trident, the 727. Sturgeon said, 'Ours [the Trident] is of a size that will match airline needs more exactly than any other coming along in the next five years.' He was completely and utterly wrong.

Across the Channel, the French were taking another tack. By the mid-50s, Sud Aviation's medium-range twinjet, the Caravelle, had emerged from Toulouse. In charge of flight testing was a brilliant French engineer and technocrat called Roger Beteille. He was to become a seminal figure in the Airbus story.

5. AIRBUS FINDS LE GENIUS

Now retired and living in Switzerland, Roger Beteille remains one of the most illustrious figures in world aviation. He is the living creator of Airbus Industrie. He remains a proud and patriotic Frenchman who has led an action-packed life. During the Second World War, a youthful Beteille took part in a French Resistance raid at Toulouse to destroy Luftwaffe planes. After the war, he became a test pilot, and survived the crash of the Armagnac, the first long-distance passenger plane built by France to compete with the Lockheed Constellation. Undaunted, he took to the air again in the prototype Caravelle and became one of the country's 'Grand Ingenieurs', a pioneer feted for being 'intrepid, tenacious and a clairvoyant'.

Building a successful commercial plane is the ultimate team game, but it requires visionary leadership, and Roger Beteille was the inspiration behind the physical creation of Airbus. Adam Brown, a Vice President for Sales and Marketing who has worked at Airbus since 1973 and is a close friend and colleague, says, 'Roger is a genius. Without him it is difficult to conceive of how Airbus would ever have taken off.'

Jürgen Thomas, the father of the Airbus A380, describes him with equal reverence: 'Without Roger, the Airbus programme would not exist. He is an engineering genius. More than this, he has always been very shrewd when dealing with the politics. He fought and won many battles over the years. But, above all, he is a commercial plane-maker.'

In mid-September, Lausanne – the refined Swiss resort on the shores of Lac Leman – is in the early throes of autumn. The sun still shines but the rain is soft and frequent. Puffs of mist shroud the Alpine peaks across the lake. Roger Beteille lives in peaceful retirement in a penthouse flat with stunning vistas. Every morning he looks out over the changing lake and in the evening he can see the twinkling lights of Evian.

He is a courteous man, and greets me wearing a white shirt and blue cardigan. He has a thick flow of white hair, and is small and slender, but a little slower on his feet. Yet still, at 84, his eyes glint with a smile and his mind flashes like a rapier across a range of subjects. The only sign of his age is when he grasps to pull a name of a long-forgotten colleague from the depths of his brain.

'I've been very lucky in my life. We all need some of it to get us through,' says the man who walked away from a test-flight crash and, perhaps more impressively, managed to negotiate his way through Airbus's politics. Airbus could have done with a measure of his *savoir faire* during the terrors of 2006.

In October 1951, the French Civil Aircraft Committee published the specification for a medium-range aircraft carrying 55 to 65 passengers. This was to become the Caravelle, and because it was to have shorter ranger than the Comet it was not seen as a direct competitor.

'In 1952, I was appointed to do the organisation and flight tests of the Caravelle up to its certification. At this time, my company was Sud Aviation [it evolved after a merger of Sud-Est and Sud-Ouest in 1957] in Toulouse and we had exceptionally good relationships with De Havilland. We were producing the De Havilland Vampire jet under licence. Relations were extremely cordial at all levels,' remembers Beteille.

'It was possible to exchange ideas and views. When I was placed in charge of the Caravelle flight test, the Comet had just started flying and I thought it was a good idea to look at what my colleagues were already doing in the United Kingdom. So I spent some time in Hatfield.'

Roger met many of the Comet's design office, where he enjoyed the English humour and the esoteric discussions about aerodynamics, using slide rules and differential calculus to compare notes. These cemented long-term relationships. Beteille would meet many of the Brits again over ten years later when he returned as head of the Airbus project. Meanwhile, he befriended John Cunningham.

'He was such a charming Englishman. John invited me to fly with him and take part in some experimental flights of the Comet. This was my first experience at the controls of a jet passenger plane. I had the opportunity to see at close quarters what the British were doing and to see the equipment they were using. It helped me understand a bit better some of the entirely new concepts and interpretations of the civil jet aircraft. At this time, we didn't even think about Boeing. It was more Douglas or Lockheed who were the American competitors for the Caravelle.'

While Sud Aviation progressed with the Caravelle, using the Comet's nose and cockpit designs, Cunningham and his colleagues began early design work on the Trident, which would attempt to steal some of the Gallic thunder. But this was of little concern to Beteille at this time, as he was engaged in his own activities. 'I had the chance to be in charge of the flight testing of the Caravelle. I flew the first thousand hours and it was an amazing experience. It was easy to fly and it was a very nice glider.'

Life was much simpler then in Toulouse. There were two French pilots, one engineer and another technician. Four people were on test flights compared with the large cast involved with the current breed of flight engineers.

The Caravelle SE210 aircraft, powered by Rolls-Royce Avon turbojets mounted at the rear, was put into production in 1953 and made its first flights from Toulouse on Sunday, 27 May 1955. Understandably, the first orders were from Air France, followed by Swedish carrier SAS.

'We had very few people involved at the time and there was no magnetic or digital recording of the plane's performance. A lot of calculations were done by writing down the numbers, using a slide-rule and a great deal of guess work, listening and looking closely at the plane. It was manual calculus.'

The twin-engine Caravelle was sleek and well made, and 280 models were sold. Then Sud Aviation signed an agreement with Donald W Douglas, the enigmatic aviator behind the legendary Douglas DC-3 Dakota. Douglas was a cautious man who had achieved world leadership with his DC-3, with over 10,600 churned out from its Santa Monica factories. Indeed, in 1985, on its 50th anniversary, nearly 2,000 workhorse DC-3s were still flying with scheduled airlines and air forces. Yet, in the late fifties, the Douglas Aircraft Company was losing its lead and needed to compete with the emerging Boeing 707. So a collaboration with Sud Aviation over a proposed Douglas DC-9, a smaller derivative of the successful DC-8, was seen as a suitable way forward. This excited Beteille as he now realised joint ventures were the only way to rival US supremacy in mass production.

'The Caravelle could have been developed for the American markets. There were discussions with Douglas where it would take care of the marketing in the US and the rest of the Americas and Sud Aviation would cover the rest of the world. Then Douglas said something had to be done to sell in the United States, specifically increasing the size of the baggage hold. The design office prepared the modification of the fuselage cross-section to increase the diameter. It came up with the development of the Double Bubble, a system in two semi-circles joined together that gives more room than a straightforward cylinder. This would give much more baggage room for the passenger.'

The Double Bubble eventually became an acceptable design for an aircraft's fuselage, and was the chosen form for both the Airbus A380 and the Boeing 787. Despite this, Douglas broke an agreement. And, while discussions with Douglas were ongoing, Beteille was headhunted to another high-profile job. He left to become the technical head of Sud Aviation's Missile Division in Cannes. With Beteille out of the equation, the Caravelle – France's most successful commercial plane – lost its chance of significantly breaking into the lucrative US market.

'Several years later, when I came back to the commercial aircraft industry, I enquired why the decision hadn't gone ahead with Douglas,' said Beteille, 'and I found out that the French government, who were providing the funds, decided not to go with the development, saying that the Caravelle was already selling well, so why spend money to try and improve it?'

There were, however, other factors at work. Sud Aviation lacked political power and money and relied on the assistance and generosity of the French government – which now seemed reluctant to deal with the Americans. This was due to something far more sexy: Concorde, the emerging Anglo-French supersonic jet project. The French officials saw Concorde as a medium-range aircraft, as a kind of Super-Caravelle. The common development between Sud and Douglas was shelved. Perhaps, in hindsight, it was just as well, for Airbus might never have existed.

Beteille's new assignment was to develop a European space and missile business in France. Beteille and his beautiful young wife, the opera singer Josette Jasmin, spent ten wonderful years on the Midi. 'When I started, there were seventy engineers, when I left there were four hundred and seventy. It was all about creating high-quality technical jobs in France. And I thought, to secure the future of this important factory at Cannes, I needed to try and find something different. Once the nuclear missiles were built, delivered and installed on the submarines, we were unable to provide work for everyone in the group. I wanted to keep this team together. Then I thought it was a good idea to use our core competencies to diversify into the emerging satellite business. We succeeded in gaining the green light to apply for the Cicero satellite, with other European partners, Standard Electric, Marconi, Alenia in Italy, and CASA in Spain,' he recalls.

The company became Alcatel Space, which merged with Finmeccanica in 2005 to create two joint-venture companies, both partners contributing their respective satellite industrial activities. Alcatel Alenia Space, of which Alcatel will hold 67 per cent, has combined the Alcatel Space and Alenia Spazio's activities.

Beteille is proud that the current company is still making space systems, satellites, payloads and instruments for civilian and military applications, including CNES, the French Space Agency and the European Space Agency. The headquarters of Alcatel Alenia Space remains in Cannes, with the group employing around 7,200 people, with sales in 2004 of €1.8bn. Quite a legacy for the Airbus founder. But that's another story . . .

Roger Beteille and his wife loved life in Cannes. It was the epitome of 60s chic, with rock stars and movie idols rubbing shoulders with successful French business people. He even designed and built his own 20 ft wooden boat which was moored in the harbour where the French glitterati would go on holiday. But, while Beteille was building boats and missiles, the Americans were reasserting their dominance in the aerospace industry.

Not for the last time, the Paris Air Show was to play a pivotal part in the evolving story of the battle between Boeing and Airbus. The show is normally a hotbed of deal-making, contract agreement, gossip and industry chatter. The company chalets that line the apron at Le Bourget Airport are where the global aviation executives grab their annual chance to meet and greet.

Back in 1965, the 26th Salon Internationale de l'Aeronautique et de l'Espace, ran from 11 to 21 June, and was larger than ever before. The crowds were treated to fearsome displays of American and Soviet military might. *Flight International* concluded, 'In the overall show scene, Russia, with a good number of aircraft and a dazzling but not entirely new space display, has undoubtedly stolen the thunder from the massive American contribution, most of which consists of familiar aircraft. Paris can be summed up in the strength and variety of French efforts in all areas, a business-like British showing (with great hopes of co-operation) and a good effort by the equipment companies.'

America's aerospace and military prowess was displayed for all to see. And it wasn't subtle. The swaggering US Navy brought across the barnstorming Blue Angels for a tour, while an array of other aircraft including the Chance Vought F-8; Douglas A-4; Grumman E-2A, A-6A, and F-11; Lockheed C-130 and P-3A; McDonnell F-4B; North American A-5A; Bell UH-1B and the Sikorsky CH-53A proudly showed off the US's military superiority.

With the Cold War at its height and the Cuban missile crisis still a tender memory for Americans, Paris was the shop window to emphasise its superpower status. The Boeing Company, which had changed its name from the Boeing Airplane Company on 3 May 1961 to recognise the increasing diversity of its products, had a few bragging rights with a real showstopper. Standing upright, and towering above the other exhibits, was a full-size Minuteman I missile, Boeing's solid propellant ballistic missile. Over 33,000 people were then working on the programme both in Seattle and in Ogden, Utah. The deadly arms were assembled and dispatched to six Air Force bases across the United States. Engineering support and test launches were the responsibility of Boeing at Cape Canaveral and Vandenberg Air Force base in California. It was a lucrative contract, worth tens of millions of pounds, and involved cutting-edge research that could be used in future commercial airplane technology.

Boeing's Minuteman was one of the most successful and best-managed strategic missile systems in history. But it didn't end there. In September 1964, the Minuteman II performed a flight from Cape Canaveral to a target in the South Atlantic. The Atlas and Agena B provided ways of powering man into outer space, while Titan II, the original Intercontinental Ballistic Missile and icon of the Cold War, was now trained on the Soviet Union, and would later become a stalwart of the Gemini space mission. The US government was able to pour huge sums into its defence and research industries. The Soviet Union wasn't lagging behind either, having recently launched its Luna 6 spacecraft on a three-and-a-half-day journey to the moon.

Increasingly, the political discussion among the intellectual elite was about continental Europe's future and closer ties with Britain. There was a sneaking admiration in the UK for what France had achieved since the end of the war. 'Immediately after the war, France, in the depths of depression and degradation, could scarcely do a thing right. French aviation became a museum of prototypes. Today, her exports of aircrafts, helicopters and missiles are a measure of the world's confidence in her dynamic and purposeful leadership,' said *Flight International* in its 10 June 1965 edition.

There was a need for rationalisation, and co-operation became the buzzword for European aviation. The American chutzpah rankled with many European statesmen and intellectuals. And one influential voice was Jean-Jacques Servan-Schreiber in his book *Le Défi Américain* (The American Challenge), which became a bestseller. An editor on *Le Monde* and founder of the news magazine *L'Express*, Servan-Schreiber highlighted Europe's post-war challenge. It was a perceptive polemic that argued that America's rapacious multinationals would overwhelm the globe and that Europe would be drowned in its wake. Even today it remains highly topical, urging Europeans to build a strong economy based on co-operation, high technology and industrial innovation. It struck a jarring chord.

Even then, France was philosophically opposed to the American model of global capitalism. President De Gaulle didn't help the tensions between the two countries by attacking the monetarist theories of the new free-market economists such as Milton Friedman. De Gaulle's model of state ownership of key industries, intervention in markets and hefty subsidies for farmers to support home-grown produce was in stark contrast to the American spirit of free enterprise.

Since 1950, France had used the state, through indicative planning of investment in the major industries and the centralisation of credit control, to stimulate a growth rate that was double that of Britain. France has a tradition of state control, or *dirigisme*, and the post-war French government built on the power of the pre-war Grande Ecoles to establish a National School of Administration (ENA). This gave France's senior civil servants management and administrative training and business skills far superior to anything available in Britain. The Civil Service in the UK were policy advisers rather than effective project managers. And the so-called *Enarch* were committed to technological development and the support of industrial projects on a grand scale.

In Britain, there were different concerns stemming from colonial decline. BOAC announced plans to cut its aircraft order book and slash its workforce. Sir Basil Smallpiece, BOAC's managing director, painted a gloomy picture. 'There is a gathering momentum in the evolution of the British Empire into the Commonwealth of independent nations. However good it may have been for those nations, it has also had a marked effect on BOAC's position in the world of aviation – an effect which we felt much more acutely in 1963 than ever before.'

When a colony became independent, the emergent nation had the right to have its own airline, and so BOAC lost its share of traffic in Ghana, Nigeria, East Africa, Malaya, India, Ceylon and the West Indies. But this had an impact on where people wanted to go. Instead of flights routed directly to London, increasingly the independent states were flying to Europe and the United States, especially New York, where the new nations were joining the United Nations.

At least the eccentric Brits were pioneering the hovercraft. 'As a nation of individualists addicted to messing around in boats, it is hardly surprising that we should make such excellent progress with the new form of air and marine transport ... although we seem to have lost our magic touch with light engines of our own design for the time being, British turbines power large numbers of foreign civil and military aircraft,' commented *Flight International* in June 1965.

While the space race was making the newsreels, an informal pow-wow of the leading European state-owned airlines, including Air France, Alitalia, BEA, Lufthansa, Sabena and SAS, was held in a quiet pavilion. There was one perplexing question on the table for the technical managers present: why was it that this group of major airlines – including BOAC – were operating 25 per cent of the global airline fleet, yet Europe's aircraft manufacturers made only about 10 per cent of commercial airplanes? Something had to be done about the overwhelming American dominance, which was at that time over 85 per cent of the market. The first session was called by Knut Hagrup, the Executive Vice President, technical and operations, for the Swedish carrier SAS. It was concluded that from 1970–71 there would be a requirement for a European-made plane with room for 150–175 passengers, flying short-haul routes within the range of 600 to 1,800 miles.

It made sense. The Swinging Sixties was an era when jet air travel was becoming the norm. The Beatles arrived in New York in 1964 on a transatlantic BOAC jet. In the first decade of jet transport from 1958 to 1968, the airline industry was piling on the passengers and, at last, making serious money for the operators. In Europe, the increasingly well-off British, West Germans, Dutch, Swedes and Danes were discovering that the Mediterranean, especially the Spanish costas, the Balearic Islands and the Algarve in Portugal, was the ideal sunshine place for a cheap two-week package holiday.

'In the mid-60s, makers of passenger airplanes and their customers saw themselves as standing at the gates of El Dorado. All forecasts of growth in passenger traffic showed a steeply rising curve; the analysts in banks, industry and government proclaimed an uninterrupted annual growth rate of 15 per cent,' said one commentator.

But the prolonged discussions would drag out for some time to come. The thorny question was: how many passengers should a European plane carry? It was a hotly disputed topic with a thousand opinions to nail down. As the meeting had suggested, there was a market for a short- to medium-size 'Airbus'. And, while there was an increasing political will, there was a desperate need for a European leader with the requisite combination of wisdom and technical skills to make it happen. Roger Beteille's name was mentioned, but why would a man enjoying the good life in Cannes want to leave such a lucrative job, with sure-fire prospects? And why take on something as dicey as a start-up business to produce a new aircraft?

More was happening though. Elsewhere, at the Paris Air Show of 1965, several French and German aircraft companies met to discuss a joint civil programme. From this, an informal group was set up called Studiengruppe Airbus. In October 1965, a further meeting was set up by the airlines, while the British and French governments got together to set up a working party. A snippet in *Flight International* on 4 November 1965 reported, 'Last week the British Aircraft Corporation confirmed that it is now working officially with Sud Aviation and Dassault on design studies for a 200–240-seater passenger, medium-range transport for service in 1972.' It was to have a range of up to 1,250 miles and a cruising speed of 550 mph. No further details were given, but the report said there were no plans for co-operation on development or construction. By late November, the Anglo-French Ministry Working Party had produced a completed report with the onus on greater co-operation between the European countries. This proposed plane was getting bigger by the month.

Meanwhile, stirred up by Concorde, America was now chasing the supersonic dream too. Juan Trippe, the legendary boss of Pan-Am, was looking at the possibilities, but this was a project so expensive that only national governments could contemplate financing it. President Kennedy was still assessing the idea and sent Najeeb Halaby, then the head of the Federal Aviation Administration, to see Trippe and tell him not to buy the Anglo-French supersonic planes until he had made up his mind about the US version.

'Trippe, too, had received conflicting advice. Lindbergh, for one, was strongly against supersonic jets on environmental grounds. Their noise figured to turn airport environs into wasteland, and for all anyone knew, they might destroy the ozone layer above the Earth. Lindbergh was opposed on economic ground also,' records the *History of Pan-Am*. Prescient comments, since the celebrated aviator raised this issue in 1965.

Britain and France were now well down the road with the Concorde project, sealed by a treaty commitment made by the Conservatives and a source of high political prestige. But Harold Wilson, the newly elected Labour Prime Minister, who came to power after the General Election in 1964, was desperately trying to balance the books and cut back on unnecessary expenditure.

He wrote to the French Premier, Georges Pompidou, on 28 October 1964, saying he 'was profoundly concerned by the magnitude of the problems that lie ahead'. He said that he did not believe that the financial outlay involved in developing a supersonic airliner was acceptable in the present economic situation.

Pompidou's curt response forced Wilson to retreat. And the UK Prime Minister wrote again to Pompidou on 18 January 1965 insisting there was no question of Britain 'unilaterally abrogating the Anglo-French agreement ... I confirm our readiness to proceed with the project.' The Labour government would have to find other savings.

In November, there was another viewpoint on the size. Lufthansa released a statement saying it was not interested in an Anglo-French airbus. 'It's too big,' said a German airline official. 'We want to see US standards of frequency and utilisation in Europe. We will buy the 170-seater 727-200, if the 727 and 737 is too small.'

Lufthansa was not representative of West Germany's aerospace business that was now flexing its power and keen for a breakthrough. Arbeitsgemeinschaft Airbus signed a contract on Thursday, 23 December 1965 with ATG Siebelwerke, Bölkow, Dornier, Flugzeug-Union Süd, HFB (Hamburger Flugzeugbau), Messerschmitt and VFW (Vereinigte Flugtechnische Werke). The pre-Christmas meeting was a huge step forward. It committed West Germany to becoming national partners in any future European programme concerned with technology in the aviation industry.

The Airbus report, published in late 1965, now came up with the concept of a 200–225-seater aircraft that would have lower operating costs than the Boeing 727-100. This would have a range of 810 nm, later increased to 1,200 nm. In France, the cabinet reached approval on the principle of the Airbus. With West Germany's industrial players behind him, Kurt Schmucker, the Minister of Economics, travelled to London in February 1966 and said that his nation would collaborate with Britain and France on the project, and a working group involving all three countries was to be set up. But the British Aircraft Corporation, part of the original Airbus study and increasingly tangled up with Concorde, made its excuses and bowed out.

This left Hawker Siddeley – building the Trident as a mainstay of the BEA fleet – as the leading British company. It forged links with Breguet and Nord of France (HBN) to pore over the ideas. Sud Aviation had just published details of the massive 269-seat Galion, which was to be designed in collaboration with Dassault. The ideas, spurred on by improvements in engine technology, were getting bigger and bolder. With its experience building the

Caravelle, the Alouette and now Concorde, Sud was happy to bring the Galion study to the table in line with the specification of the HBN designs. At last, there was real meat on the bone.

There was caution in aviation circles about the market for such a large plane. *Flight International*, on Thursday, 3 March 1966, picked up the cudgel. 'What is really needed in Europe – by passengers and shippers – is more frequency and lower, much lower, load factors. Europe has "city-pairs" just as populous and industrial as those in the United States, and yet there is no comparison between the choice of frequencies available to the public. It is frequency as much as anything else, including price, that promotes air transport – and this could be why we have not yet heard of a US market for a 200/250-seat short-haul airbus.'

In blinkered British eyes, a stretched Trident was an interim solution. 'It would be sooner and very much cheaper ... the airbus offers the best longer-term prospect of Anglo-French collaboration.'

So, in early 1966, Sud Aviation and Breguet made an agreement with Nord Aviation and Hawker Siddeley to develop a wide-body, twin-aisled aircraft for medium range. It was codenamed HBN100. It would be in two versions, a 225-seater and a 260-seater. The choice of engines would be Rolls-Royce's RB178 or the Pratt & Whitney JT 9D, which was being prepared for Boeing's new jumbo jet, the 747. At last, a proper plane was proposed, but it needed an extraordinary individual to make it happen. Roger Beteille was in the wings.

6. ROGER AGREES TO TAKE ON THE JOB

It was a command from President de Gaulle himself. 'Send for Beteille!' As a graduate of the Ecole Polytechnique, one of the grand schools that collectively trains the French elite, Roger Beteille knew one day he might be called upon to run a major government project. Now, the French President and the Premier George Pompidou requested that he take charge of Sud Aviation's latest aviation initiative.

'It was a difficult decision to take because I was very happy in Cannes. We had a lot of work. Cannes was not a bad place to live. But the business was now well established and I had mentored and prepared people of high quality to take over my job. I left without thinking this would do any damage. The company was in capable hands,' he said.

Why did he want to take on such a job? Beteille smiles enigmatically. Was it ego? Or the challenge? For Beteille, it was a heady combination of both. The Frenchman was in the prime of his life. In his mid-forties, he agreed to return and take charge of this project, but he laid down his own terms and conditions, enshrined in a formal contract.

'What was interesting for me was to be involved with a number of excellent companies right across Europe. For three years previously, I tried to organise comparative work on the European satellite project. I think it was the reason why my management asked me to take on the Airbus,' he said.

France and Britain were now under the increasingly malodorous spell of a Concorde project which was already seriously delayed and over budget, and plans for Britain's TSR2 military fighter project were mired in divisive political wrangles. He wanted a free hand to develop the Airbus plane, so there would be no political interference. And when you consider the continual changing of specification and requirements by BEA which ultimately hampered the Trident, Beteille's decision was far-sighted.

'I was one of the few people of my age able to work more or less in English. I had experience of civil design and international co-operation, even if it was only on a small scale. So I moved back to Toulouse with a team who were not directly involved in Concorde. This team was the remnants of those who were supporting the Caravelle in service and Breguet. These companies had already tried to associate themselves with other players; Breguet with Hawker-Siddeley and Sud with the nationalised British Aircraft Corporation (BAC), who were working together on the Concorde,' he continued.

The preliminary designs for the Airbus were drawn from the specific requirements of Air France, Lufthansa and BEA, who were now considering a 200–250-seat plane. None of these state-owned airlines had the resources to finance such a start-up, while BAC was still financially constrained by its ongoing Concorde commitments. In other words, the governments of Europe would have to step in to shoulder the burden. The British, French and German administrations agreed that, if there was a proven need for such a 200-seater plane, then greater pan-European co-operation was the only route to reduce the financial exposure. Breguet was soon absorbed into defence group Dassault, and so the French government decided that Sud Aviation should be the sole French partner.

Beteille had his work cut out. 'The first decision was to select a company in each country while taking care about all the precious, interconnected links in the aviation business. I was then selected by Sud to be their main man on this group.'

He was asked to give the project proper clarity. 'There were three distinct groups of people working on a relatively short- to medium-size aircraft,' he said. So on Saturday, 1 July 1967, he returned to the Sud Aviation office where he was given the spurious title of Deputy Technical Manager. It was an alias with little appreciation of the scale and gravitas of the task ahead.

'I had a very good relationship with the Technical Manager who was my teacher at the Ecole Superior Aeronautique. And then there was a meeting of the principals of the three companies on Thursday, 20 July 1967.' At this session they had to decide how to organise the initial phase. Each company had its own team leaders. But Beteille emerged as the real authority. He became a 'virtual' leader or first among equals with autonomous power delegated from his Sud Aviation boss. Beteille's immediate task was to prepare proposals to be put before the governments to build support for phase two. This was a feasibility study and a business plan of every aspect of the plane's technical definition to include a production programme, financial outlook and a delivery plan.

He was confident about the technical side, because he had considerable experience, but the Machiavellian political machinations were another matter. 'Contrary to what some people have said about me before, I had practically no political links. My job was not political. That was left to the principals and chairman of the company. I limited myself to what I had to do. When there was a high-level political delegation with ministers, that was not my job. That was the job of the chairman.'

Beteille's goal was clear: to produce the best plane possible. 'The target was: succeed, don't lose money but make something that works,' he recalls. 'But again it was about the creation of high-quality and highly skilled jobs that were sustainable. And, looking back, one of the great successes has been that we were able to create such high-quality jobs all over Europe.'

Outline funding had been agreed in May 1967 when research and development costs of £190m were to be shared 37.5 per cent by Britain, 37.5 per cent by France and 25 per cent by Germany. The French Minister of State for Foreign Affairs, André Bettencourt, the British Minister of State for Technology, John Stonehouse, and the West German Secretary of State in the ministry of economics, Dr Johann Schollhorn, agreed to £190m of development cost. Beteille was now to organise the basic split of work. Who would be doing what?

'Initially, I thought about an aircraft – or an airbus – on the basis of the jobs that could be done by my Sud Aviation team. My conclusion was that it was possible to split the job in three batches. This could meet the percentage sharing as defined by the governments and it also made industrial sense. It still remains that way. I proposed to have Sud Aviation making and working on the central part of the fuselage, the control systems and the cockpit, the British taking care of the wings outside the fuselage, and the Germans doing the main work on the fuselage.'

Beteille travelled to Hatfield and renewed old friendships, discussing his ideas with Jim Thorn, Hawker's team leader, Phil Smith, the head of research, and Alan Peters, whom he'd first met when he was seeking advice about the Comet.

'I spent two days exchanging views in Hatfield and at the end of the day they told me that they agreed with my proposal because they thought it was the right one. They were happy with the idea of working with me.'

He then made one important request that would quickly become part of the Airbus folklore. 'I thought it would be impossible to have those teams working properly together and being happy with a share of the work if they were not really interested in what was being done by all of us.'

This was the cornerstone of Airbus's future success. It was a fundamental principle that ran contrary to most accepted business practices, and it was Beteille's invention. It was the superglue that would keep *Le Grand Projet Airbus* alive during the turbulent times ahead.

'My idea was contrary to what a normal prime contractor does. I thought it completely inefficient that a prime contractor decides everything and then tells the sub-contractor how to do a job. This seemed so arrogant. It means the sub-contractor simply does the minimum and does not care about the rest of the project. I did not want this. I believe this was a difference between ourselves and Boeing. It's the way that Boeing does it. They think that they are always right. They will say, "We are Boeing and you are sub-contractors and you will do what we tell you." '

Beteille asked Thorn and his team to set up a separate group, other than the wings team, that would come and work alongside Sud Aviation in Toulouse. The same would happen with the German partners, led by Johann 'Hans' Schaffler.

'I wanted a small group of high-quality engineers whose job was just to look at what all the other partners were doing and be able to make suggestions and improvements, and become more integrated with the projects. I think that was one of the reasons why Hawker Siddeley accepted my proposal. It was also vitally important for them – and me – that they were part of the programme. I was not their boss. I was just the leader and my job was to convince people that what I told them to do was the right thing for all of us.'

Throughout his next eighteen years with Airbus, Beteille continued with this way of working and believes such regular cross-disciplinary sessions ironed out complex problems inside the business. 'I had monthly meetings with chief engineers, heads of production, and the financial teams where we discussed all the problems, across the board. It was often very tense and difficult and we would all listen to the solutions they were proposing outside their own chair as well as in their own chair.'

After this discussion, Beteille would decide. After all, this was not a committee mandate but a self-supporting system. It became the Airbus way. Jim Thorn at Hawker Siddeley understood this. Indeed, when the British government later pulled the rug, it was deeply personal relationships that kept Hawker Siddeley tethered to the Airbus dream. Without this umbilical cord, the UK's interest in the project would certainly have died.

'What surprised me was that this scepticism was not evident in Hawker Siddeley. They were much more practical and they shared my views. The problem was not to be chauvinist or to have the "not-invented-here" syndrome but to make use of everything available to succeed. They were pragmatic. That was why I always enjoyed working with them. All along.'

The next step for Beteille was to go to Munich to bond with Hans Schaffler's team. 'The Germans were less experienced in airplane production and they were more open to suggestions because of this but they eventually thought it was great to be involved in the overall project.'

Beteille stitched this together properly for an inter-government meeting in September and each government agreed to finance its own national companies. The teams began to meld together, but Beteille would need to find out more about the possible markets. Each group worked in its own design office but an international network of engineers began shuttling between France, Germany, the UK and later Spain and Italy, now a well-established part of the Airbus culture.

The early meetings were in Munich, Hatfield and Toulouse, although Beteille set up a tiny office in Paris. He built a team in the French capital with just one engineer, Jon Profel, as assistant and secretary. Beteille requested more administrative support from the partners and it grew slowly. As interest gathered, the

British, French and German governments met in September to iron out a proper agreement with representatives of Hawker Siddeley, Sud Aviation and Arbeitsgemeinschaft, for Germany. The HBN group looked at five main types, one of which was the HBN100. An HBN100 was drawn up with a 20 ft diameter, the width of the 747 fuselage.

While the governments were now committed to the idea, this put Beteille and his colleagues under increasing pressure. 'They placed an impossible target on us,' said Beteille, shaking his head in his Lausanne apartment. 'After one year, we were to have fifty orders; for a non-existing plane, made by a non-existing consortium, competing against Douglas, Lockheed and Boeing. And at a time when there was a recession in air-transport development!'

Beteille raised his eyebrow, without saying a word. Not only that, but there was Concorde to contend with too. 'And in France, Dassault was pushing with the Mercure programme. The Mercure would be very, very competitive against the Boeing 757,' he concluded. 'Finding fifty orders was a long way off, but building a system able to develop and produce a good aircraft to the requirements; that is what I thought was possible. And then we would be able to add a family of planes.'

Beteille then saw an intractable problem with BAC beginning to rear its ugly head. The British government was now being asked to fund the BAC Three-Eleven to join the One-Eleven and Two-Eleven to create a family of British-made planes at a time when enthusiasm for European co-operation was dwindling. The headlines about Concorde's delays and financial over-runs were certainly straining the Entente Cordiale. The HBN100 was picked as the design, and formal applications for funding were made on 15 October 1966. It was the same day that Conservative leader Edward Heath told his party conference that Britain must wholeheartedly embrace Europe by joining the EEC.

But the plane's specification was changing yet again and a new HBN100 was created to carry up to 320 passengers. The project was given the figure and number: A-300 or the Airbus 300-seater. 'At Sud there was no problem, I was the boss. The team in charge of looking at everything was led by my chief engineer Paul Ducasse. He was my right-hand man on the technical side. On the technical level there was no problem, people were working well together. We didn't agree on everything but after discussions it was no real problem.'

The choice of an engine was a hugely political decision. It was to be British and that meant only one thing: it must be Rolls-Royce. The initial development costs for the RB207 Turbofan – estimated at £60m but soon to be significantly more – were to be met to the tune of 75 per cent by Rolls-Royce, with the French SNECMA and the German MAN splitting the remainder. Roger Beteille was naturally cautious. And this caution turned out to be his sixth sense.

'The choice was take-it-or-leave-it. At the time in 1967, there was no competitor for Rolls. And why not? They were making good engines.' But, just nine months later, Rolls-Royce would seriously let them down.

7. BOEING, BOEING, BOEING

Boeing: confident, brash, cocky. And with good reason. In the early 1960s, Boeing was flying high, building up a commanding lead in the commercial airline market. Most surprisingly, it had all happened within the space of a decade.

In 1951, the Boeing President, Bill Allen, had flown across to the Farnborough Air Show in England to see the futuristic De Havilland Comet. He was mesmerised by its style and beauty. That night at dinner with Maynard Pennell, Boeing's chief designer, and Ken Luplow, the sales engineer, they talked about the British pacesetter.

'How did you like the Comet?' asked Allen.

'It's a very good airplane,' said Pennell.

'Do you think we could build one as good?'

'Oh, better. Much better.'

Allen's motto was: 'Act, get things done, move forward'. Six days after the first flight of the B-52 on April 1952, the Boeing board agreed to modify their military transport plane and make it fit for the passenger airline market. The company had the manpower and know-how to do the job. Now they had the approval; and they didn't hang about.

On 7 August 1955, the Gold Cup race for unlimited hydroplanes took place on the grey-blue waters of Lake Washington which laps around Seattle. It was a fine day out for picnics, boats on the lake and a chance for some corporate hoopla. A crowd of nearly 200,000 people turned up for the occasion. Boeing had been telling its people – and the local papers – all week that it would show off the company's new four-engine jet airliner, the 367-80, known as the Dash 80. A clutch of airline executives from across America had been flown in for the sparkling wine and a leisurely day by the sea.

Between the second and third heats of the Gold Cup, Boeing had arranged a special fly-past of their new four-engine jet. Behind the controls was Alvin 'Tex' Johnston, the Chief Test Pilot of Boeing, a showman to the soles of his leather-lined flying boots and one of the premier pilots of all time.

As the yellow and brown jet roared in at almost 500 mph, it swooped over the course at around 300 ft. It was so low the spectators could make out Tex's grinning face and his trademark white crash helmet. Then he pulled up hard on the throttle and, as the plane rose to 1,500 ft, he then attempted a barnstorming stunt, pushing the plane through a 360-degree barrel roll. The crowds tending the barbecues went ecstatic. And, as he turned the prototype commercial airline, he did it again.

Bill Allen was on the deck of his yacht next to the racecourse entertaining the Presidents and chief executives of most of the world's leading airlines. He'd invited them personally to come and witness this new product. His jaw dropped and he stood in stunned silence, while the airline executives queued up to slap him on the back after such a display of bravado.

The next day, Allen held an emergency board meeting of the Boeing Company. Tex was ordered to attend but turned up late as usual.

'Why did you do it, Tex?' asked Bill with a snarl.

Tex simply grinned. 'To sell your airplane,' he replied.

'You didn't have to destroy it!' countered Bill.

'I didn't. In a one-G roll, the airplane doesn't know it is right-side up, upside down or sideways. It flies as if it going straight and level.'

Bill raised his hand and pointed a finger at the flier. 'OK, smartass. You know that. We know that. Just don't ever do that with a Boeing plane again,' said the boss.

It was a sore point. Fifteen months earlier, on 14 May 1954, the shift changed at 4 p.m. at Renton. The huge hangar's doors rolled open and a new plane emerged from its secret hideaway.

The Boeing 367-80, her wing numbers bearing the name November 707, was ready for her maiden flight. A star was born and, at 72, founder William E Boeing was alive to witness a new epoch.

But there were severe problems ahead. 'When Johnston taxied the airplane a week later, he put her through some tough stops and turns. While wheeling into a final turn preparatory to take-off, the left wing suddenly dropped, the left landing gear collapsing into the wing, and the left starboard engine pod coming to rest on the taxiway,' recorded Eugene Bauer in *Boeing: The First Century*.

'The rear spar trunnion attachment for the main landing gear had fractured. In retrospect, the timing was fortunate. Had Tex not given the airplane that last severe manoeuvre, he would have taken off, with a near certain failure of the gear upon landing – a potential disaster, and a serious setback for the commercial jet age.'

The jet age demanded unyielding standards of excellence and new types of stronger steel that could cope with the rigours of flying. Boeing, with huge assistance and resources from the US Defense Department, found a new way of forging metal, resulting in the vacuum-melted steel that had excellent ductility and tensile strengths higher than any previous aircraft.

This improved technology went into all of the Boeing 707s. This plane was an outstanding achievement but the first models were too heavy and underpowered to make a non-stop transatlantic trip from New York to London. It was the BOAC's updated De Havilland Comet 4 that made the first true non-stop transatlantic flight of a civilian jet in October 1958.

Weight wasn't the prime consideration. It was the pursuit of speed. Boeing's 707 was faster and this allowed more flexible scheduling and the booming airlines liked that – even though there was a higher cost per hour in flight. This equation became an important turning point for Boeing.

The company, however, didn't have everything its own way; Douglas was right behind them. In June 1955, Donald W Douglas Sr, then in his sixties, had made the decision to go ahead with the DC-8, a more aerodynamically advanced aircraft with wings that were swept back by 30 degrees. This cut down drag as the aircraft approached Mach 1, the airspeed of an aircraft to the velocity of sound. In light of such vigorous competition, it was essential for Boeing to get Pan American to choose the Boeing 707.

Douglas had the advantage of longstanding relationships with the major airlines and considerable experience in suiting individual requirements without allowing the changes to disrupt the production line. Boeing was used to dealing with the military and tried to sell a bog-standard 707 to all of its customers. Juan Trippe, the pugnacious head of Pan American, tried to play off the two aircraft-makers against each other, wheeling and dealing between Douglas and Boeing. Boeing's 707-120 prototype was now flying well in tests, but Trippe wanted a larger plane to be powered by a new Pratt & Whitney engine, the J57. He needed it to cross the Atlantic non-stop.

Trippe, viewed as a reckless gambler, announced, 'If you won't build the plane I want, then I will find someone who will.'

Wily Bill Allen refused to budge, believing Trippe was bluffing. On 13 October 1955, Trippe threw a celebrated party at his New York HQ for airline executives. He then announced a double deal for $269m of jets. He decided to go for five DC-8s with full transatlantic range for a total of $160m. But, since the DC-8 was still on the drawing board, Pan-Am took out an insurance policy of twenty Boeing 707s for a contract of $100m.

'In Seattle, Allen read about Trippe's deal in the newspapers. As it stood, Douglas would corner the foreign market with its big, longer-range planes, and would carve out a huge piece of the domestic market as well. Commercially speaking, the current 707-120 design was doomed before it ever entered service,' says Eugene Bauer.

Allen was anxious. He rang Trippe long distance and offered to redesign the Boeing 707, using the more advanced J75 engine, and renegotiated the contract for a longer aircraft that would become the 707-320 Intercontinental. It was a deal. Within five years, this pioneering airliner sold more than the combined total of Boeing's previous 25 years. Pan-Am was hooked too. In the first quarter of 1959, 33,400 passengers were carried on the airline's new jets, with 90.8 per cent occupancy, an all-time record. Pan-Am sold its DC-8s to make its fleet all Boeing 707s. The sweetest irony for Boeing was that the order which overtook the previous record was with Air France, still keen to support a French-built product. The orders piled in. Boeing still wasn't able to say it was the top dog. That would take another eight years. But the transition from a military to commercial plane-builder was heading in the right direction.

After its late entry into the jet age, Boeing's engineering brilliance and manufacturing prowess allowed it to catch up. Soon its products would start to define the market. All of the US's scheduled carriers belonged to the Air Transport Association, set up in Chicago in 1936. It is a powerful body that has played a significant role in the safety of civil aviation, including the creation of America's air-traffic-control system. In October 1952, it could see the jet revolution approaching and decided to put down some markers.

The association issued detailed recommendations about jet transport design including the provision of carrying all fuel outside the fuselage, either in the wings, in pods on the undercarriage; wells to be designed to contain damage following a tyre explosion; the ability of a jet to land and take off in 40 mph crosswinds; and sealed electrical systems. It also determined some basic principles about jet engines that remain in place to this day. A plane must be able to fly at low speeds despite the failure of one engine in a two- or three-engine plane, or the failure of two engines in a four-engine or more aircraft.

René Francillon, author of *Boeing 707: Pioneer Jetliner*, said, 'In the light of the Comet One accidents, the Air Transport Association quite presciently favoured individual engine pods and expressed concern over cabin pressurisation problems. In the case of the power-plant, ATA considered it imperative that the engine installation . . . assured an advancement in the safety of airplanes with respect to fire over those provided by present transport airplanes. An engine fire should not jeopardise the airplane primary structure, adjacent engines, or airplane and engine controls.'

The Comet engines, buried in the wing beside the fuselage, looked sleek but it was now well understood that this was a commercial liability. What the aviation industry needed was more reliable jet engines that didn't cut out or catch fire and easier access for maintenance and repair. As it happened, the early Boeing 707 and Douglas DC-8 barely met the specifications of the ATA; but improvements were made quickly.

The introduction of the Boeing 707 was not without incident itself. On 25 February 1959, Pan American 707-121 shed an engine and pylon over France after simulating engine failure in a training flight, but landed safely in London. Another 707 landed on foam at Idlewild, New York, after losing its wheels on take-off, and a 707-123 crashed on Long Island during the simulated failure of two engines when it was in a 'dutch roll', a yawing motion that causes trouble at low speeds.

The spec improved dramatically and the 707-320, which first flew in January 1959, began a regular service from LA and San Francisco to London in August, with services across the Pacific the following month. To compete, TWA introduced their 707-320s over the Atlantic.

The mighty American industrial conglomerate General Electric – famous for its light bulbs – was applying its research and development muscle to the engine challenge too, and was beginning to power ahead. It was still classified information but GE's J-47 turbojet, the most powerful in the United States, was being rolled out by the US Air Force in increasing numbers. The engine powered the North American F-86 to a world speed record of 670 mph. However, to the Americans, in commercial aviation terms, those pesky British and their Comet jet remained a threat.

But Boeing was now spending far more on theoretical research. Professor Bill Birnbaum, who founded the US Statistical Research Laboratory in 1948, set up a school with twelve full-time professors of statistics. The university consisted of a few buildings scattered near the middle of the western shore of Lake Washington. The university embraces Seattle from the east and presses it against the inlet-filled Puget Sound, which spreads itself on the west side of the city.

Professor Wojbor Woyczynski recalled, 'We had a collaboration with the Boeing airplanes, with its headquarters and research labs located in Seattle, that lasted for a decade, mostly in the area of testing material fatigue and reliability of systems with many components. Boeing's interest was sparked by a series of crashes of the new British Comet jets. Of course, Boeing did not want to commit the same errors.

'Boeing initially retained me as a consultant for the Boeing Scientific Research Laboratories, to direct basic research – "future work", as they called it – on material fatigue and on the reliability of complex structures. With a team of mathematicians, some of them my former students, we formulated basic concepts of the mathematical theory of reliability of multi-component systems, and obtained many fundamental results.'

In the weeks after the Comet was launched, Boeing President William Allen faced even more domestic uncertainty. He was publicly opposed to moving the company's Seattle plant to another US city, saying the plant could not be moved without great loss in valuable personnel and costly facilities.

The question of moving had been aired because the US Air Force insisted that B-47 Stratojet bombers be built by Boeing's Wichita division in Kansas. Air Secretary Stuart Symington flew to Seattle to talk to Allen, but he was adamant. Allen, supported by the Democratic Senator for Washington State, Warren Magnuson, stated flatly that production of the C-97 cargo planes and B-50 bombers would not be moved from Seattle to Wichita. Boeing would be staying put. It was the prelude to a recurring debate that would break out over the next fifty years.

The company newspaper, *Boeing News*, asked Bill Allen about the future in its issue on 25 April 1957. The new Boeing 707 had set a record cross-country flight on 11 March and the cafeteria at Plant 2, at Boeing Field, was decked out in hundreds of US press stories raving about this American success. A new development centre at the south end of Boeing Field, across from Marginal Way, was being expanded to meet production. Allen was asked, 'What about the 707? Is there anything you can say about how long the company expects to be building them?'

'Well, I would say indefinitely. We will, of course, as we go along, continue to improve the airplane, develop new models, but we feel that we have a very sound product, one that will establish a new era in the transportation field. We are in the commercial business to stay and we intend to make a success of it, and that means we are going to be in the business indefinitely. We feel the airplane will prove attractive to a number of our customers and we fully expect to make substantial sales.'

Asked if he was looking into developing other types, he said, 'Well, we are constantly conducting studies involving new types. We are interested in serving the transportation industry fully . . . we recently announced a lighter version of our 707, namely the 717 which will operate in and out of smaller fields.'

Within five years, Boeing's gamble of moving into commercial jets was paying off big time. It was the premier team to beat – and this was before the launch of the jumbo jet. How could anyone knock them off their pedestal?

As ever, what is learned through misfortunes, accident and disaster proves as vital as work-bench testing when it comes to pushing the boundaries of aviation technology. And in 1962 the crash-test investigators worked flat out as Boeing planes were hit by a series of catastrophic accidents.

In March, an American Airlines 707-123B crashed after take-off from Idlewild, New York, killing all ninety people on board. This came after the crash of a Sabena 707-329 on its approach to Brussels in 1961, killing 72. Then a Continental 707-124 suffered an explosion in the toilet while cruising at 37,000 ft over Iowa, this act of sabotage costing 45 lives. Then 130 people died in an Air France 707-328 at Orly Airport, Paris, in June, while a few weeks later another Air France 707-328 was lost when it crashed into a mountain in Guadeloupe, killing 112. The final accident was when a Varig 707-441 crashed on to the Andes in Peru killing 97 people. It was all deeply disturbing, knocking public confidence in the emerging jet era. And, in France, it raised some questions about why the national carrier was buying US planes, rather than developing their own. Yet Boeing clawed itself back and only two 707s were lost the following year. The drive for absolute safety continued apace.

Flight International's technical editor said, 'The whole of this reputation has been won with a single basic design. It is a design which has established a wholly new 'plateau' of range, speed, payload, with seat-mile and ton-mile cost which are at present regarded as rock bottom. In fact, although it is ten years old as a concept, the Boeing 707 is economically impossible to beat, as its rivals know well. Nor will it be beaten, until fundamentally new designs involving extensive laminarisation, the jet-flap principle, variable geometry or high supersonic speeds come into everyday airline use.'

Boeing was stepping up its game. It now had the 727 triple-jet, with Pratt & Whitney JT8D-1 engines coming off the production and assembly lines at Renton. Mark Lambert, a pilot and air correspondent, was given a chance to fly a specimen on May 1963. 'Boeing has pushed every ounce of its vast experience with the 707 series into taming the high-performance wing it chose for the 727, and to make the aircraft reliable and easy to operate in the air and on the ground. The result is a thundering airplane that can be cruised at its limiting Mach or q from 10,000 ft to 37,000 ft, that can decelerate extremely quickly from those high cruising speeds, let down precipitately, loiter at any speed to fit other traffic, dawdle down to the runway at astonishingly low speeds and grind to a standstill in short order using high-energy wheel-brakes, spoilers and reverse thrust. And it can do this with 129 passengers in six-abreast seating in the traditionally wide and airy 707-type cabin,' said his breathless valedictory in *Flight International*. The Boeing 727 had just started service with Lufthansa and one of the earliest indications was that the Boeing plane experienced few mechanical faults. It was a superb piece of advanced engineering.

A typical flight for the Boeing 727 was Seattle to Denver, flying at 27,000 ft, followed by a continuation to Wichita, at 11,000 ft. Boeing built the plane to take a lot of punishment in daily use, but to be able to land easily to give the passengers a better ride. It took off well and was designed to land at just over 100 mph. The pilots adored it.

On the contrary, the British rival, the Trident, was not an easy plane to fly. It required three pilots in the cockpit, yet thousands of British aircrew started their careers on the plane known affectionately as the Gripper – it was so underpowered that it seemed as if it wanted to stay on the runway tarmac during take-off! Then again it was sold as an economy plane, rather than one with plenty of poke.

Yet Trident had been tailor-made to meet BEA's fickle requirements and its original incarnation could only carry 78 passengers on shorter European hops to Milan or Oslo. Export business was too tough for the stand-alone British plane-maker.

It was sandwiched between the Caravelle, still making a comfortable amount of foreign sales and into profit, and the Boeing 727, which was now cleaning up in their own backyard. The Trident 1A was aimed at American Airlines, still to make up their mind after Eastern and United ordered the 727, but American followed suit and placed an order in August 1961 for 25 727s. It was a severe blow for the British.

The Trident builders were finding it harder to please BEA, their key customer, and frustratingly so. No sooner was a modification approved and then made, than the airline requirements changed yet again. Boeing churned out dozens of 727s with little or no modifications, while Hawker Siddeley was always chasing new requirements. A more high-powered Trident 1E, with Spey engines, was produced with a lengthened airframe to take up to 110 passengers – the version most loved by the pilots. The 1C version could carry up to 93 passengers, but still the Trident lost a string of potential orders, including Alitalia, Japan Airlines and All Nippon.

John Cunningham, still acting as a test pilot, fumed after one demonstration tour to Australia, 'We have more pressing things to do than show the Trident to airlines who have bought the *other* aircraft. There's no sense in casting pearls before swine.'

JAL and ANA ordered the Boeing 727, while Alitalia ordered DC-9s and 727s. Kuwait Airways and then Pakistan International Airlines (PIA) signed deals for Tridents, with *Flight International* even suggesting that the selection by PIA of a Trident over the Boeing 727 was due in some ways to Pakistan's positive relations with China. Then, in November 1965, the very first Iraqi Airways jet airliner was a Trident 1E.

On 22 November 1965, the Minister of Aviation, John Stonehouse, confirmed to the House of Commons the UK government's support for the longer-range Trident 2E, which had an increased order from BEA. He told the MPs that £1,875,000 would be put into the project. Much of the work was to strengthen the wings and fuselage. This was promising news for the engineers at Hatfield, and John Cunningham took to the sky again flying the first Trident Two.

But serious problems were on the horizon. Writing in the *BEA Magazine* in 1966, Chairman Sir Anthony Milward said that his airline had 'a positive lack of capacity from about 1968–1969 onwards'. He then dropped a bombshell, confirming that he'd made recent visits to both Douglas and Boeing. He then added, 'This does not necessarily mean that we are looking to America for our future aircraft needs.'

This was pure brinksmanship. Milward declared BEA's inclination was to buy British, but that it could not afford to buy British if the product was not the best on the market. The options were a stretched Trident, a longer BAC One-Eleven or even a shorter 208-seater BAC VC-10. But the Boeing 727-200, the 737-200 and the DC-9-40 were all being examined.

Starting work in Hawker Siddeley's half-mile-long factory in Manchester at this time was a Manchester United fanatic following Matt Busby's great footballing side, including his heroes Bobby Charlton, George Best and Denis Law. He also watched as the wing spars left the factory en route to Germany. This young engineering apprentice, Mike Turner, would rise to become an important figure in the Airbus story. Turner later became the Chief Executive of BAE Systems, masterminding the UK company's partnership with EADS.

Milward warned the new Labour government, 'If a British aircraft was available to do this job at the right price, we would be delighted. At the moment there are no signs that such a British aircraft is available.'

It became public knowledge that BEA was seeking UK government approval to buy 35 727s and 737s for delivery from 1968. This was indeed a desperate turnaround for Hawker Siddeley Aviation who had worked so hard to accommodate BEA's ever-more capricious needs. Many people in the UK's aviation industry were astonished. John Cunningham was one: 'I found it rather hard to understand. Our lack of sales at Trident came about because BEA had insisted on a smaller aircraft for the European market, not the larger one they later demanded.'

But the political situation was delicate. The Plowden Report stated that Britain should continue to maintain an aircraft industry and Labour's election victory brought renewed interest in the merger of Hawker Siddeley and BAC with the UK government owning a major share. But there was growing discontent that Britain was dragging its feet on the Anglo-French Airbus. An open letter from a group of significant engineers, aviation experts and trade unionists in June 1966 raised serious points about the government's intention, including an order for American F1-11 jets, a failure to agree a vertical take-off plane, and the arrival of a US design organisation that was already recruiting 500 skilled UK designers. But it was the stagnation of progress on the Anglo-French Airbus that most angered the signatories.

Minister for Aviation Fred Mulley was under fire. There was no doubt that, while Mulley was a shrewd and able socialist politician, he had no experience of aviation. Britain received considerable credit facilities – around $1,250m or £450m – from the United States to buy Hercules, Phantom and F1-11 military planes. Labour and the Conservatives were staggered by the amount. Some said the figure was as high as £600m, if interest was added. Tory Sir Lionel Heald said, 'Before we allow £450m to be spent on American aircraft, the government should state its intention on the industry's future.'

On all fronts, Mulley, John Diamond, Chief Secretary to the Treasury, and Merlyn Rees, the Under-Secretary of State for Defence for the RAF, were challenged to support British aviation, rather than allow BEA to purchase American planes. Mulley needed a fudge and so announced that BEA should buy British and that a Labour government would help take steps to ensure BEA was able to operate a fully commercial fleet. Meanwhile, Mulley had other considerations on his desk. From June 1966, the Ministry of Aviation was evaluating Airbus's design proposals from the British aircraft industry. They now had a clearer idea of what was ahead with a preference for a 225–270-seater twinjet with the new Rolls-Royce RB178 engine. The Ministry expected such an Anglo-French plane to be in service by 1972.

There were also other pressing matters to deal with for Mulley. BAC offered its 99-seater BAC One-Eleven, then came up with a new version, the BAC Two-Eleven, but the British government would need to give £60m in launch aid for the development of this larger plane. In April 1967, Milward fired another broadside. 'Every week that goes by drives us nearer and nearer to buying the Boeing 727.'

Eventually, the BAC Two-Eleven was ditched and the Trident 3B, with a Rolls-Royce RB162 engine, given more support. It was BEA's *third* choice and they wanted compensation for taking the smaller British alternative and not getting the Boeing jets they really wanted.

Flight International expressed its doubts about a larger Airbus plane. 'We wonder if any European airbus should be so big. If high load factors on European routes could be reduced, which in the public interest they should be, such a very big jump in transport unit size would not be necessary. Traffic growth could be handled – and promoted – by the higher frequency that European air routes need above all.'

It was a point to chew on.

8. ENGINE FAILURE AND A US LIFELINE

Roger Beteille was still searching for his dream machine. He and his team in Toulouse were leading the design and management of the programme, but costs were escalating. Research and development outlay had jumped from £180m to £250m. And, in Derby, Rolls-Royce was still developing the programme for a brand-new engine called the RB207, which was running late. Something had to be done to get the engine project back on track.

'It was agreed between the governments that the engines were to be developed on slightly different types of co-operations,' Beteille recalled. 'Rolls-Royce was meant to be the prime contractor for the engine. It was agreed that Rolls would sub-contract certain parts. And the French and German governments would also contribute to the engine development.'

This of course led to discussion about the configuration of the engines and where they would be placed.

Beteille was adamant on this point. 'For the size of the Airbus, there was only one choice. Putting the engines in the rear, like the BAC One-Eleven, led to problems of loading the aircraft in airline operation. It is much better when the aircraft is large enough to have enough room to put the engines under the wings. There was no discussion for us.'

The partnership began working well, but the airlines were unimpressed. This new plane, the A300, was just too big – and too expensive. Air France was committed to it, but BEA was sitting on the fence. Lufthansa was also unsure and even expressed delight with its recent Boeing planes. Nobody really seemed to want it.

The grand project had nearly been killed off by one ministerial meeting after another. When the French franc collapsed and the original launch date of June 1968 was postponed, the two partners, Sud Aviation and Hawker Siddeley, were both preparing fallback options and studying smaller projects. As if to exacerbate the situation, the Rolls-Royce engine project had fallen even further behind. Rumours reached Beteille that testing at Derby wasn't going well.

'At the beginning of 1968, I felt that Rolls-Royce was not working as well as I would have liked. And the reason was simple. Rolls had a big commitment to Lockheed TriStar for the RB211 engine. They had some problems with the RB211 and my people in Derby told me that they saw some of their counterparts disappearing to help with the 211 job. It was clear to me that Rolls, like it or not, was not really putting proper efforts into my engine [the 207]. They were unable to handle both programmes together.'

Now, nearly forty years after the event, Beteille takes his time to tread very diplomatically around an issue that caused deep animosity for many years. In the early days of Airbus, there was still indecision as to which company would build the engine. The French company SNECMA had been partners with the American company Pratt & Whitney, which gave them a foothold in the deal with their proposed JT9D engine. However, Rolls-Royce made a strong argument that it was wrong to let an American manufacturer into a European deal. Rolls-Royce was arrogant, but had influence, and political clout: it secured the deal. However, now it was beginning to doubt that the French-led project was going to go anywhere. It wasn't alone.

Flight International commented, 'Something like £4 million has been spent by Britain alone on A300 studies, which have concluded that the launching cost, excluding the RB207 engine, will be £220–250 million for the fixed-price contract. This is higher than the launching cost of Lockheed's 1011. There is clearly no sense in collaboration which cannot compete with America on cost, and which is so Eurocratic that the only thing that ever flies is time.'

It was looking like a prime example of what the *Royal Aeronautical Society Journal* called the 'calamitous dissipation' of public money spent since 1951 on projects that were eventually cancelled.

'I thought at this time, perhaps if I had been in charge of Rolls-Royce I would have done the same thing,' Beteille said. 'My conclusion in May 1968 was that if I was to develop a glider I might have some success. But I needed an engine and I was far from the solution. I decided to check out my hunch, so I organised a meeting between Sir Denning Pearson of Rolls, Sir David Huddie and Maurice Papon, the President of Sud Aviation, in Derby, to really speak business.'

This meeting was going to be fiery. Beteille did his preparation and discovered the actual selling price of an RB211 engine, keeping a note of it in his pocket.

'When I finally got the price, I understood the proposition, because the two RB207 engines for my airframe would have cost me more than the three engines for the smaller RB211, which were being put on the Lockheed TriStar L1011.'

Beteille knew there was no way he was going to sell a twin-engine plane with fewer seats for more money than the Lockheed TriStar. It was crazy economics. He started to make some secret plans of his own.

'It was the end of it . . . for me,' he said. And it was also the beginning of the end of Rolls-Royce's relationship with the Airbus project. Despite its technical brilliance, the engine-maker's inherent reserve and cautious status towards Europe ultimately led to the company's bankruptcy and a later rescue by the UK government.

On 13 March 1968, Anthony Crosland, the President of the Board of Trade, announced the order of 26 Trident 3Bs valued at £83m, with options for ten more. Four months later, he made a further announcement about the compensation for not allowing BEA to take the Boeing 727. This was the 'Muliey pledge'. It cost an initial £25m and was calculated on the difference in seat-mile costs between the Boeing 727 and the Trident 3B. The £25m was transferred directly to a special account on which no interest was paid. Another £12.5m from BEA's airline borrowing could be transferred later. Milward described the settlement as 'fair but not generous'.

In a statement to the House of Commons of 10 July, Crosland said, 'The House will recall that, when the government decided not to approve BEA's original choice of American aircraft, the then Minister of Aviation gave a pledge that the government would take steps to ensure that BEA was able to operate as a fully commercial undertaking with the fleet it acquired.

'BEA subsequently chose for the first part of its requirement a fleet of 18 BAC One-Eleven aircraft, with the option for six more, and this was approved by my predecessor. For the second part of its requirement BEA eventually chose a fleet of Trident 3B aircraft . . . I have now approved a purchase of 26 Trident 3Bs at the cost of about $83 million, with the option of ten more. This aircraft is expected to come into service in 1971.'

In hindsight, this government intervention was a future lifeline for the UK industry and allowed the business to keep running in parallel with Airbus's development. If BEA had been allowed to take the US planes, Hawker Siddeley Aviation would not have been able to keep hold of its technical teams and vital future skills would have been lost for ever.

However, Boeing continued to ram home its relentless manufacturing advantage, pushing ahead even further. The first Boeing 737 for Britannia Airways was delivered to Luton Airport. The 117-seater was a stretched 737-200 heading for the charter routes. It was the first of five more to come. The deal for the first four was done through the US-Export-Import Bank who lent 80 per cent of the $15,535,000 price (then about £6.5m). The fifth was bought by Kleinwort-Benson, the London merchant bankers. The total cost was about £8m, with each plane requiring a British airworthy certificate costing £60,000. So Britain's scheduled airlines had the noisy Trident, a stalwart short-range servant for BEA for many years to come, but life was due to change.

Meanwhile, Beteille and Henri Ziegler, the newly installed Managing Director of Sud Aviation, who later became Airbus President, were ruthlessly looking at ways of making the Airbus design more cost-effective. They agreed to set up a small confidential planning unit to work up other ideas. Ziegler, then 61, was an influencer with impeccable contacts and credentials. Not only was he well regarded in British aviation circles because of his work on Concorde and his Anglophile views, but also he had been a test pilot and Deputy Director of the Centre d'Essais en Vol. Indeed, it was Ziegler who announced to the media in Paris in November that the 001 Concorde prototype would be making its first flight in May 1969.

During the Second World War, he had commanded the Free French Air Force in Britain and afterwards was Director-General of Air France until 1954. He had been Administrator-General of Breguet and was well disposed to Rolls-Royce, but he bowed to Beteille's judgement on an engine to power the new Airbus. But now the clock was ticking.

On Friday, 2 August 1968, a communiqué from the government ministers of Britain – represented by Minister for Technology, Tony Benn – France and Germany was issued in Paris. It said that Airbus would have another four months to complete its design, prune development costs and improve the operating economics. This was a broadside to Beteille and Ziegler. They had until the end of November.

Beteille didn't tell Rolls-Royce of his plans. But in his mind he was preparing for a divorce, leaving the engine-maker to pursue its American dreams. He had to take another tack and be ready to move quickly.

'We made secret proposals to continue with Airbus with the possibility of selecting another engine other than Rolls. I had in mind for some time that it was possible to develop a slightly smaller aircraft with an existing engine from perhaps Pratt & Whitney or General Electric. But these engines were not powerful enough for what I thought was properly competitive. Then around this time both decided to develop engines for the Lockheed L1011 and the McDonnell Douglas DC-10 long range. I thought the only way to develop this was to design an aircraft that can be fitted with the existing engines that somebody else can debug. So we went for this,' said Beteille. But, before he could satisfy his hunch, Beteille needed to understand the requirements of the airlines in America. After all, if this new European Airbus was ever going to outsell the Caravelle, the Trident or the BAC One-Eleven, it would need to crack America.

A few years earlier, the tough-talking Texan Frank Kolk, the Technical Director of American Airlines, had asked Boeing, McDonnell Douglas and Lockheed, the three leading US aircraft-makers, to look at a wide-bodied plane with two engines that could carry about 250 people on routes of up to 1,500 miles. The request was frowned upon by the airlines and plane-makers who thought four or at least three engines were required. Tri-jets were in vogue and Boeing's offering, Boeing 727, was a formidable competitor. Kolk persisted, saying that the airlines needed an aircraft that would carry twice as many people, twice as far as the bestselling Boeing 727. He said it was needed to lower the cost per seat per mile, so the airlines could make more money and offer cheaper flights. Kolk was an American visionary, and, with this in mind, Beteille organised a trip to visit United and American Airlines. Most of the big American airlines had large technical facilities and teams that were delighted to chew the fat with a highly regarded French aircraft designer.

'They were happy to discuss future projects and what they needed. I asked my European partners to delegate someone to go on the visit with me. Hawker Siddeley sent a marketing person, while the Germans sent Felix Kracht,' he said.

Beteille recalled with great personal pleasure the first meeting with the German engineer who played a central role in the Airbus story. 'I met him for the first time in San Francisco in the Mark Hopkins Hotel, where the United Nations treaty was signed in 1945. We went to the United Airlines building on Monday. It was the starting point. Felix and I exchanged views and we found we had a lot of ideas in common. We shared something because he was also a flight test pilot.'

It would become a renowned relationship and a bedrock for Airbus. Felix Kracht, nine years older than Beteille, was to become a soul mate and colleague committed to the European project and was duly dubbed the 'midwife' of the Airbus manufacturing system. Kracht's over-arching view was 'to execute a task once and in a single place'. It would become a signature tune for the German.

'We complemented each other. He was very good. We never put in writing our work share, we always did things by common agreement. But we worked like a team,' said Beteille.

So Beteille and his new-found friend Kracht went on to meet Frank Kolk. 'Kolk was a bit disappointed because he was a strong supporter of the twin-engine plane. Neither Douglas, Boeing or Lockheed had followed his views because they thought they had to develop tri-jets. He was very happy to meet somebody who was working on a twin-engine plane and he gave me his very detailed, technical specifications on what American Airlines would like to see as a twin. I used that and the airframe that I developed at Airbus was pretty close to that specification.'

This, according to Beteille, was why Airbus eventually succeeded in the market. 'It was slightly different from the requests expressed by the European airlines. The basic thing was: why have three engines when you can do the job with two? Of course, it has some consequences because even in the United States you have to cross the Rockies or fly coast to coast. I thought there could be an acceptable compromise between these market requirements in the United States and Europe with the exception of BEA, who were always at this time different!' he said raising his eyebrows, adding: 'Sometimes in the right things because they were asking for a two-man cockpit.'

Armed with this advice and Kolk's best wishes, Beteille returned to France. He then took one of his famous almighty gambles – he was going to design a smaller, cheaper plane, using existing engines that could be modified to get the required thrust.

On Wednesday, 11 December 1968, the 250-seater, now dubbed the A300B, was unveiled to the aviation world. In dual announcements, Sir Harry Broadhurst, the Chairman and Deputy Managing Director of Hawker Siddeley, in London, and Henri Ziegler, for Sud Aviation in Paris, said the new engine would be an RB211-28 with 47,500 lbs of static thrust. It was to be a more powerful engine and Rolls promised to offer 49,000 lbs of thrust within two years.

This created an intriguing new situation. As the plane was for 250 rather than 300 seats, it didn't need such a powerful bespoke engine, which of course had huge financial implications. Costs were normally defrayed over at least 200 aircraft sales, but, crucially, the estimated market for the A300B was up to 1,000. Now the engine that Beteille needed was more readily available.

There were some noises that the Airbus consortium was reverting back to its earlier plan of the HBN100, proposed three years earlier. But Beteille was unconcerned about such criticism. The length would now be 165 ft (rather than 176 ft 7 in), its wing span reduced to 147 ft (from 155 ft 6 in), and instead of room for 306 passengers and nine abreast, it would accommodate 252 seats, with eight abreast.

Meanwhile, Sir Harry Broadhurst, a pragmatic pro-European, and an unsung hero in the annals of Airbus, faced the newspapers and was pressed heavily by the reporters. He defended his ground admirably. He said the Germans were anxious to make the aircraft, the French were in a tough economic situation, but wanted to go ahead. And that some of the testing would be done in Hatfield. Sir Harry estimated the cost at about £170m, 10 per cent less than the A300. A saving of £20m with the national shares remaining the same.

What was Rolls's reaction to the loss of the RB207?

'You'd better ask them,' he said.

Would the smaller A300B now fit the airlines' requirements?

'We believe in it, and so do BAC,' said the Hawker man.

When was he going to talk to BAC?

'I passionately believe in European collaboration. We have got to get into bed with Europe on aircraft. We cannot get the money alone. Can BAC or ourselves raise £170m?'

The answer was no.

Would he accept co-operation with BAC if the government proposed it?

'It depends how they propose it,' he responded.

Would he be willing for BAC to have a share in the Airbus?

'We are doing the wing and the engine pods, which is quite an expensive pastime. We shall have to do a lot of spreading of work on the wing. BAC should answer that question.'

The final question was worth $64,000. Would the A300B be offered with the Pratt & Whitney JT9D engine?

'Yes,' Broadhurst said, 'the JT9D would be available if a customer with a large enough order were prepared to pay the engineering and certification costs.'

In light of the decision, Tony Benn, as Minister for Technology, was pressed to make a statement on the European Airbus. He had been a staunch supporter of Airbus at Cabinet meetings, but now he was wavering. 'The withdrawal of the A300 design presents the three governments with a new situation which they will have to consider,' he said. 'As far as Her Majesty's government is concerned, I must make it absolutely clear that I cannot in any way commit the government to give financial support to any new proposals which may be brought forward by the consortium.'

This was an ominous alarm bell from Britain. The UK government were now presented with a dilemma. Should they back the A300B or allow BAC to progress with the BAC Three-Eleven, which would be in direct competition to the Airbus and have to sell 150 to be viable?

If the British government was facing a tough decision, so was Beteille. With this new specification out in the open, Beteille had several engine options in front of him. Obviously Rolls-Royce was still in the fray, but there was competition from Pratt & Whitney's

JT9D and, coming up from the rear of the pack, the General Electric CF6-50. And it would be GE's legendary engine-designer, a German-born mechanic who had helped the Americans in China, who would eventually smooth the way.

'I think it was at this stage that the British government decided to get out,' Beteille recalled. 'There was no longer a Rolls monopoly guaranteed but the company was still in the competition. The new aircraft could have used RB 211 that was in development. But I don't think Rolls was very interested in that.'

With Rolls effectively out of the running, this then left just Pratt & Whitney and GE. Pratt had a good proposal, which was formally supported by the French government – an obviously political manoeuvre considering that Pratt was a shareholder of SNECMA. But General Electric, under the auspices of Gerhard Neumann, head of the engine department, had other ideas.

Neumann, born in 1917 in Frankfurt, Germany, was a master engine mechanic, who studied at Germany's oldest technical college, Mittweida. As an engineering student, he was saved from compulsory service during Hitler's military build-up but his mechanical talents gave him a ticket out of Germany. In May 1939, he accepted a position with a Chinese company, as an adviser in the use of German military equipment. Neumann arrived in Hong Kong to find that his contact had disappeared, and when Hitler invaded Poland, Neumann became an 'enemy alien' in the then British colony.

With some help from a Pan-Am Vice President, Neumann avoided internment and volunteered to join the Flying Tigers, an American volunteer unit of the Chinese Air Force. Neumann's amazing engineering feat was to assemble a functional Japanese Zero warplane from several damaged planes. With the information gained, US pilots improved their strategy and success rate in air combat. By the end of the war in Europe, Neumann was an American hero and was sent to Washington to report on classified material to General William 'Wild Bill' Donovan, founder of the OSS and father of the CIA. There Neumann also met his future wife, Clarice, an attorney with the Justice Department, and was granted US citizenship.

In 1948, he began a 32-year career with General Electric, where he rose to the rank of Vice President and Group Executive of the Aircraft Engine Group. At GE, he developed the variable-stator jet engine. The stator is the fixed axis of the engine. The rotors spin around this axis and draw in the vital air needed. Neumann built adjustable vanes in the stator that allowed the jet to increase air pressure in its compressor. It delivered a significant improvement in power and performance.

'We got on very well indeed,' Beteille said. 'Of course, we all had connections and stories from the Second World War. For example, I was in a small French Resistance stable that destroyed a Luftwaffe repair shop in Toulouse whose commander was a man that I met later as chairman of Lufthansa! But it was so long ago.'

Beteille decided to use Neumann's proposal as a back-up, with Neumann promising a boost to the CF6, which would deliver 47,300 lbs of thrust on take-off. This updated engine would be called the CF6-50 and be available for delivery from September 1972. However, there was still the problem of governmental intervention – which had already cost almost two years of delays. Beteille, of course, wanted to ensure this would not continue should he opt for the GE engine.

'I obtained from the officials a document that said they would refrain from interfering. That it was my industrial responsibility to take all technical decisions and all decisions including selection of avionics and the engines. But they just said that we had to get their approval for our choice. I had it in writing and I prepared it in such a way that the Germans and the French would agree.' When Neumann was told, he was delighted.

'I had always the feeling that GE were confident in the success,' Beteille said. 'They put in their money. It made a great deal of sense because the DC-10 was fitted with the same engine and they could be complementary.' Ever the pragmatist, Beteille now concluded that he really needed to look at increasing co-operation with the Americans. After all, a European plane needed to have appeal in the United States if it had any chance of breaking into this market.

So Beteille began working with Brian Rowe, the famed British engineer who ran GE's engine division and who would build up a long-standing relationship with Airbus. Rowe rose from his job as an engineering apprentice to become President of General Electric Aircraft Engines. Later he would be the leader who delivered the CFM56 engine for the Boeing 737s and Airbus A320s. However, the political manoeuvrings of one of the governments in the partnership would soon put the entire project in jeopardy.

Wednesday, 9 April 1969, was supposed to be a celebration of the greatest joint technical achievement Europe had ever known. Concorde 002, the oft-delayed offspring of French and British ingenuity, took to the air at Filton, near Bristol. Chief Test Pilot Brian Trubshaw, a household name throughout Britain, took the new plane on a 22-minute flight to RAF Fairford, Gloucestershire, which was greeted by scenes of rejoicing in the UK aviation industry. However, just 24 hours later, the up-beat atmosphere was utterly destroyed as Minister of Technology, Tony Benn, announced Britain's withdrawal from the A300B project.

Britain, according to Benn, was withdrawing because the government was not satisfied that the project would be a good investment at this stage. The total development cost was estimated at £180m – with Britain expected to underwrite £60m – and, Benn claimed, all along the UK government had stated that a go-ahead would only be taken on the basis of substantial orders; so far there were none. Tellingly, Benn added that the government was concerned at the complete lack of assurance from the other partners that a Rolls-Royce engine would be chosen. It was an assurance that would have been difficult to give, as Beteille's secret team of airframe designers had already chosen the General Electric CF6-50.

In hindsight it is easy to criticise the UK government and Tony Benn for a lack of vision over Airbus, but the calamitous fortunes of the Concorde – just fourteen planes flew commercially, seven each bought by Air France and British Airways, and sold at a production cost ten times over budget, and this was after writing off the £1,000m developmental cost – were to ultimately inform any decision on commercial aviation and European co-operation. It was fortunate that others did not give up on the European vision so easily.

Roger Beteille says he believes Hawker Siddeley Aviation remained loyal to the project because they were now tightly bound up with the Airbus concept. 'I think my idea that everyone would be involved as equals, rather than sub-contractors, played its part at this point. It increased Hawker's participation with the project after the UK government's decision to pull out. They continued because they had confidence in the system. I think they felt part of the culture that we had already. I'm not certain, but I think so. If I had been in their shoes, I would have stayed with Airbus,' he said.

Hawker Siddeley, with work on the stocks handling the Trident 3E, secured by Mulley's promise, stuck with Beteille and the Airbus consortium. With factories at Hatfield and Chester at full stretch, they felt able to risk a major investment of up to £20m working on the A300B wing.

At the sixtieth anniversary of the Paris Air Show, an event first held in 1909, Concorde took pride of place with a majestic ceremonial flypast along the Champs Elysées before landing at Le Bourget. It was a statement of immense French national pride. On Thursday, 29 May 1969, the opening day, the French and German governments, represented by French Minister of Transport, Jean Chamant, and the West German Minister for Economy, Karl Schiller, signed a new agreement, each taking a 50 per cent shareholding in Airbus Industrie, with Roger Beteille as Managing Director. Hawker Siddeley, with their advanced wing technology, chose to stay with the programme and became the major sub-contractor, signing a binding agreement with Sud Aviation and Deutsche Airbus to supply the main wing boxes for the prototypes.

A mock-up of the A300B fuselage, to be built by Airbus Industrie, was unveiled with Hawker Siddeley's logo on the side. The British Action Committee for Aerospace, a pressure group, said it believed the UK government would be throwing away an unrepeatable opportunity to redress the balance of payments if it did not invest in the project. 'It would be disastrous to have two rival airbuses in Europe, killing each other's prospects,' it said.

The UK's balance of payments deficit was a worrying phenomenon. Trade figures were so volatile that when a couple of Boeing jumbo jets were delivered to British Airways it upset the monthly trade figures just before the general election. Harold Wilson lost unexpectedly to the Conservative and pro-European Ted Heath. Even to this day Labour party strategists point to those planes as the tipping point that pushed Wilson out of Downing Street.

President Charles de Gaulle and the German government under Kurt-Georg Kiesinger gave their consent to support the construction of the prototype of the A300B. After more than 3,700 test hours using over thirty various design proposals, the very first Airbus aircraft programme entered its final design stage at the beginning of 1969. Throughout the year, Airbus continued to attempt to convince the UK to come back to the negotiation table, with no success.

Sir Ronald Edwards recommended that both BOAC and BEA, the UK's national carriers, become controlled by the single British Airways Board (BAB). But the Labour government took it further and merged the two airlines on 31 March 1974. From then on, the Tridents became a rather unloved part of the British Airways fleet, even though the planes did pioneer Autoland, an auto-pilot instrument landing system, designed by Hawker Siddeley and Smiths of Cheltenham, which helped planes land blind in fog-bound and low-visibility airports.

It was at this point that British Airways' long and fruitful relationship with Boeing began, and it would be many years before Airbus gained a foothold. In 1977 British Airways was looking at buying the Boeing 737, DC-9 or the 7X7, later to become the Boeing 757. In July 1978, British Airways placed an order for nineteen Boeing 737-200s and later signed a letter of intent for nineteen 757s. The fuel savings alone on the Boeing 757 were 40 per cent better than the Tridents.

In mid-1970 the Conservative government issued their final refusal – essentially reiterating Tony Benn's misgivings of the previous year – and added that they would support the BAC Three-Eleven. The door was closed on Airbus.

9. THE MAKING OF THE AIRBUS 300B

Feet or metres? Inches or centimetres? It's the most basic decision when fixing a stack of shelves to the wall, or laying carpet in your home. But it took some time for Airbus to decide what system of measurement was to be used.

Would it be European centimetres and metres, or Imperial feet and inches? And what language would the new company adopt? Adam Brown of Airbus said, 'We realised that if we wanted to break into the American market we had to speak English. It was going to be hard enough translating everything from centimetres into feet and inches.' So one of the first casualties was the metrification of Europe.

'It's clear that we had a very good plane from the start. Of course, we had built this plane on the basis of the experience of Hawker Siddeley, of Sud Aviation and advanced technology coming from the Concorde. Then we'd taken some of Frank Kolk's planning. Everything was possible to get things to work. It was very difficult because of the fuel crisis and a problem was the credibility of Airbus Industrie because nobody knew about us and we had no products flying. It was some kind of international system with an unknown business model.'

By the end of March 1972, Airbus Industrie – now the Paris-based management company run by Beteille for the Airbus – had only ten orders; six from Air France, four from Iberia, with options from the same airlines for ten and eight respectively. Hardly an auspicious start, particularly as, over the pond, the first two Lockheed L1011 TriStars, with the Rolls-Royce RB211 engine, were handed over to Eastern Airlines and TWA for crew training. Including an Air Canada order, 22 TriStars were due to enter service.

However, the TriStar project was not quite the success the sales suggested. Rolls-Royce desperately needed more taxpayers' money – even though they were already being funded by the British government to the tune of £190m – to make ends meet, while in America Lockheed was awarded a US government guarantee for a $250m bank loan to keep the TriStar programme viable. However, the lack of Airbus orders, and their rival's perceived successes, could not allow Beteille and his team to lose focus.

'There were two tasks. The first was to design, develop and produce a good airliner. That I thought was something I could do and one way or another I felt able to do. But the second was much more difficult. How was I going to build a system of companies, people and systems working with the same efficiency? It was impossible at this time to think about a single company. Absolutely impossible,' said Beteille.

The logistics of the early Airbus operation were mind-boggling to comprehend. The total investment in the early 1970s was more than $1bn – around £260m – half provided by the French government, slightly less than half by the Germans, with the Dutch bringing in a 6.6 per cent share and the Spanish contributing about 2 per cent. Hawker Siddeley was the UK's only investor.

Beteille now surrounded himself with people who shared his own vision, people such as Aerospatiale plant manager Bernard Dufour who was given carte blanche to get on with the day-to-day work. Dufour had worked on the Concorde project and was convinced there was a better, more direct, way of working.

'There was great pride. Bernard saw the aircraft as the most daring of European joint ventures which formed the basis of an industrially integrated Europe,' said Beteille. 'But there was a determination on the part of all of the partners to maintain strong national industries within the European context.'

Felix Kracht was quoted in *Flight International* as saying: 'At the outset the A300B programme was regarded with a certain amount of scepticism and the European aircraft industry was accused of wanting to produce a consortium aircraft for which nobody would take the responsibility when things became serious.' He said the creation of Airbus Industrie had nullified that argument.

The French side became the Aérospatiale Group, created when Nord and Sud Aviation merged on 1 January 1970, while the German partners involving Messerschmitt-Bölkow-Blohm (MBB) and VFW-Fokker, became Deutsche Airbus, founded by MBB, in order to 'enable the financing of the high production costs of the Airbus programme'. At the head of its board of directors was the then Bavarian Minister of State, Franz Josef Strauss.

This larger-than-life Bavarian statesman with a formidable mind was despised by the Social Democrats in northern Germany, but adored by his heartland. And while he fought hard for Munich and the south, he was also a committed European. He was a dedicated initiator from 1967 when negotiations about the intended new European aircraft company first took place. A controversial figure, nonetheless, he is rightfully called one of the godfathers of Airbus Industrie. Roger Beteille admired him, saying that he was a most impressive individual, capable of talking action.

Beteille's first plan was to build the largest components – such as the wings and the fuselage – in factories near a seaport. A very sensible idea. The parts from Britain and Germany would then be shipped to France and on to final assembly in Toulouse. Not only that, Toulouse is 100 miles from the sea.

Adam Brown recalls, 'It seems so normal and well-oiled now because the system works like clockwork, but at the start it was strange to have those large parts being shipped across Europe. Toulouse wasn't convenient because the ships brought the part to Bordeaux, then we used a barge up the Garonne and a road transporter.'

But the increasing congestion of a convoy of ultra-heavy vehicles on the small country roads and through the towns became too much and an alternative was needed. This was when Felix Kracht had a brainwave: a large converted air freighter to airlift the parts. He watched American pilot Jack Conway concoct an out-size transporter for NASA rockets where the nose opened up and allowed a whole fuselage or wing section to be slid on board.

'When he first proposed using a large airplane we looked at him with incredulity,' recalls Beteille. 'It was going to cost us a fortune, but then it saved us so much time. It was another touch of his brilliance. So the Airbus Super Guppy was born.' The Super Guppy, however, made the headlines for the wrong reasons. On 22 March 1972 the Super Guppy was damaged at Finkenwerder, Hamburg, when the undercarriage collapsed.

The wing components were built in Hamble, Hampshire, and Brough in Yorkshire. The wings, assembled in Chester, were then transported by the over-sized Super Guppy from Manchester Airport. The wing box which fits the wings to the fuselage was also made in Chester. The standard sections of fuselage were manufactured at Einswarden, on the north coast of Bremen, by VFW-Fokker who were headquartered in Amsterdam. The sections were shipped by barge up the Weser river to the Lemwerder plant and then flown to Toulouse. The middle of the fuselage – known as section 15 – above the wing box, which required special assembly, was built by Messerschmitt-Bölkow-Blohm. It was then shipped to St Nazaire for assembly before being transported to Toulouse.

Spain's involvement was the horizontal tail, which was built in Seville by CASA, together with some of the doors. To balance this work-sharing, the engine pylons, the strengthened brackets which hold the engine to the wings, were transferred from near Paris to the Deutsche Airbus companies in northern Germany. To rationalise its work, MBB began to concentrate its operations at Hamburg and near Stade, while the General Electric CF6-50 engines were assembled by SNECMA, in Paris and Munich.

This was the start of a unique system that has been refined to perfection over the last 35 years. But in the early 1970s it seemed like an improbable way of working. Over at Boeing there was some amusement about components being shipped halfway round the continent. The Boeing sales team used to superimpose a map of Europe over America to show the distances travelled by the Airbus manufacturers and then pose the question: 'Is this really efficient and modern airplane production?'

Boeing may have mocked – and its current 787 involves components from twenty countries shipped around the world – but the Airbus 300B was taking shape. The first prototype was complete and the first General Electric CF6-50A engines had been delivered to Toulouse from the Rohr corporation in Tula Vista, California, where they were being placed in their pods. The twin-aisled plane was then flown back to Hamburg to have the eight-abreast seats – two on each window side, four in the middle – and interiors fitted. Once completed, it was sent back to Toulouse for final test flying before delivery to the customer.

Increasingly Felix Kracht and his colleagues came up with solutions to dozens of the little technical problems that daily beset such gigantic industrial undertakings. 'There was a lot of work to undertake. It was using a lot of my time. The technical stuff was now relatively easy. The problem was that the people were not under my control. I had to have them working under my control without doing it to some extent, yet still working under the old principles of co-operation and mutual respect,' he later recalled.

The central management of the Airbus project Groupement D'Interet Economique (GIE), a joint venture according to French jurisdiction, was a system that worked well for many years. While the partners continued to exist as independent companies and were even able to compete in other markets with each other, the GIE kept the ownership rights over all developments of new products in the business area concerned. It was a coup for Beteille, and a testimony to his way of working – although its existence would eventually become a stumbling block over the planned development of the Airbus A380.

The Toulouse headquarters was owned by the GIE and while normal accounting principles were applied to the business, through a profit and loss account presented annually to the board of directors, there was no obligation to publish these accounts. This policy would form the basis of Boeing's recurring complaint about Airbus subsidies.

The administrative council had Strauss as President, representing Deutsche Airbus, with Sir Harry Broadhurst on the council as an adviser. Ziegler was the managing director, with Beteille as technical director and project co-ordinator and another Frenchman, Didier Godechot, acting as commercial and sales director. Felix Kracht completed the team as production director.

Just before Christmas 1971, the state-owned Spanish CASA (Construcciones Aeronauticas SA) joined the consortium with an increased share of 4.2 per cent, with the French and German share reduced to 47.9 per cent. Henri Ziegler, reappointed by the French Cabinet as President and Managing Director of Aerospatiale, became more passionate about European integration, particularly after the initial flight of the A-300B.

'You have 200m Americans running a large part of the wealth of the world, and as many in Russia. If we wish to stay friendly with them, but free to have our own way of life, we have to work together whether we like it or not,' he said. 'Forty months from the launching in June 1969 to the first flight is absolutely remarkable in a programme of this complexity – nobody in the United States is doing better than that. Sometimes the discussions have been very difficult but we have always reached a decision, and when the decision is reached the chief executive has implemented it.'

Those implemented decisions paid off on 28 September 1972, when a stunning white plane, with orange and yellow stripes along the length of the fuselage and Airbus's round logo on the tail, was revealed, alongside the Concorde 02, to the public in Toulouse. This was F-WUAB, the A300B1 prototype and the following month it flew for the first time. The test crew, in red boiler suits and looking like Formula One pit-stop mechanics, took to the air under the command of Max Frischl, with the young Bernard Ziegler, son of Henri, as his number two. Bernard was directing operations: 'Being a test pilot and being in charge, I was the man expected to make the first flight, but Max was a very experienced test pilot and I took the decision to put him in the captain's seat. The decision surprised the Airbus management, Roger Beteille and my father!' Later Ziegler would be Chief Pilot of the A310 and co-pilot to Pierre Baud for the flight of the first A320. It was three years and five months after the Franco-German agreement was formally signed in Paris in May 1969.

Meanwhile, Lockheed's sales continued apace with Japan's All Nippon Airlines ordering six TriStars, with 345 seats, a deal worth £55m. Japan was undergoing phenomenal passenger growth of 35–45 per cent in 1967 and the Tokyo-Osaka route was becoming the second most dense air route in the world after San Francisco to Los Angeles. There were now 11 TriStar customers with commitments to 184 aircrafts. Then Japan Airlines ordered four Boeing 747SRs – initially with 498 seats – for service on the Tokyo-Fukuoka and Toyko-Sapporo routes. What was interesting was the steady demand for larger planes. Was the A300B just too small for the future market? This was an issue that was perplexing the wine-sipping strategists and thinkers at Toulouse.

The first A300B out of production took off on 15 April 1974 and the four prototypes began the certification programmes. For a long time, Air France seemed to be the only customer who put any trust in the new plane. Between the end of 1975 and May 1977 Airbus failed to get a single order and the jokers in Toulouse urged Airbus's workers: 'Don't miss the last train out of town to Germany.'

10. A SPACEMAN'S EASTERN MAGIC

Making a plane is one thing, but finding people with deep enough pockets ready to buy it is quite another. As Airbus was to painfully find out in the early days of the A-300B. Beteille knew he had an extremely good aircraft, he just couldn't get the customers to see that. They had a problem with marketing their airplane – 'A major problem,' he recalled later – and needed a breakthrough. Eventually it came, and it was due in no small part to a former American astronaut, who'd been the command pilot of the Apollo Eight, the first space flight around the Moon.

It was the Americans who were the whizzes at sales. Their culture was built on the ability of selling all the products of the capitalist system. In the late 1960s and early 1970s, the colleges were churning our management and marketing majors who took American-made tools, cars, fridges, washing machines and whatever else was saleable around the globe.

There were patches of good sales people in Europe. 'Those who were considered really good in marketing were Hawker Siddeley, the British, people such as Brian Botting. And the others? Well, some French people were good, but very few. The Germans had no experience. And some did a very good job but they had to learn. Learning on the job is all very well but to have a real chance we had to have trained people such as Adam Brown,' said Beteille.

Adam Brown was the key to resolving many of the sales and marketing issues now facing the fledgling aircraft makers. Brown's cerebral approach was to crunch the numbers, examine the market and then present the facts. Airbus's new planes were the latest on the market. They were modern, efficient and represented value for money. But that simply wasn't going to be enough.

The selling of wide-body planes was becoming a matter of international concern. Increasingly it involved a whole gamut of government officials and ambassadors, intermediaries and middle-men, sales agents and dodgy politicians all trying to get their snouts into the trough. No international rules regulated this trade, so bribery and corruption became an accepted way of life. Doing deals was not a gentlemanly handshake after a PowerPoint presentation, it involved convoluted trading, sweeteners and 'most favoured nations' clauses – and everyone was playing the game. You wouldn't have survived long without joining in.

Even by the early 1970s Airbus was not on the radar screen at Boeing. The *realpoliltik* of the time involved the all-powerful US military-industrial lobby with McDonnell Douglas, Lockheed and Boeing, three mighty pillars of this international arms trade, selling bombs, rockets, missiles, bombers and fighters and helicop-ters to a list of friendly nations approved by the US government. But the battle for wide-bodied commercial plane sales was a significant part of their business and the big three employed the same tactics as the arms trade. Morality wasn't an issue; sales were the goal. So breaking into this American club was going to be difficult. Difficult was a severe understatement.

'The airlines were not eager to get the aircraft that we were told they wanted,' admitted Beteille. 'In fact most airlines were quite satisfied with the Boeing 727. It was a good aircraft. I don't think Boeing had any problem, I just think they significantly under-evaluated the possibilities of Airbus's success. They were making very good planes. They were selling a lot of them. They had the 747, the 737 and they made a very good start against the DC-9. They were selling a lot of Boeing 727s,' he said.

Beteille was told time and again that Airbus could not sell because it has not sold. A chicken and egg situation. 'The airlines looked at the Europeans as a consortium that cannot work except with a lot of extra cost and delays,' he said.

He would have to prove them wrong but it would take a lot more toil and cunning against the Americans. Lockheed and McDonnell Douglas were treating the contest between the TriStar L1011 and Douglas DC-10 as a strategic battleground, which was not without controversy. A series of scandals involving weapons and airplanes began to tarnish the industry. Lockheed was exposed making bribes and commissions worth $24m – half of this to persuade the Japanese government that All Nippon Airways should take the TriStar. The contest was getting ugly.

At the same time, however, there were some significant milestones for Airbus. The A300 entered commercial service on Wednesday, 23 May 1974, when Air France put the aircraft on its service from London to Paris. On its first day it completed two return trips and on the first flight all 225 economy and 26 first-class seats were full.

Meanwhile, Boeing passed through an even more significant landmark. The company announced it had delivered 2,500 commercial jets since the first Boeing 707 was handed over to Pan American in 1958. The 2,500th was a 737-200 delivered to a Dutch carrier, Transavia Holland. Boeing's total was daunting: 878 707s and 720s, 1,035 727s, 354 737s and 233 747s.

Undaunted, Airbus Industrie was now working on a new concept that would be one of its finest achievements: a family of planes that would have the unique Airbus signature stamp. The A300 B9, B10 and B11 versions were being worked up as designs. The new version would become known as the A310.

Beteille was also about to get another ally – a man he described as 'a free bird, singing outside'. Fellow Frenchman Bernard Lathiere, born in Calcutta where his father was a Michelin Tyres representative and Airbus's second President, arrived in Toulouse from the French Civil Service where he was in charge of airline policy.

'When I took over, things at Airbus were not brilliant,' he recalled. 'There were not many sales. We were losing contracts to Boeing but we learned much more from losing than from winning. We had to change the pace, the approach, the way of selling, our after-sales service. Only a few airlines really believed in us,' he recalled.

Meanwhile, the A300 was receiving some critical acclaim for its performance, proving to be cheaper than a tri-jet, with much lower fuel consumption. Even better was the news that the British Board of Trade, which monitored all landings at Heathrow Airport, found none of the Air France flights registered on its noise-level equipment. This was a quieter plane and this would become a selling point as decibel-levels around congested airports became a significant social issue. Surely Adam Brown could use this to boost sales?

'Yes, we were very pleased with the early results. Air France pulled all their statistics together to say the A300 was the most reliable aircraft it had ever introduced, even easier to introduce than the Boeing 727 they said. This was all helpful,' said Brown.

Critical acclaim was one thing, cold hard sales quite another. Orders trickled in from Lufthansa, Sabena and Iberia, although the new British Airways displayed a distinct lack of interest in both the standard A300 and the cut-back 200-seater. In the World Airline Census in December 1974, Airbus had eighteen orders, with five in service. For eighteen months Airbus did not book a single order. Airbus seemed headed for catastrophic failure.

Riding into the oil crisis, the future looked bleak – even the big three were finding it exceptionally hard. The mighty Pan-Am was on the brink of collapse as it tried to extend its credit. Between 1971 and 1976, America's five major carriers, which flew one in three of all passengers, bought only 4 per cent of the new aircraft. Boeing's orders were coming from foreign airlines. Americans began to hear the alarm bell. They needed a proper policy of working with European partners and increasing their involvement. If they wanted to win more European business, they needed to find a way of putting something back, the way GE had with SNECMA. Air Siam ordered a couple of Airbuses, then Korean Airlines ordered six, and then salesman Harry Rhoades negotiated a deal with Thai Airways International which ended a lean period when they ordered ten A300B4s.

'The sales were not going well at all. But looking back, this was a good thing. During the recession we were able to develop and introduce the aircraft so that we were really in the market when the market recovered. Otherwise I think all the airlines would have bought a lot of DC-10s and Lockheed TriStars 1011s and it would have been increasingly difficult to sell a new plane.'

Then an Airbus legend was born. The boss of Eastern Airways, Frank Borman, agreed to order four A300B4s. It nearly caused an international incident and it remained a running sore in European and US trade relations for many years. Yet Borman was a former astronaut and an all-American hero. He retired as an astronaut in 1970 at 42, and was now running Eastern Airlines. In *The Sporty Game*, Newhouse quotes Borman saying, 'In 1975–76 we were virtually bankrupt. Our bankers would not roll over a $75 million obligation due then. We had to freeze wages. Our franchise was our most important resource.'

The deregulation of US routes was just beginning and Florida to New York was a lucrative prize. It was fast becoming the Sunshine State for short-break New Yorkers who were snapping up condos on the coast. Eastern were competing with several other airlines on flights into Florida, especially National. A squabble broke out between the two airlines which became known as the 'cocktail war'.

Three days after National resumed operations after a 110-day strike it found itself entering the peak holiday season with only a few reservations. Most travellers had already booked Eastern or Delta. So National ran a provocative advert: 'I am going to fly you to Miami like you've never flown before.' The ad offered two free cocktails and free wine with a meal for those flying economy. Eastern reacted angrily and said they too would offer free drinks and that the policy would be extended to other routes as soon as possible. National blamed Delta, as during their strike Delta had offered free steak and champagne on the route. It was estimated that the free drinks alone would cost Eastern $1m on the New York–Florida route. The 'cocktail war' had begun and would soon escalate to take in almost every major airline in the world.

While the squabbles continued, Airbus pulled off an extraordinary deal. 'I was involved with the discussion with Eastern Airlines from the start,' said Bernard Lathiere. 'I was out in the United States regularly working alongside George Warde whom we hired. George was previously the technical director of American Airlines after Kolk, and chairman for a few months after that. He found out that Eastern was trying to find a 200-seater plane to complement or replace the Lockheed TriStar L1011s that they already had.'

George Warde used his connections with blue-eyed Borman to persuade the Eastern Airlines management to invite Airbus along for a discussion. Lathiere recalled, 'We appointed George and nobody in the airlines we visited anywhere in the world could say that we didn't know what it was they needed in this department. Warde knew the importance of after-sales service, spares, and that it has to work 24 hours a day, seven days a week.'

Still, as rank outsiders, any bookmaker would have been delighted to give odds of 1,000-1 at this stage, considering the Airbus team were up against Boeing, Lockheed and McDonnell Douglas. 'When we succeeded in getting the invite, George asked me to go and make the presentation. I said I was not a specialist marketing man but I knew what I was talking about. So I prepared the sales plan,' recalled Beteille.

The dark-suited Airbus team, including Beteille and Lathiere, flew across in an Air France Concorde to New York and then down to Miami. 'It happened that we were the last to give our presentation. Frank Borman and his team had listened to the others all morning and just after lunch it was Airbus's turn. And that was a chance, because we had no time limit. I put to them a convincing presentation and Borman was very interested. It ended with a proposal that we discussed internally in Airbus. Contrary to the subsequent complaints, we did not invent this kind of deal, it was something that had happened previously with Boeing for flying-boats and Amtrak for buying trains.'

Beteille offered to lease four aircraft for a test with the airlines. A few days later, the Miami sales team sent a cryptic message to Beteille and Lathiere waiting back in Paris: 'Congratulations, you have got a blue-eyed baby,' said the telegram.

'This was possible because we had four white tails [planes built and ready to fly]. And this was the start.'

This was the breakthrough. After a successful four-month trial, on 6 April 1978, the Eastern board agreed an order for 23 planes, with options for several more. It also involved Airbus taking a shareholding in Eastern. But Borman's bold move brought instant complaint.

'What I was surprised about was that the US Department of Commerce and the US government created a lot of problems for us because, in their opinion, this was a dumping, predatory policy. Yet this was something that was already being done in the United States by Boeing. This was nothing new, but we had to do a lot of lobbying just to explain that we were dumping nothing. We were just doing fair business,' said Beteille, pointing a finger to make a point.

'It was a chance for us because Frank Borman could not be considered a bad American. Two years earlier, we had a previous problem with Western Airlines when everything was decided but they were under political pressure from Washington and they had to change the decision at the last minute. It was when the chairman phoned me to say that he was very sorry but that the decision had to be changed. He called at my home and said he hoped one day that he might be able to buy Airbus,' Beteille said.

Frank became a close friend. Newhouse in *The Sporty Game* said, 'Borman's board was enthusiastic about the purchase of Airbuses because Eastern could not have bought the new airplanes it urgently required except on the remarkably generous terms which the Europeans offered.'

Borman was accused of being un-American, despite the deal being brokered on economic necessity – essentially Eastern couldn't get the planes they needed without Airbus's generous terms. He even received an angry call from Charles Forsyth, a Vice President of McDonnell Douglas, questioning his patriotism. Borman simply asked what car Forsyth drove, knowing that the answer would not be an American model. Anyway, Borman argued, the Airbus had plenty of American parts, not least of all the GE engines.

Boeing's treasurer told the House sub-committee that the Airbus sale involved 'predatory export financing schemes'. He described the Eastern sale as 'an excellent example of the extent to which European aircraft manufacturers and their governments are willing to go to penetrate new aircraft markets.'

Despite the protestations from Boeing, the floodgates were slowly creaking open for Airbus. It was a major achievement for Roger Beteille and his team. Two other American carriers, Allegheny and PSA hinted they might follow suit and in Europe the Greek state carrier Olympic and Alitalia wanted Airbus. British Airways remained the odd one out, first launching the TriStar 500, fitted with 18 first-class seats and 217 economy seats, on its transatlantic routes and then eyeing up the Boeing 757. But greater political events were unfolding.

11. THE EUROPEANS IN BED WITH BOEING

The thorny question of Britain rejoining the Airbus consortium had become a regular topic for the aviation business. Bob McKinlay, the managing director of British Aerospace Commercial Aircraft, summed up the position in a memorial lecture in 1990. 'A decade was to elapse before the opportunity was taken – and it took longer than that to heal the wound created by the lack of British government support for the European project.' That wound was gangrenous.

Bob McKinlay would remain committed to Airbus's vision throughout his career but he faced immense pressure. 'In the early days, the guy who stayed with it, which wasn't easy for him, was Bob,' says Mike Turner, of BAE Systems, which later took a 20 per cent stake in Airbus. 'He wasn't on the board but he had to keep it running. Imagine a company like British Aerospace, which was later in great difficulty because of regional aircraft, and problems with the Airbus business which was soaking up huge investment that was needed for the longer term. Imagine having to defend his position in the late 1980s and early 1990s to a board and its finance director, Richard Lapthorne, saying: "How can we afford this?" Financially things were in a poor state. Yet Bob did a brilliant job in staying with it.'

Marcel Cavaillé, the French Transport Minister, threw down conditions for the UK in June 1974. The British government would be expected to make a substantial contribution to the development costs of the A300B2 and the A300B4, possibly in the form of a share of Airbus. Then he told the National Assembly in Paris that British airlines must seriously consider buying the A300. In Britain there was plenty of suspicion about France's own reasoning.

'The British feel that the French use co-operation to further one end: French supremacy over the British in European aeronautics,' said a comment in *Flight International* in July 1976.

The British felt that the French military policy was selfish – it was not a member of the North Atlantic Treaty Organisation and built its own nuclear weapons – while the French believed the British aircraft industry was overmanned, arrogant about its technical ability (especially in engines) and lacking at government-al level in aviation will and spirit. The British only became co-operative, the French said, when their own selfish policies failed. It was all terribly sour.

But the Martin Gruner report on West German aerospace, a beleaguered industry facing a 25 per cent reduction in state funding, repeated the call, recommending that Airbus Industrie be expanded to include Britain and Italy. Germany's aerospace industry was a quarter of the size of the UK's, yet the country's GNP was much larger (£176bn to the UK's £74bn). The aerospace industry was tough across the board. In the UK, Rolls-Royce was slashing back jobs and closing factories in its engine division. In California, Lockheed's TriStar programme was toiling as losses were mounting, while McDonnell Douglas had failed to sell a single DC10-10 in the mid-1970s. The gas-guzzling tri-jets were beginning to lose out to the twin-engine Airbus. The second-hand sales business was, however, booming with desert parking lots filled up with used aircraft. 'Psst, wanna buy a used TriStar? Only one careful owner . . .'

The British Aircraft Corporation was about to merge with Hawker Siddeley, and it would be a while before the industry was able to shake itself out. Meantime, the BAC One-Eleven was a steady income stream, although it was now facing a stiff challenge against the Boeing 737. Currency shifts made it hard at times, but the rise of the dollar gave it a temporary cost advantage.

On 13 April 1976, Eric Varley, the Secretary of Trade for Industry, appointed the members of the organising committee for British Aerospace, the new nationalised company formed from

Hawker Siddeley and BAC, under the chairmanship of Lord Beswick. Allen Greenwood, the chairman of BAC, was to become full-time deputy chairman, with Les Buck, a leading trade unionist, Dr William Pearce, chairman of Esso Petroleum, Sir George Rowland Jefferson, of BAC, and two Hawker Siddeley representatives, Eric Rubython and John Stamper on board. They were all first-class people; they had a mammoth mountain to climb.

Lord Beswick said, 'It would have been impossible for Britain to have succeeded in the civil-transport area with two airframe companies competing with each other – there would have been no future for the civil aircraft in this country if it had been left in the hands of private companies. I have said that everywhere I have been – and I have been right around the industry – and I have never heard it contradicted.'

On the stocks was another idea. The French Air Minister Cavaillé was looking for British support for the Mercure 200, a 150–170-seater concept being created by the French military plane-makers, Dassault, and McDonnell Douglas. The American manufacturers were now serious about wooing more European partners. Its President John Brizendine headed across to the Farnborough Air Show and held private sessions with several key British partners, although BAC and Hawker Siddeley, and the German partners, VFW-Fokker and MBB, were not sure that the Mercure was the right plane for the job. Once again there were rather a lot of options and while Britain appeared keen not to shut the door on the Mercure, it was also considering the BAC X-Eleven and a possible collaboration with Boeing on the 7N7.

They weren't the only ones considering their options. Aerospatiale, frustrated by Britain's lack of action, opened talks with Boeing about the 7N7-100, a stretched 160-seater 737 with a new wing made by the French. The discussions were a blow for those still intent on European integration and co-operation. But Aerospatiale was under severe political pressure to stem the £40m a year losses from civil aircraft and to get some returns. The exposure, shared with the Germans, on the A300 was £300m and the figure for Concorde was just too astronomical to contemplate. It was a black hole of public funding that just got deeper and darker.

Aerospatiale President General Jacques Mitterrand, brother of the new French President, Francois, handed out a tid-bit to

Britain, saying the A300BB10 might have a Rolls-Royce RB211, assuming British Airways showed goodwill.

'Aerospatiale's deal with Boeing comes as no surprise to France's European partners . . . it is clear that the deal is not just a negotiating ploy, a firm letter of intent has been signed with Boeing, and senior British and Germans aerospace people are reconciling themselves to the fact that the French have actually decided on an Atlantic rather than European civil transport policy,' reported *Flight International* in 1976.

A year after the formation of British Aerospace, the new company was being urged to make a firm commitment to Europe. And so another European plane was taken into consideration by Britain: the Jet.

'Most of Europe wants Britain to lead the Jet airframe. The Rolls-Royce 432 powered Super F28 could be the best Jet 1,' said veteran aviation commentary Bill Sweetman. 'The Jet needs Britain . . . the political muscle of Rolls-Royce is behind £250m for the Boeing 757's engine, and British Aerospace's only firm proposal to the UK government concerns the HS146 [a proposed 70–84 seat jet, which eventually became BAe's 146. It first flew in 1981]. Europeans are beginning to ask themselves whether the HS146 is a hoarding while BAe itself goes into business with Boeing.'

British Aerospace had also been in a cosy tête-à-tête with Boeing over the impending development of the Boeing 757. In August 1976, a joint BAC/Hawker Siddeley team had visited Seattle to look at taking over the detailed design and manufacture of the wing, undercarriage and pods for the 7N7 as full partners. Then, in July 1977, it was agreed that it was not practical to set up a joint venture on lines acceptable to both parties.

But Boeing President Tex Boullioun told Lord Beswick he was still waiting for BAe's proposals. Boeing laid down the opportunity of engineering work, production of a new wing, landing gear and nacelles for the RB211-535 engine. Boullioun also said the Brits could have the flight-testing and final assembly 'if this makes business sense, though I can't understand why anybody would want the problems of final assembly'.

Final assembly was seven per cent of the hours spent and 97 per cent of the problems. But Boullioun was now looking at the 767-200, which United Airlines was expecting for delivery in 1982. Boullioun was bullish.

'I believe we'll kill the Europeans in the open market. We'll sell a thousand 757s and they'll sell perhaps fifty to a hundred Jets.' He wasn't far off. Boeing delivered the last of 1,048 757s in April 2005 to Shanghai Airlines.

According to the Boeing boss, the UK investment in the Boeing 757 would be between £150m and £200m, while the Rolls-Royce RB211-535 development would be another £250m. The ebullient Boullioun predicted the deal would be worth £1bn to the UK, though the plane would still be known as a Boeing 757. One British Minister told the Boeing boss he wanted the Americans to give business to British equipment suppliers. 'I suggested that he send some of them over to knock on doors rather than waiting in the store for somebody to show up,' said Tex.

So, despite the cultural difference, a real deal was on the table. Now the clock was ticking for British Aerospace. Which way would they jump? British Aerospace was extremely cautious. This was high-stakes poker playing with the future of Britain's high-tech industries.

BAe said it was assessing the situation. The company was keeping the industry on tenterhooks, especially as Lord Beswick intensely disliked the French way of working and was not rushing to rejoin Airbus Industrie. He regarded it as a French-based, French-dominated overmanned company and an over-centralised way of running a wider European airline family. The British wanted Jet 1 to be made with European co-operation in the United Kingdom.

British Airways was keen on the Boeing 757 and thought the Jet 1 was a non-starter – and neither was it too sure about British Aerospace. While the success of the A300 went some way to prove that Europe could make fine planes, there were some at British Airways who were less than convinced. 'Airbus still has to make a profit. We feel nervous when British Aerospace says it may have difficulty making wings to match Boeing prices,' said one senior executive.

There were, however, political pressures attendant on BA's decision. Ken Gill, the general-secretary of Tass, described then as the white-collar section of the Amalgamated Union of Engineering Workers, was a powerful trade unionist and just one of many voices who roundly condemned BA's request to purchase the Boeing 737.

For the British government, with unemployment reaching record levels and public services such as hospitals, schools and transport, in a run-down and dilapidated state, the consequences of 'Going Boeing' were huge. It wasn't just about the French – there was no doubt the West Germans, Dutch and the rest of Europe would have been deeply offended by a renunciation of Europe. Sure, the French had flirted with Boeing in 1976, but this decision would shake Europe to its core. The British could argue that this was not a European Treaty matter and that it was purely business rather than politics – however it clearly wasn't. The European aviation industry had soaked up vast amounts of taxpayers' money and constant political interference was the price to pay for this. Anybody who wanted to see the spirit of the EEC destroyed would be advocating an Anglo-American Boeing 757 deal supported by British Aerospace, Rolls-Royce – who were dependent on the deal for their RB211-535 engine – and British Airways. But the Airbus A310 was on its way.

Phil Smith, then Hawker Siddeley's Director and Chief Engineer, recalled the course of events at the time of the birth of the A310: 'Lufthansa was the first airline to say they had a requirement for a 200-seater optimised for their short stages of under 1,000 miles, in addition to the A300Bs they had already ordered. Hawker Siddeley was in a position to design a much more efficient wing than on the A300B. This involved higher launch costs and, as it was a major step forward, with no full-scale flight experience, there was a considerable risk involved. Every possibility of using a modified version of the existing wing was explored. However, the French and German designers did not like this approach, so the new wing went ahead. In the end, its performance was considerably better than predicted, giving a cruise fuel burn at Mach 0.8 which was 6.5 per cent below estimates. There was a problem devising a wing which would enable a 2,000-mile stage requirement (one interested airline wanted to fly between Europe and West Africa) to be met, by development of the A310, without compromising the economics of Lufthansa's short stages, and the wing area was increased slightly to ensure that the long-range requirements would be met. The Hawker Siddeley aerodynamicists concerned, notably Don Dykins, who was responsible for the company's contribution to Airbus aerodynamics, were given the Esso Energy Award for their work.'

Wing concepts had been under development at Hatfield, but Filton, near Bristol, was emerging as a true centre of excellence, with Broughton, in North Wales, becoming a manufacturing facility. This legacy would become a vital ingredient for the challenges of the A380.

At the time when the A310 – then called the B10 – was first mooted, Phil Smith was part of Hawker Siddeley's team visiting Boeing in Seattle. He was there to hear what Boeing was prepared to offer in the development and manufacturing of the 757. He returned and wrote a report which came out in favour of continuing with the B10, and this was accepted by the board of British Aerospace. He said, 'In the end, British Airways ordered the Boeing 757, even though its seat-mile costs did not match those of the A310, even when no allowance was made for the freight capacity of the A310.' At last, Airbus was proving to be a formidable player in the aerospace arena.

12. A JUMBO ICON SHRINKS THE GLOBE

Joseph Sutter now enjoys his retirement. But he was once given a task that literally changed the world. As one of America's leading aeronautical engineers he led the development of the Boeing 747 jumbo jet.

Boeing made a pact to build the jumbo after Juan Trippe of Pan American Airways said he would buy it. But Bill Allen, the head of Boeing, knew the plane would cost much more than they could afford. Much, much more. At a board meeting in October 1965, Allen turned to John Yeasting, the Vice President of the Commercial Plane Division.

'I have been going all over the country saying how impossible it would be to undertake the supersonic transport (SST) without government support. This will cost us at least half of what the SST development will cost.'

Yeasting didn't like to contradict his boss. Not on this one. The 747 was going to be Boeing's second entry into the 'Sporty Game', betting the whole business on one single project. It had done it once before with the Boeing 707. And won. Now the company's net worth was $762m, so Allen tripled its authorised capital stock to pay for the plane. Failure would mean certain catastrophe for Boeing.

'It was the beginning of the most heroic venture ever made in the civil aviation business. It would take four years and $2 billion to complete, and it brought Boeing to the very edge of bankruptcy. In giving the go-ahead Bill Allen was quite literally "betting the company" ', says Stephen Aris in his book *Close to the Sun*.

But Boeing's high-rollers seemed game for the gamble on the roulette wheel. Sales of the 707 and 727 were going well and the space and missile business was literally booming.

Joe Sutter, who retired in 1986 and is still a consultant, recalled, 'This was one heck of a commitment for them to make, particularly since Pan-Am wanted its big airplanes quickly. I got a phone call from the Chief Engineer of Boeing Commercial Airplane Division to go and see him.' In the meeting Dick Rouzie asked Joe if he'd lead the development of the new plane. Sutter continued: 'The question thrilled me. I was 44 at the time and I had been with Boeing for twenty years. I had no way of knowing how achievable this new assignment might be or where it might lead.'

Without a moment's hesitation Sutter agreed and immediately started putting together an engineering team to define the new plane. He visited Pan-Am to find out what exactly they wanted. They told him they wanted a really *big* airliner. Not only that, they wanted it now. Sutter needed to sound out some others. He went to see Cathay Pacific Airways, British Airways, Japan Airlines and TWA and several other airlines. They were all clamouring for something bigger.

'We worked up the preliminary basic weights, performance parameters, and operating economics for three different airplane sizes – a 250-seater, a 300-seater and a 350-seater – and asked them which one they wanted us to build. I was amazed to see that every one of these carriers voted for 350 seats. The Boeing 707 carried about 140 passengers. This meant the world's airlines wanted to build a massive jet two-and-a-half times bigger than anything in existence.'

This was a quantum leap, considering today's A380 is about one-third bigger than an existing 747-400. 'When the topic of a very big airliner arose, everybody immediately thought in terms of a 'double-decker'. You could only stretch a jet's fuselage so far, so the logical and obvious way to double the capacity of an airplane was to design it with two full decks, one above the other. That was how you achieved seat counts.'

Sutter says this was Trippe's initial thinking. The Pan-Am boss still had a romantic notion and loved the idea of the tea clippers that once crossed the seven seas. Before the war, Pan American's Clipper service used Boeing 314 flying boats to take pampered passengers to Europe. Trippe expected his new plane to have tall sides and two full rows of windows like the portholes of a ship. On 2 December 1965, Pan American, Boeing and Pratt & Whitney signed a letter of their intentions. It would be $22m a plane, four times the cost of a Boeing 707-320. It meant some swift action.

Construction on a new complex at Boeing's Paine Field, alongside the Snohomish County Airport and close to Everett, a town nearly thirty miles north of Seattle, was approved within weeks, and the ground for this 780-acre site was brokered in June 1966. The world's biggest manufacturing operation was ready by January the following year.

'We drew up one double-decker after another, but for a number of reasons none of these fuselage cross sections satisfied us. First, there was the worrisome issues of how to safely evacuate passengers on the ground from that very high upper deck, Secondly, a double-decker has proportionately less room in its lower holds for passengers baggage and revenue cargo. Thirdly, double-deckers make lousy freighters,' said Sutter.

At the start, the new jumbo was being designed for both passengers and paying cargo. The original 747 was not expected to sell very well because of the dash for supersonic flight. Concorde was on the stocks, and the US and the Soviet Union were developing their own supersonic transports (SST). Boeing was building the US SST and this had priority on the Seattle drawing boards. This was the sexy stuff for the Boeing wizards. The jumbo jet? Well, it was viewed as an interim project and the Boeing marketing team predicted that it would sell about fifty. Not for the first time they were way off beam. The Boeing 747 was being designed predominantly as a cargo plane until the SST project was shelved in 1971.

'We saw at once that it would be difficult for airlines to load and unload cargo from a double-decker's upper level. Stowing high density air freight in a tall, narrow fuselage brought special structural problems. And operators would want to move this freight through their systems in shipping containers or pallets. What kind of container and pallet could work on both levels of a double-decker without sacrificing too much of the plane's available volume?'

So the designers changed tack and began to think about a standard size pallet used by the trucking and railway companies, sized 8 feet by 8 feet (2.44 metres by 2.44 metres), and wondered whether two of these pallets could sit side by side in an airplane. Sutter explained: 'It was this reasoning that led to the 747's final fuselage cross section, which was derived by drawing a circle around two of the industry-standard pallets side by side on the main deck.'

This defined the size of the plane, giving more room. This was also enough for nine or even ten economy seats in a row. And so the concept of the twin-aisle or wide-body jet was born. As innovative as this was, there was a further piece of distinctive design that defined the jumbo jet: its famous hump.

Again it was all about cargo. It was easier to load freight through a landing door at the front of the plane, with a hinged nose to allow pallets to be loaded more quickly and efficiently – just as every 747 is loaded today. This did, however, mean that the flight deck had to be above the main deck so as to allow the front cargo door to be raised. So for aerodynamic reasons a dome was added behind the elevated cockpit. This was its trademark and also where first-class passengers would eventually sit. Joe Sutter's initial idea, however, was to use the extra space as a crew rest-area, but Juan Trippe scoffed. He knew the cost of real estate in the air. He wanted revenue and asked for first-class passengers upstairs. And so the hump was extended to make room for 44 premium fare-payers. The plane was an encyclopaedia of superlatives: wing span of 195 ft 8 in (59.64 m), a length of 231 ft 4 in (70.51 m), a maximum take-off weight of 680,000 lbs (308,448 kg). The original engines were four Pratt & Whitney JT9D-1 engines. These were large and had 41,000 lbs (18,598 kg) of thrust, which would give the plane a cruising speed of 600 mph (966 km) at 40,000 ft.

This, for Joe Sutter, was a big issue. Was there enough power to get this titan off the ground? More changes in the specification increased the weight, so the JT9D-1 engine was not powerful enough. Pan-Am and Boeing were now faced with a take-off weight of nearly 310,000 kg (310 tonnes) – forty tonnes more than anticipated. Boeing now needed an engine with 43,500 lbs (19,732 kg) of thrust. The answer was the JT9D-3 which could deliver the 45,000 lbs (20,142 kg) now demanded. This was a tough call for Pratt & Whitney, but Boeing was pushy and insistent, mindful of Trippe's expectations.

Just how tough was illustrated by the lateness of the engines' delivery. As the first flight loomed, Boeing 747s were coming off the production line with two concrete weights on each wing awaiting the engines. Mal Stamper, the 747 programme director, commented blackly: 'We're rolling out gliders instead of air-planes.'

Boeing had to stump up compensation to Pan-Am. So while the jumbo jet was now selling with gusto – with nearly 200 orders worth $1.8bn – and the Everett mechanics were churning out an exceptional seven aircraft a month, the losses were mounting. Boeing had legal commitments to produce on time, yet reported a loss in 1969, its first in over 20 years. The hold-ups got worse. More engine delays, and then a recession, gradually forced Boeing to the edge of the abyss. But the 70s would be a whole new chapter for the jumbo jet.

Who says the 1970s were boring? The Boeing 747 became front-page news on Thursday, 15 January 1970, when Pat Nixon, the wife of President Richard Nixon christened the first jumbo, *Clipper Young America*, at Dulles Airport in Washington DC. It wasn't the smoothest of starts. One of the engines overheated and every one of the 324 passengers was evacuated. Six hours later, after 1 a.m., they boarded another plane and instead of going to Paris, headed off to London.

Over the course of the year, Pan American took delivery of 25 jumbos, introducing them on the other transatlantic routes from New York to Amsterdam, Barcelona, Brussels, Frankfurt, Lisbon, Paris and Rome, plus Chicago to London and Frankfurt, San Francisco to London and Paris. There was even a Polar route taking the Great Circle over the North Pole from LA and San Francisco to Paris and London. As more aircraft were delivered, the jumbo stretched out from LA and San Francisco to Honolulu, Tokyo and Hong Kong and San Juan, in Puerto Rico. TWA became the first to introduce coast-to-coast 747s across America, with American Airlines following suit. Lufthansa was the first non-American customers on the Frankfurt route, with Air France and Alitalia using this new record-breaking plane.

The era of the jumbo jet had arrived. This single plane defined the public's attitudes to travel, heralding a boom in popular travel and shrinking the globe. It was an antidote to the elitist fuel-guzzling Concorde that carried so few passengers. It was the embodiment of the American Dream. Pan-Am, Coca-Cola and the

Boeing jumbo jet. For the next 36 years it would be unchallenged as the world's biggest passenger plane, and already they had 200 orders. However, there was something not quite right, in fact very wrong, at Boeing. They were going bust.

To stem the tide, and buy some time, Boeing was forced to go to the markets to raise a loan from America's bankers. It was the largest amount ever raised to prop up a multi-national American corporation, but it wouldn't last forever. Boeing needed surgery and someone would have to operate.

Thornton Arnold Wilson, known as T, volunteered to do the bloody hatchet work. In a desperate bid to save money, he cut $100m from the commercial aircraft division budget. 'The logic was simple. If I don't do it, the board will bring some guy from outside who will.' It was an unprecedented bloodbath. Over 86,000 jobs were slashed in three years. Factories were closed, routine maintenance halted and research curtailed. Unemployment in Seattle hit a staggering 17 per cent, yet it saved Boeing – and the jumbo jet.

Affairs over at Boeing's rival, McDonnell Douglas, were also in disarray. A series of tragic airline accidents marred the reputation of the three-engine DC-10 and there were even indications that the design was fatally flawed. In June 1972 an American Airlines DC10 hit a problem at 12,000 ft on a flight to Detroit from Buffalo. The cargo door blew off, followed by decompression, with the rear deck of the plane collapsing and damaging control cables. The pilot did a brilliant job landing the DC10 safely but investigators found the door had not closed properly. The condition was not fixed properly and in March 1974, another DC10, a Hava Yollari, a Turkish airline, with 346 people on board, crashed thirty miles north-east of Paris. All were killed. The DC10 programme never recovered. Questions began to be raised over the effectiveness of triple-engine planes and Boeing took full advantage of the lapses.

Flash-forward 36 years and the jumbo is still earning its keep, and Boeing are determined to make sure that it continues to do so – even in the face of the A380's competition. Boeing isn't willing to relinquish the 747's history, its value and its massive contribution to the company's profits without a fight. And Randy Baseler, Boeing's combative Vice President of Marketing, punches like a veteran heavyweight when discussing Airbus's whipper-snapper challenge.

'The 747 and larger market forecast is about 900 airplanes during the next twenty years. The 400–500-seat market is about half of that at 450 airplanes. The 747 works in today's infrastructure making it the most versatile jumbo jet.'

He was certain its supremacy could continue over the new titan talking to the sky. 'Unlike the A380 – which is planned to land at fewer than 30 major hubs by the year 2009 – the 747 family flies to more than 210 airports worldwide. The 747 is the perfect airplane for multiple applications. Its flexibility allows airlines to use the 747 in hub-to-hub or hub-to-point operations, or even in point-to-point high-density markets.'

The irony is that the 747's prolonged life is due to its cargo capabilities. Boeing's 747-400F and the 747-400ERF continue to be the mainstay of the world's freighter industry, with the 747-400F providing over 50 per cent of the world's freighter capacity. Baseler says customers are still asking for the passenger version of the 747-400, and is dismissive of Airbus's chances.

'Even though the 747 has about 130 fewer seats, the A380 operating weight per passenger is about 21 per cent heavier than the 747. Plus, the A380 trip costs are about 25 per cent higher than the 747. The A380 increases the risk to airlines during an industry downturn. The much larger A380 has an only marginally better seat-mile cost of 3 per cent and much higher infrastructure costs. This makes the A380 a very risky gamble for airlines versus the proven performance of the 747.'

This proven performance could be enhanced by the launch of the 747-8, which will have 450 seats, 8,000 nm (14,800 km) of non-stop range and lower seat-mile costs than the A380. New high-bypass engines being developing by GEnx for the 787 Dreamliner will be used on a new 747-8 Intercontinental. This will reduce fuel consumption – 15 per cent lower than the 747-400 – and make the model quieter and more acceptable to an environmental lobby increasingly blaming aviation fuel – and the jumbo jet – for global warming. The 747-8's aerodynamics will feature raked wingtips that reduce cruise drag, dampen noise and increase efficiency. Advanced aluminium alloys will reduce weight and help to make the new variant more efficient. But Baseler was more determined to sell its benefits.

'Flying at mach 0.85, the 747-8 will be the fastest commercial airplane in the sky. The new 747-8 will be e-enabled. Compared to the 747-400, the 747-8 will have 8 per cent more capacity with only marginally higher trip costs yet nearly 6 per cent lower seat-mile costs.'

For operators, the choice is whether to stick with the 747 they know, or operate with the risks associated with the A380. The airlines are also shrewd and know that the jumbo jet is still nearly 40 years old. If Boeing isn't encouraged to build a new big jet, then technology might stand still; after all, the A380 will still have 92 more seats than the 747-8, and consume about 12 per cent less fuel per seat. But despite full-page glossy newspaper adverts, the airlines didn't seem to want this updated jumbo by the summer of 2007.

Less fuel consumption means fewer pollutants. Furthermore, the 747-8 will be the quietest jumbo and would be able to meet the stringent London-Heathrow QC2 requirement. 'How do we claim that the 747-8 is more efficient than the all-new A380? After all, the 747-8 is a derivative. Like most comparisons, you have to go back to the basics and in this case, it is the efficiency measures of airplane design: aerodynamic, propulsion and structural,' says Baseler.

Aerodynamically, the A380 will have an advantage. After all, it is all new. But, the 747-8 is not far behind as Boeing has been improving the aerodynamics of the existing 747 wing with tweaks such as raked wing tips that reduce cruise drag, dampen noise and increase efficiency.

Baseler takes his blunderbuss out and takes another shot at the A380. 'Larger airplanes with more seating capacity should be more efficient. The A380 has over 30 per cent more seats than the 747-400, yet has very little efficiency gains. This lack of efficiency gain can be attributed mainly to its excessive weight.'

Boeing's decision to launch its first major derivative of the 747 in nearly twenty years was a bold blocking move. The launch customer for the 747-8 Freighter was Cargolux, who ordered ten to be delivered between 2009 and 2012. What sold it to Cargolux was the plane's capacity and the ability to turn around a fully-laden 747 in less than an hour – time, after all, is money.

One thing is clear: the Boeing jumbo jet in all its guises will be here for a long while to come. It will be up to Airbus to make sure it becomes obsolete as quickly as possible.

13. AIRBUS IN THE FAMILY WAY

The eventual sale of A300s to Eastern Airlines in April 1978 created a trade dispute between the United States and Europe that continues to this day. Boeing would not forget the debacle in a hurry. Nor would legions of flag-waving American protectionists, petrified about the future.

What was becoming clear was that it wasn't simply the improving quality of the jet planes and their engines that was selling to the airlines, but more the spicy deals being offered and secured in smoke-filled rooms. Airbus was accused of providing $96m of its own money to secure the Eastern Airlines deal. But the fact that engine-maker General Electric extended $45m in credit was overlooked by everyone except an angry Pratt & Whitney. Harry Gray, the vociferous chairman of United Technologies, Pratt's parent company, told a shareholders' meeting that it was evidence that his company was competing against foreign state treasuries and not foreign companies.

The negative reaction to the Airbus deal was fanned by another deal, a British credit agreement which helped Pan-Am. The British government, via its Export Credit Guarantee Department, gave Pan-Am a fifteen-year 100 per cent loan to purchase Rolls-Royce RB211 engines for the TriStar L1011. Rolls was still in intensive care, recovering from its spectacular collapse into bankruptcy in 1971. It was again facing a precarious race for survival, and leading British politicians, including the Prime Minister, James Callaghan, were under pressure to prop it up again.

The development costs for the RB211 engine had bounced out of control at Derby. The UK engine-maker, tied to a stiff contract, had been forced to take the hit on the chin and had been bailed out by the UK government. Similarly, Lockheed had descended into deep trouble. The L1011 was not selling well and was locked in a death-or-glory competition with McDonnell Douglas's DC10. After Rolls-Royce spurned any work with Airbus, it was viewed as staunchly pro-American and desperately needed to hang on to its relationship with Lockheed. This was put into severe jeopardy when General Electric offered a fifteen-year finance agreement for its engines and Rolls were given an ultimatum to beat this. Callaghan was forced to make a snap judgement to back the British engine-maker. He agreed to put up the money. He said later, 'I talked to Jimmy Carter about it. It was a very political affair. I was worried about the overall impact on Anglo-American co-operation.'

When Democrat Jimmy Carter was sworn in as US President on 20 January 1977, America was increasingly concerned about predatory exports from all kinds of industries, including car- and steel-making. So a venerable institution, set up during the Great Depression, was revitalised: the Export-Import Bank. Through a change known as the 'Harry Gray amendment', the bank was now able to give loans for development projects. In 1977 the bank handed out $700m in credit to aid US businesses; the following year that had jumped to a staggering $2.8bn. It now financed $731m worth of US jets, making no secret of its policy of aggressively promoting US exports. It would act to match any terms offered by Airbus's consortium governments. One company benefited more than most: Boeing.

Boeing complained that it had lost a 747 deal to the Airbus A300 after the buyer, Pakistan International Airlines, was promised long-term financing that it couldn't match. Gradually, Boeing began to use more and more loans from Eximbank. The loans became so successful and regular that the bank became know as 'the Boeing Bank' or 'Boeing Savings and Loans'. Increasingly, there was even disquiet in America about the huge influence the Seattle company had on the bank, a view vigorously rejected by the bank's officials.

Later on, a deal in Australia caused uproar. Boeing sold 25 aircraft to Ansett Airlines in 1980, 12 767s were part of the order, with the rest 727s and 737s. The terms from Eximbank were far better than Airbus's. Airbus was trying to sell twelve A300s and promised export finance support, with a loan over twelve years at an interest rate of 7.99 per cent. Boeing called in Eximbank and urged them to beat this rate. This broke a convention of matching, rather than beating, an offer, and it placed America in hot water with the Organisation for Economic Co-operation and Development, which was trying to improve trade arrangements.

This American defensiveness coincided with pressure on Britain to return to the Airbus fold. In 1978, Prime Minister Callaghan said he did not want to interfere in the decisions of the newly created and government-owned British Aerospace, but he faced pressure from his German and French counterparts to rejoin the consortium. For six months, the question of Airbus's future was debated intensely among politicians and the news media. In July, Airbus announced the launch of the A310 and needed more financial help.

'The situation was intensely political,' said James Callaghan in *The Sporty Game*. 'Had we not gone into Airbus, it would have been interpreted as a political act. Valery Giscard d'Estaing, the French President, would have used it against us and Helmut Schmidt [the German Chancellor] would have drawn a similar conclusion. On the other hand, we wanted Anglo-American co-operation.'

Boeing had been actively wooing the new British ambassador to the United States, Peter Jay. He was invited out to Seattle over Thanksgiving Weekend in 1977 where Tex Boullioun, the hard-drinking, crop-haired and characteristically blunt leader of Boeing's Commercial Plane Division, offered to give British Aerospace half the work if British Airways would be a launch partner for the 757.

Events came to a climax in August 1978 with the announcement that British Airways would indeed buy 19 Boeing 757s, to be equipped with Rolls-Royce RB211-535 engines. But, at the same time, British Aerospace was allowed to join Airbus Industrie with an entrance fee of £25m and a loan for its proportion of the A310.

The French were determined that British Airways should take the Airbus before BAe could join the consortium. Giscard d'Estaing was annoyed with Callaghan, then moved off on a statesman's tour of the Middle East to win new friends and build influence for Airbus. It was Freddie Laker who saved the day for Callaghan, when he announced he would buy ten A300B4s for his low-cost Skytrain service.

On Tuesday, 24 October 1978, France, Germany and Britain officially announced the new agreement to make BAe a full partner from 1 January 1979, with a 20 per cent stake in the consortium. There were some horse-trading and concessions as Aerospatiale and Deutsche Airbus reduced their holding by 10 per cent each to 37.9 per cent, with the CASA share remaining at 4.2 per cent. But, most importantly, BAe were given responsibility for the A310 wing. It might have been skill, more likely a stroke of luck, but British Aerospace emerged strongly from the deal.

The Airbus sales strategy, devised by Bernard Lathiere and sales director Dan Krook, was typically flamboyant. They dreamed up the Silk Road sales pitch along the ancient routes of adventurer Marco Polo. Countries such as the Philippines, Malaysia and Indonesia, and into the Middle East, India, Iran and Pakistan, were being wooed. Airbus sales teams were scouring for any emerging opportunities where there was no relationship with Boeing – or even strong anti-American feelings that could be used for better leverage. But the exotic nature of the Silk Road strategy smacked of desperation. The consortium was grateful for buyers anywhere. Thankfully for Airbus, they were gradually winning interest – and orders.

Bernard Lathiere was also into his stride. He was an al-together very different character than Roger Beteille and Henri Ziegler. He was more outgoing and gregarious; he loved Habanas, the rarest Clarets and was truly larger-than-life. He had managed to steal an Indian contract in Delhi from under the noses of Boeing and Lockheed, with Air Chief Marshall PC Lal, the President and chairman of Air India, eating out of his hand and singing: 'Happy Birthday, dear Bernard' when a huge cake arrived. His *piéce de résistance* was to pull out a battered black and white photograph of Mahatma Gandhi, an elderly woman and a small boy and then ask his Indian hosts to name the trio. They recognised Gandhi, and the lady was a well-known Indian poet, but the boy? They were all stumped. Lathiere would then declare with alacrity: 'That boy is me.' It was quite an act and Boeing and Lockheed had no reply.

The straight-shooting Tex Boullioun decided to mix it for some fun at Airbus's expense. He offered to co-operate saying both companies should work together on the Airbus B10 and the Boeing 767. But the talks collapsed. Beteille recalled, 'It didn't work because Boeing didn't want it to. If we had accepted their offer we would simply have become sub-contractors.'

Beteille said Airbus was not ready to give up the secrets of his fuselage. That would have been the equivalent of giving up the crown jewels. And while the Boeing 757 struggled to inspire sales, especially with its Rolls-Royce engines, by the end of 1979 Airbus had sold 256 wide-bodied planes – a record for a European plane-maker.

There was also an intriguing development in America: deregulation. Jimmy Carter abolished the Civil Aeronautics Board in America which opened the door to a new breed of air entrepreneurs who set up instant airlines that could undercut the traditional carriers on their profitable routes. Before 1978, the CAB was a cartel which enforced a fare structure that had kept prices artificially high. Now there would be a backlash as companies, such as Braniff, the Texas-based airline, collapsed. The new players would cherry-pick the most profitable routes to cream off the profits.

When the price war heated up on the transatlantic routes, the traditional airlines moved away from the smaller internal routes to concentrate on protecting their key revenue-earning routes out of the larger hub airports. And a whole range of regional airlines sprung up to deposit local passengers into these hubs. This was the birth of 'hub and spoke', a network which would cover North America, Europe and Asia. All of the biggest airlines now used a hub: TWA in Kansas City, British Airways at Heathrow, Northwest Orient in Minneapolis, KLM at Amsterdam, Schipol, and Delta at Atlanta.

Randy Baseler, of Boeing, points to a significant intercontinental shift. 'The dramatic effect of both market liberalisation and the availability of smaller airplanes, such as the Airbus A320 and Boeing 767, on the North Atlantic market, changed things. In 1985, when the 767 began service on the North Atlantic, these smaller airplanes addressed passenger desires for more non-stop flights and frequency choices, despite having higher seat-mile costs.'

In the future, this would be the core of Boeing's argument against the need for the titanic A380. The Seattle pundits said that the average airplane size had dropped dramatically. 'All air travel growth was accommodated by increases in frequencies and non-stops to meet the desires of air travellers,' suggested Baseler.

In 1984, 62 per cent of the flights across the North Atlantic were on Boeing 747s but this dropped to only 16 per cent in 2004. The dinosaur airlines that didn't adapt became extinct. Pan-Am chose to maintain a foolhardy strategy of low seat-mile cost – and stuck with its fleet of Boeing 747s – connecting passengers through hubs, such as its New York gateway at JFK. But, increasingly, passengers didn't want this and the once-mighty giant, hit by the fallout from the Lockerbie bombing over Scotland, eventually folded.

Adam Brown, of Airbus, said, 'By the early 1980s, Boeing was sitting up and paying attention to us a bit more. There was no doubt that Boeing was beginning to bear the brunt of our successful campaigning at Airbus. Not only was the A300 an excellent match for the Boeing 747 on some routes, we had the smaller A310 and this was a good plane too.'

While the political squabbling in Europe was still going on, Airbus was now showing a distinct technical and organisational lead in producing airplanes. The painstaking structures of Roger Beteille and Felix Kracht were paying off. 'Each participant was completely responsible for the elements that they brought to the plane,' said Brown. Beteille's system based on the integration in Toulouse of the large sub-assemblies of wing, fuselage, engine and tail fins that were near completion was proving to be most effective.

'Each firm was required to specify the precise components of their portion and to give us a proper price and delivery schedules for these parts. This involved a great deal of dialogue and discussion about how we put a price on every single time,' said Beteille.

The Airbus GIE system acted like a moderator and sometimes a judge and jury so that detailed contracts between the partners could be agreed. In reality, the GIE acted as a general contractor and purchased the components from the members. 'We kept a meticulous set of accounts for ourselves and each partner, which tracked the delivery of components and the payment of funds. Invoices were reconciled every ten days and the monies then sent to the partners,' he recalled.

However, critics increasingly slated the GIE system saying it was not transparent, that no accounts were published and that contractors were actually concealing their profit and loss on Airbus work in their own balance sheets. All this raised huge suspicion among some Americans who believed that Airbus was purely a politically motivated agency with the sinister aim of destroying American capitalism.

Airbus's decision to launch the A320 exacerbated the tensions in transatlantic relations. In the summer of 1987, the four national governments – France, Germany, Spain and the UK – appointed a commission to review the Airbus Industrie structure. Jacques Benichou, President of Groupement des Industries Francaises Aeronautiques et Spatiales (GIFAS) and head of engine-maker SNECMA, was the French representative; Peter Pfeiffer, a Bayerische Vereinsbank director and on the board of MBB and Deutsche Airbus, was the German representative; Emilio Gonzalez Garcia, a former aero engineer, banker and board member of Iberia Airlines, represented Spain, and Sir Jeffrey Stirling, the chairman of Peninsular and Oriental Steam Navigation Company was the British representative.

In early 1988 the 'four wise men' issued a damning report. They found that Airbus's administrative body was too large and followed rules that made prompt action almost impossible. The report noted the absence of a consolidated balance sheet showing the financial status of the consortium's entire operations. It called for a financial officer to be appointed to create and manage a more rational accounting system. It identified a complete divide between marketing and production functions within Airbus, with the sales team negotiating deals without an accurate picture of the cost of production. The four partners fixed the costs of their part in the process without telling the other members the actual costs. The 'wise men' recommended that a fully integrated civil aerospace company should be created, even a public limited company.

This was a step too far. So a fudge was suggested, that the GIE structure be strengthened, making management more efficient and giving the partners more oversight into the daily operations of Airbus. The Supervisory Board should be slimmed from twenty members down to five, and both the President and other members should devote their full attention to the consortium's business. They also suggested a seven-person Executive Board with real authority, able to make binding decisions, with a managing director chairing the executive board. The financial director would become an important part of this set up. Such sensible reforms, following mainstream business organisations, met with resistance from Europe's civil servants and it was another year before they even started to consider the reforms.

The death of Franz-Josef Strauss, chairman of the Airbus's Supervisory Board, in October 1988, left a hiatus in the reforms and Hans Friderichs, a German banker and politician with something of a chequered career, was chosen to fill Strauss's shoes. One of his first tasks was to implement the changes. This he did. Most changes were made in 1989, but not all of them. The reconstituted Supervisory Board was cut back to Vice President Henri Martre, chairman and Chief Executive Officer of Aerospatiale; Hans-Arnt Vogels, President and Chief Executive Officer of MBB; Sir Raymond Lygo, Chief Executive Officer of BAe; and Javier Alvarez Vara, President of CASA.

Jean Pierson, the President and Chief Executive Officer of Airbus Industrie, was named managing director and was joined by the heads of the consortium's aircraft divisions, including an assiduous financial director, Robert Smith, formerly of BAe's Royal Ordnance subsidiary who was sent to Airbus in 1989. Smith became very frustrated because the partners did not want to divulge their financial information and were not eager to act like a fully fledged Anglo-Saxon-style PLC.

Problems were brewing. Henri Martre, the head of Aerospatiale, was already objecting strongly to any moves towards becoming a PLC, saying that such a status would weaken the business and that it would be far too small to compete with Boeing. Martre said he was willing to continue with the current system where members were major subcontractors and the AI didn't have to reveal its costs. He didn't want to open the books either. 'I have never come across a company where the financial director has authority over everybody else. That would make him a managing director, not financial director,' he is quoted as saying in Ian McIntyre's book, *Dogfight: The Transatlantic Battle Over Airbus*.

Not surprisingly, Jean Pierson was also in agreement with Martre's sentiment. Martre thought financial transparency was an artificial idea. Frustrated, Smith quit in December. Airbus wasn't ready for change. But it would be one day.

The A300 had taken seven years from being a few sketches on paper to its first commercial flight. The next major step would take almost as long, but the A320 would be worth the wait. Over the next ten years Airbus would be getting much closer to Boeing, and Roger Beteille's vision of a 'Family' of European commercial airplane models would take an amazing leap forward.

Elsewhere Boeing was not hanging around. The company was preparing to play catch-up with the 767 and its companion, the Boeing 757. This was a new direction for Boeing and the first all-new aircraft designed by the company in 15 years. The 767 would also have a lot of input from abroad, with 30 per cent of the work subcontracted to Europe and Japan. But this was another expensive project, costing $2bn to develop.

Adam Brown has no doubt about Airbus's right now to sit at the top table. 'The A320 was a major achievement for us. We did not believe that it would become such a successful plane for us,' he says. It was intended to be ready by 1982, but wasn't launched until two years later, didn't fly until 1987, and didn't enter service until 1988. 'When we look back, the lengthy delays actually helped the A320.'

Roger Beteille had asked one of Airbus's brilliant Polish-born engineers, Hartmut Mehdorn, head of Deutsche Airbus and a member of the Supervisory Board for twenty years, to become involved with the project. But there was a serious rift to resolve first. Nothing too drastic: just that Germany wanted to pull the plug on Airbus. There were some heated opinions on whether to go with the A320, favoured by the French, or the larger A340, the preferred choice of Lufthansa. Mehdorn says that Airbus had to attack Boeing money-spinner, the 727, with over 1,700 flying around the globe, and the 737. Airbus needed to move its battle tactics into the narrow-body market.

The idea was to expand the family with a smaller, short-medium, single-aisle, twin-engine aircraft to compete with the larger Boeing 737 variants that were being hatched in Seattle. The A320 was to offer seating for 150–180 passengers and would be built with more carbon-fibre composite. And it would feature the new 'fly-by-wire' control system.

The French government backed the project at the Paris Air Show in June 1981, and Air France set the ball rolling with an order for 25 jets. But the British and Germans were still unsure. The engine-makers were undecided too. General Electric and SNECMA were to develop an engine for the A320 but it needed more thrust than the existing CFM56. It was only after the International Aero Engines consortium was created by Pratt &

Whitney and Rolls-Royce, that GE/SNECMA upgraded the CFM56.

While the arguments and bickering about the workload went on, the technicians were developing the technology that would become a paradigm shift for commercial aviation. The fly-by-wire system featured five main computers which operated the hydraulic jacks and all the primary and secondary flight controls. The system was so advanced that it would not permit the pilot to exceed the aircraft's limitations. This included preventing the pilots exceeding g-force limitations.

This was a revolution. The international pilot community were going to take some persuading that they should relinquish control in the cockpit. The argument against it was that the captain was no longer in full control of the aircraft, but simply a servant. A new phrase was adopted by the pilots and crews in the cockpits: 'flight management'. Now the computers could judge more clearly the differences between a good take-off that burned less fuel, and an average one. It allowed the aircraft to trim itself more easily and efficiently in the air.

On 2 March 1984, Airbus announced it was to proceed with the A320, the initial version named the A320-100. However, only 21 versions of this model were made before the A320-200 became available in 1988. The later version had fuel tanks in the centre section of the wings which increased the take-off weight. And it had winglets. The plane flew for the first time on 22 February 1987, while Air France took delivery of the first A320-200 on 28 March 1988, with British Airways receiving, ironically, its first aircraft three days later.

There are some who believed that BA's initials did not stand for British Airways, but *Boeing Always*. But when BA took over British Caledonian in 1988 it inherited ten A320s which were on order from the former British carrier. By default, BA ended up with five of the A320-100s and the A320-200s. As one airline commentator, Robbie Shaw, said, 'It is understood that the airline would like to dispose of the aircraft, were it not for their popularity with passengers.'

1989 was a momentous year. It was the year the Berlin Wall came down, unifying East and West Germany in an outpouring of global euphoria that would soon evaporate in Germany into the realities of merging two rather alien nations. For Airbus it was also a momentous year. Orders were especially good: in the

United States, Northwest Airlines had ordered ten of the new A330 models on top of the twenty A340s they'd already committed to, while TWA requested forty A330s. In the Far East, the award-winning airline Cathay Pacific – known for its style and comfort, and its support for Boeing – asked for ten A330s. It had gas-guzzling TriStar L-1011s which it now wanted replaced with new-generation, more efficient planes. Even Aeroflot, the Soviet airline which supported its own state-owned plane builders, bought five A310-300s with options for more.

The Paris Air Show was a thrilling week for the Airbus people with orders for all Airbus types reaching 1,153 from 77 customers during the show. The only black spot on the horizon was a prolonged strike by BAe's workforce in the UK which created a backlog, running into March 1990, and cost the consortium £200m. But, by the end of the year, Airbus had booked 421 firm orders with a backlog value of $34bn. Throughout the year, the consortium delivered 105 aircraft with revenues in the region of $5bn. It seemed almost too good to be true. It was.

The invasion of Kuwait by Iraq on 2 August 1990 threw the aviation business into turmoil. Optimism went out of the window as traffic plummeted and revenue forecasts were thrown into disarray. Aviation fuel prices soared, but, more damaging in the long-term, it had a psychological impact on passengers and a fear of terrorist action. Air travel is a highly sensitive activity. And in 1991 the number of people travelling by plane dropped for the first time since the advent of jet travel. The situation would be prolonged and lasting.

Around the world, airlines began to see their revenues and passenger numbers tumbling. At best, this meant delayed delivery of new planes or the cancellation of options, at worst the cancellation of firm orders. Airbus was dealt such a blow in December 1992, when Northwest cancelled its order for 24 A340s and 50 A320s.

There was a deepening fondness for Airbus. As the 'Family' of Airbus types grew steadily, the airlines found the *commonality* of the planes rather compelling. The similarity of pilot's controls in the cockpit between the different types of Airbus planes allowed a concept called 'Mixed Fleet Flying'. Boeing tried to ignore this, branding it a marketing gimmick, but really it had no answer to this innovation. Again this was the genius of Roger Beteille. He had imagined a world where a pilot could fly one type of airplane, perhaps a 300-seater, and then the next day fly a 100-seater without having to relearn the layout and controls. Gradually, as Airbus built up to ten different models, it could offer serious savings in terms of pilot training. It was a winning formula.

Typically it took 25 working days for a highly paid pilot to learn about a different type of aircraft, how it handled and where the controls were. Training pilots, putting them through refresher courses and regular simulator updates, was a big expense. A Boeing 737 was completely different from a jumbo jet and required different classifications of licence and insurance. Not only that, but a Boeing 737-600 pilot had to go on refresher courses to fly a 737-700, or a 737-800. Airbus's 'fly-by-wire' planes were all designed with characteristics that were virtually the same; there was very little difference between models and the advanced computer system compensated for the weights and sizes. The single aisles had a similar type rating, and so did the twin aisles. There was very little difference between the A318/A319/A320 and A321.

Jürgen Thomas, the father of the A380, said it was vitally important to retain this commonality: 'You must have somebody guarding against changing this because engineers always want to invent something new for everything; even if it is very useful sometimes. If it was a gadget that could spoil the commonality, it wouldn't get on the plane. I was the biggest defender of commonality and so was the head of our training centre.'

With pilot salaries one of the most expensive assets on the balance sheet, it was better to keep them flying, especially in the low-cost sector. The airlines with perhaps a short-range and long-haul fleet would be able to use Airbus's Mixed Fleet Flying. This was possible with a much shortened training programme and Airbus's Cross Crew Qualifications, which meant more variety for pilots and greater flexibility for the airline's operations manager when selecting pilots.

Furthermore, when a captain retired, the cost of moving everyone up the ladder was huge. Airbus worked out that a captain retiring triggered off a cascade of eight staff movements, each requiring new rounds of training. This cost around $300,000 per person. The Airbus Family offered enormous productivity savings with less dead time. Airbus calculated that its Mixed Fleet Flying could save an airline $1m a year, per aircraft – it was no surprise that the airlines were interested.

For all their innovations, however, Airbus were still judged by the same yardstick as every other aerospace manufacturer – how safe are the planes? And for the first time in the company's history, serious questions were being asked about their reliability. In 1994, the German news weekly *Der Spiegel* interviewed Bernard Ziegler, the Director of Airbus Industrie, who was now responsible for the flight test and certification of all Airbus aircraft.

The interview was conducted in the light of several crashes. The first was at Bangalore, in February 1990, when an A320 landed short of the runway in clear weather killing 92; then in January 1992 in Strasbourg an A320 descended into a hill in clouds on approach to the airport, with 87 lives claimed; the following September an A320, landing in a thunderstorm, overran the runway at Warsaw, killing two people and injuring many more, and at Nagoya, in April 1994, an A300, with the co-pilot and autopilot in conflict, crashed tail first onto the ground, killing 246. This all came on top of the disaster in June 1994 when seven were killed – including Airbus's Chief Test Pilot.

Maiden flights were becoming safer and safer, although Airbus was stunned in 1994, when test pilot Nick Warner and six others were killed on the A330 prototype as they conducted a simulated engine failure exercise at Blagnac. It was a horror that jarred many people in Toulouse on the ground as they watched colleagues and friends perish. It was a difficult but not a dangerous test, and questions were raised later about the computerised autopilot in Airbus's 'fly-by-wire' planes. The autopilot was mistakenly left on at 2,000 ft but should have been at 7,000 ft, according to a checklist. This fundamental error meant that the crew allowed a situation to unfold where the plane's nose was too high for too long during a low-speed run. There was momentary confusion on the flight deck between the test engineer and Nick Warner, then the Chief Test Pilot of Airbus.

Warner had engaged the autopilot and deliberately 'failed' the left engine to test the plane. The crew then expected the Flight Management System to kick in and return the aircraft to a precise pitch. A two-second delay caused a disaster. The airspeed dropped rapidly since the nose did not go down, and the A330 was unable to maintain control and yawed and rolled. Warner tried desperately to throttle back the right engine to regain control, trying to make the wings and the nose level. But the plane hit the ground. It was a tragedy that shocked Toulouse.

The magazine wanted to know just how much the electronic technology on the planes had contributed to the disasters. Were technical failures contributing to the series of accidents? Or were pilots over-extended by the 'flying computers'?

Ziegler pointed out that Airbus had had a streak of bad luck and said that they had had fourteen accident-free years, although the downing of an Iranian Airbus shot down by the US Navy was not included. Ziegler told *Spiegel* that the A320's record compared favourably with the Boeing 727, 737 or DC9 when they were introduced.

He said that Airbus was 30 per cent better than the average of all builders – but he wanted it to be 100 per cent better. Again the technology was questioned – was the fly-by-wire philosophy of taking over some of the pilot's tasks by computer seriously flawed? Again Ziegler rebuffed the suggestion and added that all of the new technology developed by Airbus, from the glass cockpit displays to the new types of autopilot, was being followed by all the other manufacturers – Boeing included. Ziegler also emphasised that the pilot still had the last decision. 'Whoever suggests the contrary doesn't know what they're talking about,' he insisted. Ziegler was then pressed about the involvement of Airbus's autopilot in the Nagoya disaster. Why had Airbus not modified all the autopilots of these types?

He replied that requiring expensive modifications is not a simple matter, and would need to be investigated. He noted that Boeing had waited twelve years before recommending modifications in one particular case. Airbus developed an autopilot modification and recommended that the A300-600 customers use it. After the Moscow incident, Airbus had once again notified all airlines about the correct use of the autopilot. After the Nagoya accident, Airbus decided that the modifications they had recommended to A300-600 and A310 aircraft should be mandatory. It took two years and $60m to alter the fleet.

Airbus steadily increased the proportion of advanced composite material in the A320 since it first used glass fibre reinforced plastic fairings on the A300 in 1972. Today the A320's vertical fin, horizontal tailplane, engine cowls and wing control surfaces are composed of carbon-fibre reinforced plastic. The A380 has even more.

14. TRIPLE SEVEN UP

S uzanna Darcy-Hennemann is a stunning woman. With her curly blonde hair and trim figure, she is instantly recognisable on the tarmac at Boeing Field. Darcy-Hennemann is the Chief Test Pilot for Boeing's 777 programme. She is polite and personable and keen to answer questions on her pet subject – Boeing airplanes.

She joined Boeing in 1974 and spent her first seven years in the engineering department. She then became a trainer for airline pilots and in 1985 was named a Boeing production test pilot, becoming the first woman hired in this capacity. In 1989 she became the first woman to be rated as a captain on the 747-400, then the 737, 757 and 767. Her latest accomplishment in 2005 was the completion of testing of the second of two airplanes in the 777-200LR flight test programmes. As lead pilot, she spent nearly 600 flight hours testing overall engineering performance in different environments and under a host of conditions.

'I'm never apprehensive about being the first person to fly a new airplane off the production line because I'm totally confident that everyone at Boeing has done their job,' she says. 'We have the best people in the world putting our airplanes together and our crews have extensive training.'

In June 2005 in Paris she was on the first stage of a promotional tour for the 777-200LR, the latest iteration of the plane dubbed

The Twenty-first Century Jet. 'For ten years now, the 777 has had tremendous capabilities,' says her colleague Lars Andersen, Boeing's Vice President of the 777 programme. The 777 is a twin-engine aircraft. And two has become the new magic number for Boeing.

Essentially, airline engines have become dramatically more reliable, and, as a consequence, the need for four or three engines on long-haul flights is being superseded by something called ETOPS – or Extended-range Twin-engine Operations. Airbus said that in the entire history of jet transport there has never been an accident as a result of multiple engine failure due to two different causes. Yet only twenty years ago when airline chiefs were evaluating the DC10s and Lockheed L1011 TriStars, they insisted on three engines to fly over the Rocky Mountains.

The US Federal Aviation Administration insisted that a two-engine plane must be within sixty minutes of a diversionary airport if one engine failed. Of course, that made flying across oceans virtually impossible. So the A330 and the 777 were designed from the start with ETOPS in mind. The plane-builders wanted authority to fly 180 minutes from an airport. Boeing spent a great deal of time and huge amounts of testing on the Boeing 777 to achieve this. It has done this, making it one of the most versatile twin-engine planes in the world. Boeing even negotiated a 27-minute extension to the 180 rule on the North Pacific flying over Alaska, the Bering Sea and northern Russia, where there are few airports suitable for diversions. This was a significant breakthrough for Boeing – and one that would soon give them a commercial advantage.

Back in 1992 five senior Boeing Vice Presidents would meet every Tuesday at Renton for what was known as the Muffin Meeting. There were no rules, no written agenda and no minutes taken. Phil Condit, then head of commercial planes, was the unofficial chairman, and Dale Hougardy, head of 777 operations, would sit in with Alan Mulally, Neil Standal and Rudy Schad. It was in these informal meetings that strategies and ideas were mooted that would result in a plane that would have more computer technology and next-generation composite material than any other plane flying.

Alan Mulally, explaining in the early 1990s how the 777 was going to be a completely different beast, said, 'With earlier digital computers, we didn't have enough computational capacity to simulate the design of an airplane. We've been able to use computers for parts of the task – the best example is the flight-crew training simulators, where we simulated lots of the airplane's flying characteristics as well as the systems to teach pilots how to fly. But as digital computers became larger and could handle more capacity, the next step was to see how much we could make use of them as a design tool.'

In the past, full mock-ups of the eventual plane were made of plywood. Indeed, little had changed since the days of the Comet. But in the early 1990s, computer-aided design was the opening salvo in the Boeing revolution. The miracle in airplane design was possible because Boeing joined together two massive systems: CATIA – or the Computer-graphics Aided Three-dimensional Interactive Application – and EPIC, Electronic Preassembly. CATIA was already known by the plane-maker in France because it was used by Dassault.

'In the past, where we had to mock-up parts and try to figure out how to fit them together, now we were able to actually simulate the parts and assemblies and we can see ourselves all the parts are there and if they fit before we release them to all the makers around the world,' said Mulally.

This allowed different components – some minute – to be designed on screen by a qualified aircraft designer and then integrated into one single computer simulation of the plane. For the 777 project, Boeing bought over 2,000 computer terminals for the design teams and connected them to the world's largest group of IBM mainframe computers.

The arrival of the Internet also helped. Key partners in the process in Japan, and engine-makers in America and in the UK now had immediate access to the data and were kept up-to-speed on a daily basis with changes as soon as they had been approved by Boeing.

The Muffin meeting would debate whether aluminium-lithium was strong enough and light enough for major parts on the plane; they would examine in detail the rival A330/340 and look at its alloys and weights; they would discuss whether fly-by-wire was now the way to go for Boeing. It was all up for grabs.

The challenges to Boeing's engineers were immense. Walt Gillette, chief engineer in charge of systems, had the job of assessing fly-by-wire over the conventional cable-controlled systems.

'We wanted to adopt a far more up-to-the-minute computer technology but we worked very hard not to turn the 777 into a plane that is flown by reading computer screens rather than feeling the plane. Most commercial pilots have spent all their flying live in planes in which the feel of the controls and their senses combine with the sight and sounds of the cockpit. This gives them all-around feedback. We wanted Boeing pilots to have control to override the system if necessary.'

The plane was given the go-ahead and a new final assembly facility was built at Everett, 30 miles north of Renton. But this plane would have major input from Japan with 20 per cent contracted out to four main companies; Mitsubishi, Kawasaki, Fuji and the smaller company Nippi. Instead of a partnership with Japan taking 25 per cent equity, the big Japanese companies became subcontractors, making fuselage panels, floor beams and doors. Japan's companies put up about 10 per cent of the start-up costs for the $3billion venture, far less than expected.

But it worried the indigenous American worker. In Seattle, on 5 October 1995, members from the powerful International Association of Machinists and Aerospace Workers rejected a new contract. In a vote, the union reported that 19,905 employees – or 76 per cent – overwhelmingly voted to reject the Boeing offer while 20,553 – or 78 per cent – voted for strike action. A total of 26,304 ballots were cast in Puget Sound, Wichita, Portland and Spokane, or more than 80 per cent of the union's total membership. It was a kick in the head for Boeing.

A ten-week machinist strike by the 32,000 workers in Washington, Oregon and Kansas played havoc with production. There were some bitter and nasty exchanges that left a legacy for many years. But it ended on 14 December 1995 when the union members returned to their work stations. They had ratified a new four-year contract but it had been a painful disruption for Boeing.

Apart from the improved pay and health care conditions, a major element was to look at subcontracting and other commitments that would affect security of employment. There were genuine fears that Japan was coming across to Seattle and learning all about making planes, in what was known as the 'Open Kimono' policy of sharing information with the Japanese. Management and unions agreed to meet at least twice a year to discuss subcontracting and agreed that employees would not be laid off because of subcontracting. If Boeing was to remain competitive against its increasingly aggressive French-based competitor, it had to control its costs. When the dispute was settled, Boeing chairman Frank Shrontz and Phil Condit faced the media and admitted they had learned some lessons.

'Here's what's going on. Here's why it's going on. Here's why we've got to make the changes we're making. It's going to take a lot of communication, a lot of understanding of what it means for us to be competitive. It means being willing to sit down and talk,' said Condit. 'We certainly did not seek this strike ... It is disruptive, it does antagonise customers ... and it clearly causes us to incur costs.'

As New Year approached, Schrontz said 1995 had been a rollercoaster for the company, but said the first deliveries of the 777 and the progress on the design of the next-generation 737, were real highlights. Indeed British Airways flew home its first Boeing 777, powered by a General Electric GE90 engine, on Saturday, 15 November 1995. It was the culmination of a five-year Working Together Partnership between BA, Boeing and GE.

Alistair Cumming, BA's managing director of engineering, said the airplane was designed with intensive input from the airlines and BA was pleased to have been a part of the design. Earlier in the summer, the launch customer had flown the 777 for the first time when United Airlines Flight 921 flew from London Heathrow to Dulles International in Washington, a week after its delivery. Taking off at 11.40 a.m. it arrived in the US capital at 2.15 p.m. local time. United had also been a key partner in Boeing's Working Together programme.

'It is one thing to build an airplane that flies very well, but inside the tube of the airplane fuselage everything has to be working right for the passenger,' said Gordon McKinzie, United Airlines 777 programme manager. 'One of the drivers was that it had to be wider than a DC-10, and it had to have more storage capacity in the overhead bins. We wanted the bins to pull down more easily so the passengers could get access to them more easily.'

At the Paris Air Show in June 1995, Ron Woodard, President of Boeing Commercial Airplane Group, gave the much-needed business a fillip. He announced that four major carriers – All Nippon, Cathay Pacific, Korean Airlines and Thai Airways International – all with existing orders for the 777, had placed 31 orders for the new 777-300X. This was a stretched version capable of carrying 20 per cent – or 368 passengers – more than the 200 version. He told a press conference at Le Bourget this would be in three classes up to 5,700 nautical miles and ready for delivering in 1998. The Boeing 777-300ER (Extended Range) was unveiled on 14 November 2002 and took to the air on 24 February 2003. Engine efficiency had improved so much that the FAA increased the ETOPS rating to 240 minutes, which could be increased beyond this time once operational experience had been established. This was all excellent news for Boeing.

Woodard said, 'Even if Airbus stretched the A330, it could only do so by compounding the A330's existing range disadvantage. By our estimates, the 777-300X would offer significantly greater range than a stretched A330 and still carry more passengers.'

He added that a shortened version, the 777-100X, carrying 259 passengers in three classes would have a range of 8,600 nautical miles. 'It will fly farther than any other airplane today and up to 600 to 800 nautical miles farther than the proposed Airbus A340-800.'

Despite this, Larry Clarkson, Boeing's senior Vice President for planning and international development, was still forced to defend the decision to use suppliers from outside of the US, especially China. 'The way I see it, 80 per cent of something is better than 100 per cent of nothing. With every international deal that we've completed, we have created or maintained jobs in the Puget Sound area, in Wichita and in Philadelphia. Without these [overseas] deals, we would not have had those jobs. Nearly 70 per cent of our airplanes are sold overseas, yet more than 80 per cent of the jobs created by our sales stay here in the US. Clearly, the balance is in our favour,' he said in an interview with *Boeing News*, 7 July 1995.

At the time, China was not a member of the world trade body, GATT, and so Boeing had an offset arrangement to take certain parts so that it could sell commercial airplanes. Under a contract China was due to build a section of the 737 aft section, while aluminium and titanium forgings were also supplied by the Chinese.

Indeed, China was emerging as a significant market with 200 Boeing planes flying with seventeen airlines. One in every seven planes built by Boeing was being delivered to China. To keep up, Boeing had established a centre in Beijing in 1994 and set up a new subsidiary, Boeing China Inc.

Back in Seattle, however, union resentment was simmering. A no-win game of hardball was being played out, while executives in Toulouse watched with interest. Airbus weren't the only people interested in the drama. Best-selling author Michael Crichton, the creator of *ER* and *Jurassic Park*, thought it would make a suitable story for a bestseller, *Airframe* in 1997. He invented an airline thriller where industrial sabotage was used to halt an American aircraft deal going to China!

Flight International gave the Boeing 777, the largest-ever, twin-engine plane, a glowing report in its Flight Test in the April 26–2 May issue in 1995. Harry Hopkins, flying with Chief Test Pilot John Cashman, took the plane for a spin out from a gloomy day at Boeing Field. 'The cockpit is the most spacious of any airliners yet. The electrically powered seats run very smoothly and rudder-pedal adjustment is in a handy raised position. Large, opening windows give a wide-angle side view.'

It is a heavy beast though. The plane's weight at take-off is 202,250 kg (202.2 tonnes), with 117,345 litres of fuel, weighing 61,000 kg. By comparison, a typical on-the-road saloon car, such as a Volkswagen Golf, weighs over one tonne, at 1,320 kgs. The Pratt & Whitney PW4077 engines now give off 77,000 lbs of thrust. The Boeing 777 was also available with the slightly smaller, Rolls-Royce Trent 800, and the larger GE90-85B. Jets need a vast amount of fuel to get them off the ground and at lower levels; the 777 burns 8,600 kg an hour at 5,000 ft, then 6,900 kg an hour at 17,500 ft, and about 4,500 kg per hour when it levels out at 35,000 ft. The climb takes 20 minutes and it burns 4,900 kg of fuel. With the plane now weighting 197,350 kg, it can cruise at its optimal altitude of 38,000 ft, with a fuel flow of 3,300 kg an hour. The certified ceiling is 43,100 ft which is achievable near the end of the flight when the plane's weight has dropped to around 175,000 kg.

This was Boeing's first plane mirroring Airbus's fly-by-wire flight controls. Hopkins's verdict: 'At times the 777 is almost too agile; it responds best to a light touch on the controls, rather than a grip, taking full advantage of pitch trim. It is sweet in normal operation at scheduled speeds, with pilot-friendly reminders of speed and altitude limits. You always feel in contact with the airplane, mainly by virtue of the actuator-produced speed stability. In contrast, the Airbus feels a little more distant. I would not say that the 777 is easier to fly than the Airbus fly-by-wire types, but perhaps easier to learn to fly if you come from a conventional type.'

Boeing rediscovered its *raison d'etre* with the 777. It could not have been better timing because the flying public was rapidly losing the thrill of flying. The mystique was evaporating under the stress of herding thousands of people on an off a plane every day. While the bus concept was good, it was devaluing the experience of flying. Now Boeing became evangelical ... and it was good news. Boeing says the 777 is the fastest-selling twin-aisle plane in the history of aviation. Its long range and ETOPS rating has made it popular. With 693 firm orders and 517 in service in the middle of 2005, it was hard to disagree with Boeing's verdict.

A bonus was the 777 Freighter sales, with each plane priced at $240 million. Boeing's sales pitch was that it offered more capacity than any other twin-engine freighter and the lowest trip cost of any large freighter. The 777 Freighter has a payload capability of 229,000 lbs or around 104 metric tonnes with a range of 4,885 nms (9,045 km). The first 777 Freighters are due to be delivered in late 2008. By the middle of 2007, 78 777 Freighters, worth about $18.5 billion, had been sold to 10 customers around the world.

Anita Polt, the Regional Director, Marketing, of Boeing Commercial Airplanes, is one of Boeing's new breed of believers. A smart young ambassador who wants her business to go places, she says of the 777-200ER: 'It's a lot lighter. Over 28 tonnes lighter on take-off weight. And that means a lot of fuel-burn per seat. Everybody has fuel-burn on the brain these days. Everyone is watching the price of barrels of oil. So a lot of airlines when they are making their fleet decisions are looking at the airplane that burns less fuel. It's the smart business choice,' she said at a presentation in Boeing's Commercial Airplane HQ in Seattle.

Since the demise of the Anglo-French Concorde, the fastest plane in the sky today is the Boeing 747-400. An amazing statistic considering its age. The Boeing 787 will be about the same speed, and the 777 is slightly slower. But, in Seattle, they feel that it's a selling point that they are roughly as fast as each other.

'This really matters on the longer-range flights. When you've got a faster airplane, honest-to-goodness, air traffic controllers will give priority clearance because they want to get them out of the patterns as quickly as possible!'

Polt explains that the Triple Seven flies out of Vancouver a little bit later than the A340 but still gets in faster to its Asia destination and that means passengers are through customs much sooner.

'We try to make our airplanes very structurally and aerodynamically efficient. That's not just a neat thing. It has a huge impact on fuel burn and the bottom line of airline,' enthuses Polt.

A Boeing 777-200LR, with two GE GE90-110B1 engines with 110,100 lbs of take-off thrust, has a fuel capacity of 47,890 US gal (181,280 l). It has a maximum range of 9,240 nms, using extra fuel tanks in the lower hold instead of cargo. It carries 301 passengers and Boeing says its relative seat-mile cost is 15 per cent less than a four-engine Airbus 340-500, with 280 seats, over 5,000 nms. Although the more modern A340-600, now being used on a lot of across-Asia routes, is substantially more efficient and carries 323 passengers.

Polt says the empty weight of the airplane is divided by the number of seats to get the relative seat-mile costs. 'It's a very meaningful measure of structural efficiency,' she says. 'It's not the kind of thing we make up because it looks good. It has real meaning. We are talking about a 13 to 26 per cent less fuel burn on a Boeing 777 airplane than an Airbus,' says Polt. Extra weight creates so many extra costs, including the wear and tear on the tyres and brakes, the throttle and the engine, pilot and crew pay, landing fees and fuel burn.

So a challenge was thrown out to the industrial designers scattered around Seattle to make it a comfortable ride for the twenty-first-century passenger. They came up with some smart goods: 'The Signature Interior is a breakthrough in industrial design. It was first introduced on the 777 and has expanded across our twin-aisle airplanes. What we have created is a curved, upswept architecture in the cabin providing a more spacious and pleasing appearance. With wider seats and aisles, vast headroom and sidewall clearance, there is a full view of the cabin, and continuous streams of light and ceiling architecture. So the passengers are given a greater sense of space,' says Polt.

The overhead bins are increasingly an essential factor in aircraft design. The discerning traveller now has more hand-luggage and takes more bags on board. So the new planes have to be designed to handle larger carry-on hold-alls, computer bags and suitcases.

'We've designed them so that when they close, they virtually disappear into the ceiling. We've also increased stowage space with passengers gaining more than 100 per cent more space for carry-on bags,' she says.

Independent surveys show three out of four people like flying on the Boeing 777s. The interior design is now a big selling point, allowing the airlines to choose different architecture that will help them with branding. In a tough market, this differentiation will be vital.

Boeing says the 777-200LR can fly the same range as the A340-500 without auxiliary fuel tanks. If an airline goes for the three extra fuel tanks it can fly another 700 nautical miles but doesn't have the room for cargo. This is a trade-off for the extra range.

The 777's success gave Boeing a spring in its step. Boeing's Renton plant is on the lake, a twenty-minute cab ride from Seattle-Tacoma Airport. It is a massive manufacturing facility deeply etched in Boeing's history. Three times a day, a plane revs up on the nearby runway and takes to the air before landing a few miles down the road at Boeing Field, the home of Boeing's test flight centre. The final documents are exchanged, credit details finalised and it is then handed over to its new owners, any one of a hundred world airlines.

'It's like a baby leaving the nest,' says Mary Jean Olsen, communications manager with Boeing Commercial Planes, now retired. 'Every time I see a plane rising up into the clouds, I go ka-ching, ka-ching,' she says pressing her fingers on an imaginary till.

Like so many people here in Seattle, Mary Jean loves Boeing. It has been her career, her family and her life. Now, as she enjoys her leisure time, she reflects on her time with the business. 'Yep, there have been many ups and downs. Times when it hasn't been so great up here, but Boeing is a fabulous company and a great business. The ordinary people who work here are committed to one thing: making the best and safest commercial planes that can possibly fly.'

Mary Jean leads a small party through a side door into the production hall of the Boeing 737 Next Generation. It is a vast cavern with scaffolding, work stations and roof cranes. There are dismembered planes in various stages of assembly and, at a faraway door, one completed plane, ready to taxi out to the runway. This is one of the world's largest indoor spaces, pipped only by Boeing's factory further north at Everett where the Boeing

747 is produced. But what Everett has in terms of size, is dwarfed by the importance of this new production line. This modern system is the future, and is currently in use on the 737NG, but more crucially will be the template for the production of the Boeing 787 Dreamliner. It has taken a lot of toil and sweat to get to this point. Airplane designers, production managers, executives, the unions and the mechanics have all had to change the way they think and work.

'When we began to realise that Airbus were whipping our asses, we had to do something to prove we were still the world's best at making commercial airplanes,' says one of the mechanics as he painstakingly countersinks screws into a section of fuselage.

Boeing's wake-up call has reverberated to its most sleepy nooks and crannies and has roused almost everyone. *Almost* everyone. As far back as 1991, Boeing knew that they faced an uphill struggle. Frank Shrontz had identified the problem himself. Complacency. Pure and utter complacency. Speaking to the Seattle Chamber of Commerce on Friday, 27 September 1991, the Boeing boss knew something was up. He said Boeing was determined to regain its competitive edge.

'At times, that may require taking tough stands on sensitive issues – like higher wages – and keeping our wage and benefit structure under control,' he said. 'Could Puget Sound [an area of Seattle where Boeing is based] turn into an aerospace rust-belt in the twenty-first century – complete with padlocked factories, unemployment lines and urban blight?'

He paused and looked at his audience of business people. He could see their heads shaking. 'Yes, it could. Boeing is subject to the same kind of cost and market pressure as any other American manufacturer. Each year the competition gets a little stronger. And that means each year we've got to get a little better, or one day we're going to get beaten. It's as simple as that.'

Honest words, but it took a long time to convince Boeing's own people. Even in 2005, when the company was still fighting to keep its costs down, another damaging dispute flared causing more lost days – and plane delays – through strike action.

By the end of 1999, Boeing had fallen behind its rival, with Airbus capturing 70 per cent of the orders during the year. While Boeing has made continual improvements to its planes, upgrading each model, it forgot about how to produce them more effectively. Orders were late, production slipped and delivery became depressingly unreliable. Airlines were complaining, but the criticisms seemed to fall on deaf ears. The only form of censure came from crippling compensation payments.

One British aircraft executive said, 'It was awful at Boeing. You had no idea about delivery or when you could make plans for the arrival of a new plane. It was pretty shoddy in terms of customer service. The people at Boeing made great planes, yes. But their attitude? It was all wrong.'

Even El Al, the Israeli state-owned airline, a loyal friend and supporter of the American aerospace industry, announced it was considering the purchase of some Airbus planes for the first time, though the actual order has yet to materialise. The commercial plane business needed another radical rethink. It had to look again at the whole shooting match.

Randy Baseler said, 'We learned so much by making the 777. This was a plane designed and built using the best digital technology. Now we needed to improve our ability to make planes at lower costs by cutting out all the extra changes, making fewer mistakes in design and production and with fewer requirements to make last-minute changes.'

While Boeing had a dominant market share it didn't really matter as long as the planes were the best. Certainly Boeing products were safe and reliable but the production system remained remarkably inefficient. Sandy Angers knows every inch of the shed at Renton, where each plane is constructed, and all its quiet little backwaters where an errant worker can squeeze in a sly break. Like Mary Jean, she is a Boeing woman to the core, and speaks with evangelical zeal about Boeing's new-found religion of lean production and just-in-time delivery – though she is similarly candid about the production difficulties of previous years.

'Making a plane was a very time-consuming process,' she explains. 'Production work only happened in the first of three shifts of the day. The second shift was used to pull away all the tooling from all the airplanes. The third shift was used to tow out the last airplane and jockey all the planes up one position.'

All in all, this practice ensured that Boeing was only able to use one *third* of the day to actually build commercial airplanes, meaning that work on new planes only went on for four months of the year. It was a nasty hangover from the earliest days of the hand-crafted production of US bombers. It was hardly state-of-the-art Japanese modern car-plant production. The whole operation was languid and fraught with debilitating flaws. One guy leaving his monkey wrench in the men's room could mean hours of lost production, as the chain would be broken, and then getting the momentum going again took an age. In the meantime, orders slipped. Excuses were made to customers and Boeing began to get their awful reputation for delivery.

'At one time, if you ordered a new Airbus A320 you were told when it was coming and it was delivered right on time. But a Boeing? Well, it became rather ridiculous. It wasn't a joke. You'd have thought they were doing you a goddamn favour,' said one leasor who has invested in both Boeing and Airbus.

Boeing's products were high quality, but production was lagging way behind. The problem stemmed from Boeing's insistence on doing everything and having their way about everything, says one American industry sub-contractor. 'I talked to a Goodrich guy [who make the landing gear for Boeing and Airbus models] who said Boeing has 140 design engineers for landing gear. He said, 'We make landing gear, that is what we do. Yet Boeing has 140 landing gear engineers and they have never made landing gear. We had no idea what they did except to meddle in our business.'

It is his belief that Boeing is still overstaffed and delegates far too little to outside contractors. 'Most of the suppliers I deal with prefer to deal with Airbus. Sure they drive a hard bargain, but once you have cut the deal they leave you alone. Just make sure it's on our loading dock when we say it's going to be there. We are going to squeeze you by 3 per cent every year, that's the deal,' he says.

But the transformation did eventually come to Boeing, driven by Alan Mulally, the hero of the Boeing 777. Bringing a new broom and a fresh management credo, Mulally was determined to change the old ways of working. On 1 September 1998, Boeing announced the sweeping changes. Chairman Phil Condit dropped Ron Woodard as head of the Commercial Airplane Group and brought the blue-eyed boy who delivered the 777 back from his spell as President of Information and Defence Systems. Woodward's tenure had ended in desperate problems with production as Boeing tried to increase output from 22 to 40 aircraft a month. It had been a disaster.

Along with Mulally came Fred Mitchell, Walt Gillette and Scott Carson, as group financial officer. But a changing mindset also

Above Giant of the sky: The four-engined A380 is now the world's largest commercial airplane capable of carrying over 555 passengers (© Airbus S.A.S 2005)

Below The challenger: Boeing's new 787 has two engines and aims to fly passengers directly to their destinations and avoid the hub airports (© The Boeing Company)

Above Jet pioneers: John Cunningham, the Comet's Test Pilot, with Sir Frank Whittle, the designer of the jet engine, and Major Frank Holroyd (© Getty Images)

Below left President and Chairman of Boeing, William M Allen, who staked the company on building the Boeing 707 (© The Boeing Company)

Below right The Airbus genius: Roger Beteille (© Airbus S.A.S 2005)

Above The British leader: The De Havilland Comet, here being captained by John Cunningham in 1958, was the world's first passenger jet – well ahead of the Americans – but lost its lead after a series of disasters knocked confidence (© Hulton-Deutsch Collection/CORBIS)

Below Beautiful beast: The Boeing 707. More than 760 planes were built by Boeing making it one of the world's most successful commercial airplanes (© The Boeing Company)

Above left The Gallic dynamo: Noel Forgeard, former Chief Executive Officer of EADS, which owns Airbus. Forgeard staked his reputation on the A380's success (© Airbus S.A.S 2005)

Above right Father of the A380: Jürgen Thomas, the German engineer, was given the task of getting the plans for the super jumbo jet off the drawing board (© Airbus S.A.S 2005)

Left Super salesman: John Leahy, now one of Airbus's Chief Operating Officers, has built a ferocious reputation for his ability to sell Airbus's planes (© Airbus S.A.S 2005)

Right Boeing to the core: Alan Mulally was the project leader of the 777 which broke the mould with new technology. Now he is head of Boeing's Commercial Plane Division (© The Boeing Company)

Below left A turbulent time: Phil Condit was revered as one of Boeing's finest business leaders, but he was forced to quit after taking the company in the wrong direction (© The Boeing Company)

Below right Boeing's new boss: James McNerney's arrival in June 2005 has given the US planemaker a new-found zest in its battle with Airbus (© The Boeing Company)

Above An icon of the sky: The Boeing 747 has been the market leader since going into service with Pan Am – now it faces a challenge from the A380. But a newer version – the 747-8 – promises more new technology and fuel efficiency (© The Boeing Company)

Below A European success story: The Airbus A300B, the B was later dropped, was able to capture a large share of the market and allow the Airbus Industrie consortium to challenge the Americans (© Airbus S.A.S 2005)

Above Seattle view: Boeing's manufacturing plant at Renton, outside Seattle. Its other main facility at Everett is where the Boeing 787 is now being built (© The Boeing Company)

Below French connections: Toulouse is the main assembly plant for the mammoth A380. Completed parts are brought from across Europe, including the wings from Broughton, South Wales, and the fuselage from Hamburg (© Airbus S.A.S 2005)

Left Paris Fashion: President Chirac and French ministers, along with Airbus's executives, including Noel Forgeard, visiting the A380 at the Paris Air Show in June 2005. The A380 was the star performer at the show (© Kenny Kemp)

Above New kid on the blocks: Airbus's announcement that it is to launch the twin-engined A350 has re-opened a trade rift between America and Europe (© Airbus S.A.S 2005)

Left Record breakers: Captains Suzanna Darcy-Henneman and Frank Santoni after the world record 13,000 miles non-stop flight from Hong Kong to London flying east by Boeing 777-200LR Worldliner in November 2005 (© The Boeing Company) requires the wholehearted support of the unions and that in itself was a gargantuan task. Unsurprisingly, it hasn't been an easy ride and even in 2005 the Seattle production lines were halted again by a damaging union dispute.

When Mulally took over, Boeing was facing unprecedented production problems in every department. There were large write-offs because of late deliveries and compensation payments, not to mention the money lost after the merger with McDonnell Douglas. These financial pressures lead to Boeing reporting its first annual loss in history in 1997. It was Woodard who carried the can.

Condit admitted: 'We have experienced unsatisfactory financial performance with our commercial aircraft operations. Our expectations are that commercial aircraft operations produce significant double-digit operating margins. We concluded there must be significant changes in the composition of the management team.'

Sandy Angers explains more of the manufacturing transformation. 'Today, with nose-to-tail straight line configuration, we don't have to do the jockeying, so the production work occurs on two shifts. Now the third shift is done to replenish all the tool and parts kits that we provide to the mechanics,' she explains. The first shift starts at 6 a.m. and ends around 2.30 p.m., then there is a two-hour buffer and the second shift starts at 4.30 p.m.

'That was intentional. The reason we put in a two-hour buffer was to allow any work teams to finish their jobs if they got behind. They could finish without getting in the way of the second shift.' This prevents 'travelling' or the work jumping out of sequence. In one interview, Mulally said, 'Some people think it is between five and fifteen times the cost when it is out of sequence.'

The second shift finishes after midnight, and the third shift is now much smaller, dealing with the clean up and replenishing tool kit and parts kits. They also take the tug that pulls the last airplane and then recycle the tug to the back of the production line again. Boeing has identified key lean manufacturing processes to improve airplane production. 'We follow this in our production system and it has allowed us to increase our quality and efficiency and reduce the flow time and level of inventory that we hold,' explains Angers, as the group is driven in a four-seater electric car deeper into the shed.

For instance, back in 1999, it used to take 22 days from the time the fuselage arrived from the Wichita plant by train until it went out the door as a completed plane. The train journey bringing the fuselage section took eight days to cover the 2,000 miles. The Classic 737 fuselage used to be delivered in two pieces and once they arrived in Seattle they would be joined together. But now Wichita delivers a single piece. By June 2005, the Renton workforce had cut the 22 days down from receipt of fuselage to completion to just eleven. This is a stunning statistic. Boeing is now able to produce an airplane in half the time. The amount of inventory kept in stores has been reduced by 60 per cent too. 'We're moving towards a just-in-time delivery system where parts are delivered to us as they are needed. Instead of carrying two years' worth of inventory, or twenty airplanes, we now carry just two airplanes worth of inventory,' says Sandy, 'We want to get it down to one,' she adds decisively.

In 1999, there were steel towers and gantries alongside the production line that were piled high with parts and tools. But improvements have meant they can clear out all the towers and renovate the space. Now Boeing's workforce have offices over-looking the plant. This may seem a small point, but it is crucial to Boeing's new way of working.

Boeing had become a huge and amorphous organisation, and had almost become removed from what it actually did. The marketing and sales people, the communications professionals, the human resources teams, even the design engineers were so far removed from the real-life washers-and-screws production, that for most Boeing employees the business could have been making chocolate-chip cookies rather than airplanes. But now 2,500 people have moved into the renovated space so the human resources department and the number crunchers can view the product as it moves along to completion.

'Every time you go to the john, you get a glimpse of the action down on the floor,' says one marketing executive. 'And while it doesn't often look as if there is a huge amount of action. You can tell by the painted tailfins of the airlines that we are making something special.'

But this is more than just having some fine offices overlooking the shop front, affording occasional glimpses of the manufactur-ing process. It has brought problem-solving into the twenty-first century. 'The mechanics on the factory floor love the fact they can go up to an engineer and say: "Hey, I've got a problem with your drawing. Help me fix it,"' says Sandy Angers.

'Under the old way, the design engineers with their planes and blueprints were based miles away in another Boeing complex and good luck trying to find them. Their phone numbers were always engaged or they were in a meeting. Or out to lunch. The mechanics couldn't leave the building, so the engineers would have to come to the factory.' Their proximity now allows a much smoother operation.

Once a fuselage arrives from Wichita, the first job is to put temporary floorboards inside so the mechanics can move around easily. The insulation blankets, the air ducts and the 36 miles of wiring are then tagged and fixed to the inside walls. Every task is checked, crosschecked, then inspected again before the next stage can go ahead.

On this day in June 2005, most of the 737NGs are earmarked for familiar airlines, though their bodies are bright green, coated with a new protective layer, which is currently being tested. During its time in what is known as first position, the mechanics and electricians work inside on securing the ducts to the bulkhead and weaving the coloured cabling through the spaces in the ceiling and the floors. The cockpit is taking shape but is still a mess of colourful spaghetti with gap sites for computer hardware. But the scene changes quickly. Once the fuselage has gone through its first position it is lifted gently and put into second position.

'The fuselage stays up for about four days in the assembly area where the fuselage and cockpit are built up before being placed into a new position called the Wing to Body Joint. That's pretty self-explanatory. This is where the long metal tube begins to look like a real airplane,' shouts Angers over the wailing sound of a cacophony of power drills.

'This is where the fuselage gets not only its wings but its feet. The landing gear and the nose gear are fixed and then it is able to move onto the moving tug line where it is pulled along the factory floor at two centimetres per minute.'

After the 737NG leaves this second position it is then able to move on its own landing gear. 'Not only is the airplane digitally designed on computer but so is all the major tooling for manufacturing. All the light green tools are all designed on computer, so we can get a much more accurate fit.'

The laser tooling enables the wing and fuselage to be joined to within a thousandth of an inch. Then to ensure the precise alignment of wing to fuselage, lasers are used. 'The straighter the alignment, the straighter the airplane will be in flight and the more fuel-efficient it will be,' explains Sandy.

In 1999, it took two days to join the wings to the body in this position. Now it takes a single day. 'They are attaching the wings, the landing gear and now the nose gear,' explains the Boeing host. 'Once it leaves this position it joins the moving line. It is attached to the self-guided automated tug that is hooked onto the nose gear of the 737.'

Everything around the production line is now on wheels. Boxes, pipes, tool holdalls, all have rollers. In its final phase, the 737 is hooked by the nose gear to the self-guided automated tug. Two sensors follow the airplane down the line so if it starts to wander it is automatically brought back into alignment. Renton now employs lean manufacturing. 'The basic philosophy is to rely on your employees. We consider them the experts in our production system because they work with these processes day in and day out. We've asked our employees to figure out new ways of manufacturing based on a full production, just-in-time system.'

The Boeing mechanics, all members of the International Association of Machinists, view themselves as American artisans – the aristocracy of labour. They are a skilled labour force that has fought hard for its conditions over many years. But they have strongly resisted change and now there is an acute problem of attracting enough young mechanics into the trade. In the downturns, Boeing has often shed thousands of people and it has always been the case of last in, first out. As the century closed, the workers were looking for a reason for their problems, and found an obvious target.

In November 1999, the International Association of Machinists District Lodge 751 – which represents more than 30,000 Boeing workers – found a new complaint. That the playing field in the aerospace industry now favoured Airbus Industrie. The lodge claimed European governments were funnelling subsidies to Airbus, hurting Boeing sales and threatening the company's workers. Lodge officials were also worried about countries drawing work contracts from Boeing in exchange for purchasing the company's products.

'We feel that Airbus has an unfair advantage. Being subsidised, they can basically give an airplane away,' said District Lodge 751 President Bill Johnson in an interview with the local *Seattle-Post-Intelligencer* newspaper. 'I think the ground rules need to be equal.'

Local Lodge 751 was only a tiny labour voice heard in Seattle that week as anti-globalisation campaigners gathered to protest at the power of the World Trade Organisation, holding its members' meeting in Seattle. Leaders from more than 130 nations, including President Clinton, were attending with 5,000 delegates, but the city was shocked when the anti-capitalist protests turned violent and nasty with pitched battles in the street. Washington State Governor Gary Locke was urged by Secretary of State Madeleine Albright to call out the National Guard to clear the streets. Police used tear gas and rubber bullets in scenes that this liberal and tolerant city hadn't witnessed before. The riots became headline news beamed around the globe. And Seattle became a by-word for anti-globalisation. At Boeing, there were concerns that the larger protest threatened to drown out the voice of the local union.

The AFL-CIO and other unions hoped to flood the airwaves and newspapers with their demands, including a provision that future WTO trade pacts comply with core labour standards. Union leaders also wanted their representatives on future trade negotiating teams said Thomas Buffenbarger, the President of the International Association of Machinists and Aerospace Workers, the parent union of District Lodge 751.

President Clinton, who had upset organised labour by championing free trade policies, tried to ease labour's concerns by pushing for the creation of a World Trade Organisation Working Group on Trade and Labour. But, the President wasn't doing enough, said Buffenbarger. 'We are beyond the working group stage. Put us at the table. Give us a vote.'

Government subsidies were top of Lodge 751's concerns. Johnson argued that Airbus's advantage translated into fewer sales for Boeing and possibly fewer jobs for District Lodge 751 workers. He said that even when Boeing sells airplanes and other products Puget Sound Machinists say they can still lose.

Johnson also demanded a halt to 'offsets', where foreign companies would be given parts of the complete work in exchange for airplane orders. Some aerospace insiders felt the union leader must be living on planet Zog. Indeed the 737NG involves intensive input from Japanese suppliers: Mitsubishi Heavy Industries, Kawasaki Heavy Industries and Fuji Heavy Industries all have binding agreements with Boeing for major parts.

By 2006, there was a better appreciation of the reasons for all of this. Now the American mechanics work in teams with their own names such as Royal Lights, Raiders, Wildcats, Cable Hawks and Tankers. They have made uncomfortable changes, indeed they have claimed it was all one-way traffic on their side. Before the changes, the mechanics bought all their own tools. They would often have their own favourite tools hidden away; a hammer to bang in a stubborn screw, or a set of pliers to trim a loose piece of wiring. But this made it hard to find out if the tools were properly certified or even calibrated correctly. This was coupled with the inefficiency of the system whereby when the mechanics picked up their tools they then wandered over to another part of the factory to get the parts they needed for the day.

'It could be anything between 20 and 45 minutes before the Boeing mechanic even touched the airplane,' explains Angers. This threw everything out of sequence and it had to stop. Walt Gillette, the veteran Boeing engineer, set up 'process councils' to analyse every part of the engineering process and came up with a resolution. It required more arduous negotiations around the table until an agreement was banged out.

So there was a revolution. Today when the mechanics arrive, everything that they need to do the job for the day is provided right where they need it and when they need it; all calibrated and checked and bought by Boeing. At the end of 1999, there were large work crews at Renton with anything between 12 and 25 people with one leader. Everyone on that crew had a specific job that they were trained to do. And few people knew exactly how to do that job, so if they were on holiday or sick, the production line faced problems. This had to end. So again, more prolonged sessions to resolve this. If there was a problem you would approach the leader and the team would all work together to resolve any issues. Indeed *Working Together* became the Mulally Motto. Today, the work teams are broken down into teams of six with a quality assurance person assigned to each team. Each team was able to choose a name and design their own individual logos with the aim of getting everyone on the team cross-trained so they can all help each other out if one falls behind.

'Under the old system, we never knew we had a problem until the whole line shut down. Today, there is a visual control system in place – a bank of large-scale television screens where each job is lit up when it is completed. Green for completion means the next phase can go ahead. Green means everything is fine,' says Sandy Angers. This morning everything is a comforting green.

If a mechanic in the Wildcats has a problem, he logs in at the computer on the production floor and indicates what is happening. This immediately turns the box on the visual control system to orange. The support service team beside the screens will call up the people needed to get help. It could be a manufacturing engineer, part control area or quality assurance.

'These folks work at getting the right person down here as soon as possible. The response time now is fifteen minutes. Under the old system all the engineers were located in a building south of Renton. And the response was: 'Maybe, I'll make it down there in an hour or two . . . or even tomorrow.' That was if you could find the right guy,' says Angers. 'Today everyone can see the movement of the plane and see what is causing the line to stop. So they are motivated to get any hold-ups sorted out within fifteen minutes,' she adds.

The moving production line was set up to create a sense of urgency at the factory, so that everyone knows that they had to keep it moving. There is no obvious sense of urgency as the mechanics, some wearing colourful bandanas and many wearing Lodge 751 T-shirts, wander into each area and fix their component. There's plenty of banter, and only a few suspicious looks at the besuited strangers on the shop floor. The flashing screens also give the mechanics a far clearer idea of how they are doing. All the changes were negotiated, step-by-step. On either side of the display board the work teams can see how they are doing. In America, fixated with baseball, basketball and football statistics, this is a winner in keeping interest and motivation going.

'On this system we can see all the problems and issues of this airplane and its exact status,' she points out. 'We can see where we are with resolving these problems, and, on the left side, that represents how many jobs have to be completed and how many yet to go.' These metrics were unavailable just a few years ago. So the mechanics – and the management – had little idea of how they were doing throughout the course of the day. Now they are able to judge their performance and progress and the status of every job.

'So the guys on the production floor have been given ownership of the full production of the Boeing 737NG as it progresses towards completion,' she explains. The change in tooling was a major part of the huge improvements in productivity at Boeing. For each individual task, and there are thousands on a plane, there is a plastic crate about eighteen inches deep with a number of pigeon holes marked with letters and numbers. For instance, in every flight deck installation kit there is a slot for every piece needed for the job, such as 'the marking template for the number three window' or MTW3. It's based on the old wooden scissors boxes used in infant school. The numbers represented a job number. Everything the mechanic needs is in that kit. And the kits were designed by mechanics. The people doing the job have worked out how to set out the tools and they are presented in a more functional, easy-to-use way. The time savings have been huge.

Everything is colour-coded, with blue representing all the tools, green for chemicals or hazardous materials, and grey for the smaller parts such as nuts, bolts and screws. Inside the fuselage the wiring trails are like long, long, coloured strands of plastic spaghetti, all tucked in neatly to the insulated bulkheads. Sandy Angers points at a tool crate with a few gaps. 'It's easy to see that at the end of the shift if this tool kit is brought back to the 'tool jail' you know immediately if something is missing.' After the shift, each kit goes back to kit jail and the supervisor and the mechanic cannot release this back into the kitting area until all the tools are accounted for. 'They have to go back and find this piece of equipment before they can go home,' she says. This is so that it hasn't been left in the fuselage or the wing – Boeing abounds with apocryphal stories of jumbo jets rattling with screwdrivers or a hammer.

Now the Boeing 737-800 plane is taking shape. Its list price is $54m but large orders secure substantial discounts. Standing on the concrete floor and looking up, it still looks large with its painted tail-fin. The swept-back wings span 117 ft 5 in (35.7 m) with their beautifully distinctive blended winglets. The plane is only slightly longer than the span, at 129 ft 6 in (39.47 m).

The Auxiliary Power Unit is like a metal funnel sticking out of the end of the plane; it is made from titanium. The APU gives the airplane power before it takes off, helping the start-up ignition and keeping the lights on in the cabin, before the engine power kicks in. Titanium alloy is being increasingly used by both Boeing and Airbus. While most people know about it for dental root implants and artificial knee and hip joints, 65 per cent of the world's production is used in commercial and military aerospace. The 777 has around 8 per cent titanium, while this has jumped to 20–22 per cent for the 787 Dreamliner. There are continuing concerns about its supply in this very fickle market, especially when the ore is mined in politically turbulent regions.

Boeing is supplied by the Russian giant, VSMPO, which developed its use in Soviet subs and spaceships, and weapons and warships, and is one of the major commercial suppliers for Boeing. But one of the key Russian subcontractors, Volnogorsk GOK, in the Ukraine, which provides an essential ore for titanium, has had a chequered history with its Russian client.

Titanium is the ninth most common element in the Earth's crust and is recovered from deposits of rutile, leucoxene and ilmenite ore from which titanium dioxide is extracted. Australia, India and South Africa are the leading suppliers but Russia and China are the regular suppliers for the aviation business, because the cost of extraction is high. This is vital for VSMPO who make the completed titanium forgings for the Boeing APUs and parts of the landing gear.

The metal is very different from other light metals, such as aluminium and magnesium, because it allows the formation of alloys and is a good bonding metal. High-quality alloys have a tensile strength and toughness, are more fatigue-crack resistant than other metals, and are resistant to oxidation and corrosion. For example, the hydraulic fluids in an Airbus and Boeing landing gear are highly corrosive, so the use of titanium prevents any damage to this vital part of the aircraft.

With all the time savings, Boeing is paying a backhanded compliment to Airbus's methods of production. Far more of the components were pre-prepared before they arrived at Renton, just like Toulouse. One example is the construction and installation of fuel-tubes which takes fuel from the wings and pumps it around a system of pipes through the engines. Fixing them into a plane is a very delicate operation. Sandy Angers explains. 'Before, you would take 900 little pieces and the mechanic would go into the confined wing area and assemble it in a very small and confined place. It was very hard on the body. It was a tough job and time-consuming. We took that work right out of the aircraft. It's now undertaken by a feeder line mechanic. So instead of 900 parts an installation mechanic gets 120 parts. He spends less time in the wing, so it is better for their physical state and it improves the quality and improves the flow time.'

The Moonshine teams, who were encouraged to break the rules and come up with innovation and time-saving devices, had a gang member brought up on a farm in eastern Washington State. He came up with one wacky idea that earned him a bonus. He was driving home one evening and witnessed a mechanical hayloader stacking bales in a field. It was a genuine eureka moment. On the production line, it took two eight-hour shifts to load all the seats onto a jet and then screw them in place. But by converting a hayloader to lift the seats, it now takes 25 minutes. In the final position, adjacent to the huge sliding doors that stand ajar, two planes are waiting, prepared to be taken out for their final paint job and then over for flight testing. One is ready for Shandong Airlines in China and the other for Virgin Blue in Australia. Before they go there is one more job. 'We hang the engines last because they are the most expensive part of the airplane and they account for one third of the value. You don't want to hang onto that kind of inventory for very long,' says Angers.

Boeing is continuing to do it better. And this means the 777 and the new 787 will be more efficient commercial propositions too, borrowing from the 737NG experience.

In 2005, Suzanna Darcy-Hennemann undertook the flight test programme of the 777-200LR. 'In the flight programme we have two planes, Blue Baby One and Blue Baby Two. Blue Baby Two was taken on a sixty-day world tour, including a trip to the Paris Air Show, before returning for environmental testing, while the other plane is being tested in Seattle. The tests so far have been flutter, initial airworthiness, flight control and aerodynamic performance. It's the first plane to have the GE90-115B engine, with 110,000 lbs on each side and racked wing tips. We've done the first stall test to find the landing speed of the plane and she handled brilliantly.

'I've flown a lot of planes in my time, but this is just one of the smoothest and most comfortable. It is like walking on air, and the passengers will enjoy it too,' she coos. In November 2005, with Darcy-Hennemann and Santoni at the controls, the 777-200LR broke the world record for a commercial aircraft flying non-stop from Hong Kong to London eastward. Boeing's renaissance will push Airbus. But the four-engine A380 was still making bigger headlines as it arrived in Singapore and Australia.

15. AN AIRBUS DEAL IS BOLTED TOGETHER

One fact is clear. The Airbus A380 would never have taken off without some political and industrial shenanigans. The aircraft designs might have been out-of-this-world, but it needed action to break the European inertia. Here was a multi-dimensional Gordian knot that no one could untie. It would take a no-nonsense Northern bruiser to came along and slash at the strands. That individual was Mike Turner.

For mere mortals, it is hard to comprehend the lies and deceit that went on at an international level for many years. With the full connivance of international governments and their civil servants in Europe, these exceptionally well-paid players undertook a series of alliances and counter-alliances that were hard to fathom. It was all a rather complex, interconnected web of international egos and industrial aspirations that was forged into the making the A380.

The New Year's Eve party of 1990 was a happy one for Dick Evans. Earlier that day he had been appointed the Chief Executive of British Aerospace, the culmination of a career in the aerospace business. BAe was a young company, cobbled together by the nationalisation of half a dozen defence and aerospace firms in 1977. Two years later, it was the first government-owned company launched by Margaret Thatcher's privatisation programme. But the problems were rife. It needed drastic surgery.

'I remember the ATP [Advanced TurboProp, a 65–68-seater, of which less than fifty are in service], which was a disaster,' says Mike Turner, now the Chief Executive Officer of BAE Systems. 'As part of the deal that Sir Austen Pearce [chairman of British Aerospace and former Esso boss] and Raymond Lygo made, I was party to the discussions with the Prime Minister and Norman Tebbit, the Industry Secretary. Although I wasn't actually there myself, I was aware of all that was going on.'

Margaret Thatcher's government desperately wanted to avoid another Concorde debacle and the Tory government, culturally opposed to state intervention, was extremely cautious about launching the A320 with taxpayers' money. And while Norman Lamont, the Aerospace Minister, knew the reasons, he simply sat on the fence, refusing to give an answer.

In 1984, however, Thatcher was put under intense pressure at a summit meeting with President Mitterrand of France and Chancellor Kohl of Germany. If Britain didn't want to join the A320 project, then the French and Germans would go it alone. As ever, Thatcher drove a hard bargain. She agreed to £250m launch aid, with £50m repaid even if the A320 was a flop. BAe would fork out £200m of its own money to support the project. Mitterrand's government was more generous, meeting 75 per cent of Aerospatiale's costs and giving an interest-free loan of 380m francs until the A320 was flying. Later, Margaret Thatcher would approve a further UK government loans for BAe for work on the A330 and the A340; however, this was not the lifeline it appeared.

'I don't think it was sufficient for all the wing work but I know the deal was not to keep it in the UK,' says Turner. 'And that's why a lot of it was subcontracted to America. US firms picked up a lot of wing work because they agreed to bear the non-recurring debt as a company, simply to get a seat at the table. At the time Airbus was looking for some dollar content to give it more clout in the United States. The UK government hadn't given all the repayable launch investment needed to keep all the work in the UK, which was a mistake.'

With BAe, hit with the ATP costs and the new Airbus project, in crisis mode, Turner was offered a dirty job. He had made his mark running the military aircraft division in the south of England, Kingston, Dunstable and Weybridge, which he closed as part of the rationalisation of the business. Then he and Dick Evans, the former marketing director, had successfully exported a lot of Hawk trainers. He had a reputation as a tough guy who could put together very successful teams.

In December 1991 he had lunch with Dick at Cheekys, a favourite London restaurant. The conversation was apocalyptic, and with good reason. With Rover, whom BAe owned, consuming £2bn of precious bank funding, and General Electric rumoured to be preparing a hostile take-over, things look grim. Evans admitted that there was no way that BAe could currently afford the business, and unless something drastic happened, it was inevitable that British Aerospace would go under. Dick wanted that drastic something to be Mike Turner. To Dick's relief, Turner accepted the offer, despite his only knowledge of commercial aviation being a short stint as an apprentice at Hawker Siddeley in the 1960s.

Initially Turner went in to look at the regional aircraft on British Aerospace's roster: the 146, which by then had become the RJ, the Jetstream (in its initial incarnation a small 19-seater, later to be a 29-seater in its 41 guise) and the ATP. The business was not in good shape. Propeller planes were already falling out of vogue and, more importantly, the market was too small and too fiercely competitive to be profitable. BAe were up against Fokker, Saab, Beech, Shorts and others in each of these markets. The lack of success of the ATP proved that the situation was unsustainable. 'Clearly it was a business that we had to manage our way out of,' says Turner 'Which we did. And it cost £3.5bn over a ten-year period.'

It was a record write-off but Dick Evans was grateful to be easing out of regional aviation. In January 1994, the Rover car business was sold to BMW. Then, in 1994, on the back of making a success of sorting out the regional commercial aircraft, Turner was given the extra responsibility of dealing with Airbus.

'At the time it was not clear to the British Aerospace board that Airbus was as big a mess as BAe's regional aircraft. While there were problems in our regional aircraft side, and they would continue, we were at least sorting this out. There was a lot of scepticism at British Aerospace board level about Airbus, particularly by Richard Lapthorne, the finance director,' says Turner. Lapthorne, later BAe vice-chairman, understood British Aerospace's huge investments in Airbus over many years was a deep, black hole. They had invested £2bn, with nothing coming back.

'We were still investing in Airbus's family concept of the A300, A310, A320 and by then deep into the A330 and A340. I found myself having to defend Airbus to the board as something that we should stay with. But it became clear to me that the only way Airbus could be successful was with major changes. I think I got Dick on side but I'm don't think I ever got Richard Lapthorne. We did have discussions at the board between Dick and Richard. On my side I had Tony Rice, who had done a good job in showing what could be done if we got the financial situation right with Airbus,' says Turner.

For Turner and his BAe colleagues getting it right meant two things: creating a single corporate structure for Airbus and launching the A3XX, which would became the A380. 'We needed to take that Boeing monopoly away,' he says.

At the time the original GIE structure, set up by Ziegler and Beteille, was still in force. Dick Evans had been on the Supervisory Board from 1990 until 1994. 'I started attending Supervisory Board meetings. It became clear to me that the whole thing was an absolute mess. There was no way that this business, which had outgrown the GIE structure, with partners being shareholders and subcontractors, was working. It was just hopeless. It was no way to run a modern business. The Supervisory Board, headed by Manfred Bischoff, was ridiculous.'

Turner knew it needed sorting out. He wasn't alone. Even Manfred Bischoff – head of not only the Supervisory Board, but also of DASA – had realised it was unwieldy. In December 1996, the German government began looking seriously at its funding for aviation research and the launch of the A3XX. Its package of 600DM ($400 million) a year was due to run out in 1998. Future funding, said the Germans, was dependent on the launch of the A3XX, but the restructuring of Airbus as a commercial company was also essential.

For Bischoff, Europe's various rules on taxation and employment were emerging as a stumbling block. Company taxes, which were at the time paid in each of the four partner countries, would end up all being paid in one country if the new business was set up and based there. This was a real issue for all concerned.

'This is not a game: this is the first real European company which will be set up. If we make a mistake due to time pressure, then we may create problems later,' said Bischoff.

'It was so fiendishly complex, we just couldn't find a way of sorting it out,' says Turner. 'We still hadn't agreed what the pay-out would be from the proceeds of the sales of the A330 and the A340. It was clear to me that with a big aircraft such as the A3XX coming along, this couldn't be allowed to continue. If we couldn't agree on the A330 and A340 after many years of trying, what hope did we have of agreeing the contractual rule on the A380 unless we could create a single entity.'

It was indeed an impasse that would stop the progress of Airbus.

Across in Seattle, Boeing's Airbus watchers began to take the threat of the double-decker super jumbo plane more seriously and responded with plans to launch a new version of the 747 capable of taking 660 people. This caused concern in Toulouse. Jürgen Thomas remembers: 'When we heard about this it caused us some consternation. We still had a huge amount of development on our plane, and Boeing would have been able to steal a march on us, because their stretch version was another jumbo jet derivative.'

The biggest issue for Airbus was the wings. Noel Forgeard headed across to Filton to hear from Iain Gray, the managing director of Airbus UK, and his colleagues what was happening.

'He came across and gave us a very hard time,' recalls Gray, an Aberdeen University engineering graduate who joined British Aerospace at Filton in 1979. 'We had to produce a wing that would cut operating costs by 15 to 20 per cent. This was the target if the A3XX was to be attractive to airlines. Noel kept telling us to push harder and harder. It took us a while to find the right solution.'

In the United States, defence issues were front-page news. Lockheed Martin had sealed a deal in July 1997 to buy Northrop Grumman for $11.6bn, but the US Justice Department, egged on by the Pentagon, argued that this new combo would create a monopoly in electronic hardware such as early warning radar. The US attorney-general Janet Reno said, 'Our nation cannot afford anything less than full-blooded competition.'

The sale was barred by Washington, and with McDonnell Douglas now a part of Boeing, BAe was eyeing up the lucrative opportunities opening up in the United States. The question was whether the Pentagon would allow a foreign company to buy sensitive assets such as Northrop's Stealth bomber technology.

'When it's all over we probably ought to sit down and devise a computer or board game for it all. It could be the twenty-first-century version of Diplomacy,' joked Weston, the Chief Executive who took over from Dick Evans.

Meanwhile, the Airbus advisory board was continuing to go through its convolutions and contortions. They began work on a valuation dossier to establish the worth of Airbus, then looked at the company's composition, at one stage leaving Spain out as their haughty behaviour had seen them object to everything. Further tension, this time on the manufacturing side, was rising between the Germans and the British over the wing. The Germans, with a technological lead in new polymers, wanted to use far more carbon composite in the wing, but the Filton designers preferred to keep a higher proportion of aluminium. The British argued that, while the composite was lighter, it was more difficult to blend with other materials and therefore far more expensive. This attitude would eventually allow Boeing to overtake on composites with its all-new composite plane.

These shenanigans were played out against a background of rumours concerning a possible merger between British Aerospace and DASA. Indeed, John Weston and Manfred Bischoff were, throughout the early summer of 1998, in discreet discussions about a full-scale merger. It was a high-wire strategy. DASA Airbus employed 13,000 people at five plants in Germany, while BAe Airbus had 6,500 people and was worth an estimated £1bn. If the deal had been concluded it would have significantly changed the whole balance of power in Europe, giving the Anglo-German group 58 per cent of the Airbus share, with 38 per cent to Aerospatiale.

Weston had already tipped off Peter Mandelson, the then Secretary of State for Department of Trade and Industry, but the story managed to leak out to the French media during the holiday month of August. The French were spitting with rage when they found out. Jean-Claude Gayssot, the French Transport Minister, warned that any merger between BAe and DASA could jeopardise plans to turn Airbus into a single corporate entity. Aerospatiale President Yves Michot moaned: 'I don't know what BAe and DASA are trying to achieve . . . the current climate does not give rise to an atmosphere of great mutual confidence.'

'Over my dead body,' vowed Jean-Louis Gergorin, when he heard the news. He simply wouldn't allow the Germans and the Brits to have majority control. Gergorin was well disposed to the British, but this was beyond the pale. As a former Professor at

France's Institute of Political Studies, he had moved seamlessly, like so many Gallic academics, into the senior echelons of industry as Director of Strategy with Matra Hautes Technologies.

Jean-Louis Gergorin was now Chief Strategist and would mastermind the creation of EADS with Jean-Luc Lagardère. Lagardère was the leader of the French defence and military conglomerate which carried his name. In July 1998, the French government announced a significant step in Airbus's history when it merged Aerospatiale with Matra Hautes Technologies, the defence arm of Lagardère's private company. Jean-Luc Lagardère had his heart and soul in the French aircraft industry, having sat next to the legendary designer, Marcel Dassault, at the drawing board. But now, as head of Aerospatiale, he had huge doubts about the A3XX, a staggering project set to cost $11bn.

'If you think it's vital for the future, you'd better convince him,' Turner was told by Dick Evans. So Lagardère flew across to Filton along with Noel Forgeard and the A380's chief designer. There were a number of presentations.

'Frankly, the key to the A380 is the wing and the aerodynamics and the performance. Could we give it the right performance and advantages over a Boeing 747-400? But Jean-Luc had to know that 17 to 18 per cent improvement that we quoted over a jumbo was right,' says Turner.

It was a tense session as he witnessed how Airbus in the UK was doing on the design side. Chris Geoghegan was running BAe Airbus at the time and explained why the project was essential for Europe and not a reckless risk.

'I said at the time: even if we don't make a penny, and we will. Bischoff and myself said we expected a 20 per cent return on the A3XX – and the business case is still very sound on this – but if we didn't, it would still be worth it because it would stop Boeing having a monopoly with the 747. Boeing makes $30 to 40m on each plane which can cross-subsidise the rest of their fleet making them cheaper against our other products.'

After his UK trip, Lagardère went to Hamburg and Madrid, and was by then convinced it should go ahead. He lobbied CASA chairman Alberto Fernandez, who wanted to keep a minimum of 4.2 per cent in the new entity. 'Airbus is the wonder programme of Europe and everyone wants to be on board,' said Fernandez. With Lagardère talking 33 per cent of the new Aerospatiale-Matra and the French government's holding reduced to 44 per cent, 20 per cent was available for private investors, while the final 3 per cent was for the workforce. At last, the French had effectively privatised its aerospace industry.

The Lex column in the *Financial Times*, on 8 September 1998, said, 'Just as the barriers to Airbus's transition to normal company status seemed to be coming down, the French government is once again throwing spanners in the works. Clearly British Aerospace's merger talks with Daimler-Benz's Deutsche Aerospace subsidiary have raised French fears of being pushed about by its British and French partners. Its response in threatening Airbus's long-awaited re-organisation is a shame. It is important that Airbus takes advantage of Boeing's current turmoil to improve its own internal organisation and profitability.'

The day before, at the Farnborough Air Show, BAe announced it was close to a deal with Boeing on a link-up to supply parts for the massive Globemaster C-17 transport plane, and there was the prospect of further contracts on commercial planes; while at a separate press event, Noel Forgeard announced Airbus was moving into the regional jet market with a 100-seater, A318.

Prime Minister Tony Blair, accompanied by Peter Mandelson, also urged the industry to move toward consolidation. 'Over the last year, the aerospace industry has made important progress on restructuring in order to beat the growing challenge ... I have strongly supported this,' he said.

But Airbus Industrie pulled off its biggest ever coup – a record-breaking deal with British Airways. The order for up to 188 A320s came after a decisive battle with Boeing. For thirty years, British Airways was one of the American firm's most loyal and feted customers. This single deal would have strategic and long-term implications, and would ultimately clear the path for the A380. Noel Forgeard described the deal as a 'crowning achievement' of an excellent year for Airbus. Phil Condit, the Boeing boss, was incandescent with rage. This was the final straw. Heads were about to roll – and the guillotine was about to fall on the head of hapless Boeing commercial planes boss, Ron Woodard.

While there were celebrations at Airbus and carnage at Boeing, British Aerospace was edging towards an incredible move. The DASA deal, which had so broken French hearts, was now on ice. This was partly due to Jürgen Schrempp, then the head of Daimler-Benz, applying some arduous conditions. He wanted too much control, says Turner, and a veto of a defence business that was a sideshow to his central motor interests.

'There was not a chance of that,' says Turner. 'So we took another direction. We rightly consolidated the UK defence industry between British Aerospace and Marconi.'

On Tuesday, 19 January 1999, BAe and GEC announced a £7.7bn ($12.3bn) deal to create a defence business based in the UK. It would make BAe the third biggest among the global aerospace companies in terms of sales behind Boeing and Lockheed Martin.

Marconi was yet to become a swearword for the destruction of shareholder value and in early 1999, Lord George Simpson, a former head of Rover cars when it was owned by BAe, and John Mayo, an investment banker turned deal-maker, were at the helm – and riding on the crest of the dot.com wave. One of Britain's most successful post-war industrial businesses, GEC-Marconi, had become a cash-rich business right at the heart of Britain's defence business, However, Simpson and Mayo wanted to create a New Economy business for the developing Internet age. While the defence side was the cream of the crop, the two men believed they had seen the future and made the strategic decision to put the Marconi Defence Systems division up for sale. It was a woeful error that still haunts both Simpson and Mayo and sees them scuttling for cover years later.

'Buying the Marconi defence interests was the right thing to do and I argued very strongly for this at the BAe board,' says Mike Turner. 'The non-executives were very supportive. We had to consolidate our position in the UK before then deciding what we do about the rest of Europe. That really pissed off the Germans, and forced them to get together with the French, and eventually the Spanish.' The new company is now called BAE Systems.

There was huge mistrust and back-stabbing. German commentators accused the British of deceit and lies. Tony Blair didn't like it either saying it was 'too British'. Months later, Schrempp was still fuming, blaming the UK and French domestic consolidation for killing off the idea of the EADC. It wasn't too far from the truth. But more twists were still to come.

John Weston and Turner's green eyes were looking enviously at the Pentagon business. 'With Marconi, we got access into America. Clearly, to a number of us, the way America was going on defence was more attractive than locking ourselves in with continental Europe. The way the US Congress feels about some of the continental Europeans could have blocked our path on America. This was dangerous for BAe. The market for us was in the United States, there wasn't enough money in defence in Europe.

'Were we just sitting on the Titanic by staying in Europe rather than taking the opportunity we now had because of the Marconi merger. After our Marconi deal there were rumours. I had heard the Germans and French were talking again and I had a conversation with Bernard Taylor, at the merchant bankers Flemings, who were acting for Lagardère,' he recalls.

Turner could sense the angry backlash in Europe. 'I went to see Bernard and said, "I know you are going to create this company" and we want to negotiate our part in all of this, especially Airbus. Let's talk.'

BAE Systems Chief Executive John Weston had already been openly discussing a company with the title of European and Aerospace Defence Company (EADC). In the *Financial Times*, 3 September 1998, he said, 'We are seeing the first moves towards globalisation, where we have two or three big players globally.'

Then the French and Germans thought they were rubbing the British noses in it by calling the new entity EADS. But BAe refused to rise to the bait; Turner said he wanted to be supportive. 'Frankly, it was the right thing to do,' says Turner. 'Jean-Louis and I got very close through this process. And Bernard Taylor too. We all began to trust each other.'

It still came as a shock. A few days before the announcement in mid-October, Turner was asked to go to a meeting in Paris with Bernard and Jean-Louis. A dinner was arranged at Le Train Bleu at Gare de Lyon when the bombshell was dropped in Turner's lap like a bowl of scalding soup.

The hosts delivered their news with perfect politeness. They were setting up a joint business. Was BAe in or out? Please make your mind up. This was the ultimatum over supper. 'Look Mike, this is going to happen. Do you want to join?' said Taylor.

Turner thought for a moment. 'No, thanks, I appreciate the offer, but I don't think this is the right deal or the right time for British Aerospace.'

Weston and Turner were still busy swallowing the Marconi deal and they weren't sure how the integration would evolve. 'I still wasn't sure if Europe on defence was the right way to go,' admits Turner. British Aerospace was still keen to build the A380, but wanted proper remuneration for the wing work that was essential to the project. Turner, Mike Taylor and George Rose had calculated that it was worth more than 20 per cent of the new plane and wanted to ensure they were properly paid for the work.

'The good news was I got very close to Jean-Louis and we then decided very shortly after EADS was mooted that we all sit down and agree the single corporate entity. Clearly they needed it.'

Bernard Taylor put his holiday home in Provence at their disposal and some all-day sessions went on al fresco around the veranda table overlooking the swimming pool.

'If EADS was going to work, it had to have a way through with BAe's agreement. It was the only way forward for Airbus. Although Jean-Louis had difficulties with it all, I believed that the right thing was to create the AIC (the single corporate entity) and at the same time we would go forward and launch the A380. But, without the single corporate entity, there was no chance of launching the A380.'

It was all very complex and financially technical. 'I don't know how Jean-Louis and his number two, Marwan Lahoud, his right-hand man, managed to keep the French, the Germans and Spanish at the EADS end together. It was difficult enough for him to cope with me, George Rose [BAe's finance director] and Michael Leicester and what we were demanding.'

Noel Forgeard, increasingly impatient and desperate to make an announcement about the A3XX, adopted a few Napoleonic traits. He wanted urgent action on the centralised structure. 'Boeing has just finished reorganising and will seize the initiative. We must advance at a forced march,' he told the French aviation press club on 10 November.

'Jean-Louis had to concede things to us, then I felt sorry for him because he had to go back to the French and Germans and defend what he had done. It was difficult for Jean-Louis, but he was fantastic. Without him, we would never have done this. How he carried the others with him I will never know. I think it was a nightmare for him and shortly after he was ill because of the stress,' says Turner. 'He did the right thing for the continental Europeans and I and George Rose and Michael Leicester did the right thing for BAE Systems.' The deal was concluded. 'We all agreed and we then went on to launch the A3XX and that would never have happened without the AIC.

BAE Systems believed it was in a very strong position now and played their trumps to gain certain rights and privileges with the new single corporate entity (SCE). Following major gains from selling non-core activities, BAe made a net profit of £692m that it disclosed in its 1998 figures. But how much was it making working with Airbus? This was almost impossible to tell. Heavy discounting by Airbus meant an operating loss of £125m for the group, so BAe would be expected to take its share of this loss. BAe also repaid aid to the UK government of £122m in 1998, up from £66m in 1997. 'We've never made a big profit out of Airbus,' says Turner in 2005. 'The UK government has made more than we have,' he added.

It was now agreed that the to-be-announced consortium, EADS, would have 80 per cent of Airbus, with BAE Systems holding 20 per cent of the Airbus Integrated Company (AIC). There were some final details to sort out before the announcement in the Grand Hotel in Paris on Friday, 23 June 2000 in Paris.

The previous day was Ladies Day at Royal Ascot, one of the premier days in the UK's horse-racing calendar, and Mike Turner joined Taylor and Marwan Lahoud in Robert Fleming's corporate box. It was champagne, canapés and constant calls.

There were still some highly significant issues to deal with throughout lunch in the Fleming's hospitality box. After several phone calls to Philippe Camus and Gergorin between the second and third races, it was agreed that while BAE Systems would not have a veto, there would be a get-out clause that said the British company could sell their stake at any time after 2003.

That evening the Ascot party flew by private jet to Paris for the announcement the following day. One of the sticking points was the name: the Germans wanted to call the new company EADS Airbus but Turner refused saying that it was Airbus, an EADS joint venture company with BAE Systems.

'We had huge discussions about that,' says Turner. 'But I just dug my heels in and said it's not going to be called EADS Airbus.'

Then Sir Dick Evans had a minor political problem. Stephen Byers, the Trade Minister from the Department of Trade and Industry, phoned to say he was concerned about the deal and what it would mean for the UK.

'Even although Jean-Louis and I had worked with the DTI throughout to comfort them that there were certain safeguards in the agreement, the UK government was anxious. If BAE Systems decided to sell its 20 per cent stake, that it would still stay within EADS on obligation of keeping wing design and manufacturing work in the UK.'

Byers was still concerned. But, sitting in Evans's hotel room in the Intercontinental at 3 a.m., Turner and his chairman, with a few changes of words in the final agreement, managed to convince the Minister to accept the deal. After some final horse-trading, EADS was set up on 10 July 2000, when it evolved from the link-up of Aerospatiale Matra, Construcciones Aeronáuticas S.A. and Daimler-Chrysler Aerospace. It was the largest partner in the new Airbus consortium with 80 per cent of the shares while BAE Systems held a 20 per cent stake. Now it was clear to support the biggest decision on commercial planes, which was announced in December. The A380 now had the go-ahead.

'The A380 is set to become the flagship of Europe's aerospace industry,' said the joint chairmen of EADS Board, Manfred Bischoff and Jean-Luc Lagardère. The Co-Chief Executive Officers of EADS, Philippe Camus and Rainer Hertrich, added: 'EADS is the indispensable prerequisite for the promising A380 business case. By integrating the Franco-German-Spanish national champions in aerospace into EADS we have achieved the technological and financial basis for such a challenging programme. We are fully committed to make the A380 a success. It will help lead EADS into a new dimension of profitable growth.' Maybe so, but it wouldn't stop the bickering. But perhaps that was all an essential part of European life.

Turner says, 'I think the UK government finally caught up with the story. While they were very supportive about creating a single corporate entity, they suddenly realised that they were now in a competitive situation with the rest of Europe in keeping the work in the UK.'

Here Britain was entering a new phase with Airbus. The politicians couldn't expect to rely on BAE Systems, because it was in its own interest to look after the wing work in the UK. But as a shareholder in the entity, whichever government made the best offer in support of Airbus, BAE Systems had to go along with that. And for the UK government – which forever had been telling us we had to be competitive in defence, design and making wings – they now had to be competitive too in the support that they offered Airbus, particularly when it comes to new models, says Turner.

Turner argues there was a danger that wing engineering, design and manufacturer might migrate somewhere else. Indeed, this was a central issue for the British government over the aid for the launch of the Airbus A350.

'The UK government has to be competitive in offering a level of support to Airbus that other countries are prepared to do. It would be fine if Boeing didn't get support from the US government and Japan and Italy and all the rest, but they are getting that support. So Airbus has to get that support on a level playing field. And if Airbus isn't getting that support from Britain, it will have no alternative but to go elsewhere. And that will cost the UK in the longer term. Once these hi-tech jobs go, it is nearly impossible to get them back,' he says.

On the technical front, Iain Gray and his teams at Filton were still battling to find the best wing characteristics for the A380s. It was a complex process, taking their finest engineering brains. The scale was enormous; a complete pair of wings are the length of a football pitch – nearly 80 metres (261 ft 4 in) – and made up of 30,000 major parts. The engineers wondered how they could make the tight commitment on weight and also hit Toulouse's punishing schedule. It was extremely tense and self-doubt crept in. How were they going to fit all the components, including the fuel tanks, into the wings?

They held long meetings that stretched into the night to try to solve all the issues – all this with Forgeard breathing down their necks. That they managed it is a testament to their dogged determinism and their engineering excellence. Indeed, the A380 wings alone are an engineering wonder of the world.

It wasn't always a dead-cert for BAE Systems. The £2bn spent by the company over many decades was a lot just to be a semi-detached part of the Airbus family. 'It is huge success. Now the complete family is with the A380. And you've seen the way Boeing has to respond. But it was by no means a no-brainer for the British Aerospace board that I joined in 1994 to stay with Airbus. Tony Rice helped me put the arguments to the board on a single corporate entity and the benefits that would flow to our shareholders. The financial guys were questioning: how long do we have to keep putting money in the business.' How long, indeed. Now, with the proper backing of the European governments and a better business structure, there was a European business capable of standing up to Boeing.

16. THE CONCEPTION, BIRTH AND FLIGHT OF THE A380

Jacques Rosay woke as usual at 6.00 a.m.; the warm southern French sun already streaming through his comfortable, six-roomed townhouse in Toulouse. He showered, shaved, shared a breakfast of fresh crepes, oranges and English tea with his wife and two teenage daughters, then called his friend and co-pilot Claude Lelaie. They spoke briefly, and with a certain note of excitement. Today, Lelaie said, they would make history.

This was something special. An historic day for European pride as, at last, the world's biggest passenger plane would take to the skies. Lelaie has always loved the thrill and the freedom of flying. Back in 1970 he had arrived at the Centre d'Essais en Vol, the French flight test centre at Istres, in Provence. Then he was responsible for military aircraft. It was an extreme profession testing military jets. In the 1950s, a test pilot, diving in a Mach 2 fighter, actually went faster than the shells from his cannons and shot himself down. Or so the legend goes. He was also part of Les Porthos, the aerobatic team that performs in displays all over Europe. But today there would be no theatrics. What was required of him and Rosay was a perfect take-off and a serene landing for MSN001.

Soon the two men were on the road to Toulouse-Blagnac Airport, weaving in and out of the abnormally busy traffic. Both listened to the excited voice on the radio discussing the historic nature of what they were about to do. The announcer wasn't the only one whose interest was piqued; almost 20,000 people were expected to throng to catch a glimpse of the A380's maiden flight. Much of Europe and, indeed, a horde of American flight buffs, would be following it with huge interest.

On arrival at the airport, Rosay headed for the Airbus operations room to convene an informal meeting. A former project pilot on the Dassault Mirage 2000 and the Rafale A, he had tested more than 150 types of military and civil aircraft, yet was often ribbed as being the 'new boy' at Airbus. Since 1997 he had been the project pilot for the A380. In the earliest blueprint stages he sat with the engineers shaping the cockpit design. Rosay was composed. The previous months of computer testing and flight simulation had gone exceptionally well, the state-of-the-art avionics were brilliantly responsive, and the runway taxiing manoeuvres a week earlier had been fine.

Lelaie, who spent the evening with his wife in the nearby Sofitel Hotel to avoid the traffic, arrived at Blagnac centre just before 7 a.m. and was waved through security. He was one of the most well-known and popular people in the vast complex. The pilot went to his office in Airbus Operations and sent some emails, including the corrected French version of the press release. He changed into his orange flying suit and went across to Operations where he greeted Rosay with a bear hug. The two pilots checked over some test notes and enjoyed a coffee and croissant as they were joined by the others. On the first flight were four Frenchmen, one German and a Spaniard. The Spaniard, Fernando Alonso was Vice President of Airbus's Flight Division and he would be leading his team of flight engineers, Jacky Joye and Manfred Birnfeld. Also on board would be another test engineer Gérard Desbois.

The inaugural flight was the culmination of a gruelling schedule of ground tests, which started nine months earlier when the plane's electrical power was switched on for the first time. Since then, engineers in Toulouse, Germany and the UK had systematically and exhaustively tested all A380 systems, from hydraulics to electrics, and all parts of the airframe structure, including static testing and wing and fuselage load testing. The extensive nature of the tests meant that maiden flights were becoming safer and safer, although Airbus veterans remembered the terrible crash eleven years before. Nick Warner and six others had been killed on an A330 prototype as they conducted a simulated engine failure exercise.

On this sunny Wednesday, 27 April 2005, this all seemed such a long, long time ago. Yet it was still an accumulated Airbus memory and an accident still at the back of many test crew's minds. Safety is the priority for test pilots working on civil aviation projects; that's their job.

Just after 8.30 a.m., all the office checks were concluded and the six headed out to the runway. At 8.40 a.m. the crew climbed the steps up onto the plane as a crowd of Airbus engineers and colleagues clapped and cheered. The six put on white helmets and their parachutes; a precaution taken by all Airbus test pilots.

What surprised them all was the mounting media interest. Already, just after 7 a.m., a scrum of journalists, photographers and television camera crews were milling around in a stepped stand and enclosure, cordoned off by security staff. Outside the French crowds were vying for suitable spots along the perimeter wire fence to witness this unique occasion.

Just after 9 a.m. the crew carried out the final flight tests, checking the critical systems. This was the culmination of months of practice. Test pilots have an ethos of camaraderie that they represent the thousands of pilots who will fly the planes for decades to come. The sun was glinting on the cockpit windscreen at 10.29 a.m. The four Rolls-Royce Trent 900 were powered up and the A380, with the appropriate registration F-WWOW, began its final taxi out to the main runway.

Jacques Rosay pulled back the palm-size joystick, a control familiar to millions of Play Station games players. This simple movement increased the engines' throttle and the A380 rolled forward quickly gaining speed to hit its take-off speed of 150 nm (nautical miles) an hour. The plane glided along the runway and, for a spilt-second, hovered as it lifted off the tarmac. The engines powered up to maximum taking the full weight of the 421 tonnes (928,300 lbs). It was the heaviest civil aircraft ever to take-off, although well below its maximum weight of 560 tonnes (1,232,000 lbs).

On board were barrels of water, set out in rows like liquid passengers and clamped to the floor to be used as ballasts, alongside banks of flight-test instrumentation that would measure, in real-time, the in-flight performance. As the world's first double-decker Airbus, this test plane was fitted with a twin set of instruments and work stations, one on the main deck and another on the upper deck. When Rosay pushed the A380 control stick to either side, the fly-by-wire computers let the plane bank left or right, but only so far. The Airbus computer software stops the aircraft from exceeding its structural limitation, bringing in a far higher level of aircraft safety.

Airbus was the pioneer of 'fly-by-wire' technology in 1988, and it is now used extensively in the A380. The powerful and sophisticated computers actually tell the pilots how to fly more effectively. In early years, it wasn't such a popular idea with every self-respecting pilot preferring to use his or her own skill and reaction, but 'fly-by-wire' systems are now the norm in both Airbus and Boeing.

Accompanying the A380 was an SN601 Corvett twinjet. This six-seater chase plane, built in the 1970s for Aerospatiale, would provide the stunning blue and white colour images and the crystal clear digital film footage that would soon be routed around the world.

They reached 10,000 ft and began cruising towards the nearby Pyrénées mountains. One of Rosay's first manoeuvres was to retract and then extend the hydraulic landing gear with its twenty giant tyres several times. The A380 was fitted with four sets of landing gear, that would drop down with gravity in an emergency if all systems failed.

During the flight, the crew explored the aircraft's flight envelope and tested handling using both direct and normal flight control laws with the landing gear up and down, the twin-tyred nose landing gear, and with all flaps and slats settings during the part of the flight at cruise altitude.

Over the intercom, Lelaie spoke to the control centre, confirming that the handling was wonderful and the take-off perfect. His comments were greeted by a boisterous cheer which went up from the crowd. Champagne corks popped as the titanic bird climbed into the French skies, soaring away, before disappearing as it headed south-west towards the snow-capped peaks.

When the plane returned to base it came in slow to fly over the Blagnac Airport, its front lights shining. Then, in a moment of vanity, the plane turned around in a wide, full circle and approached the runway once more with a landing speed of 138 knots an hour, slower than Airbus's four-engine A340-600. It gave the massive crowd another opportunity to cheer and shout: 'Vive le Airbus!'

Rosay brought the A380 back in for a perfect landing at Toulouse-Blagnac International Airport at 2.23 p.m. local time after successfully completing the four-hour flight. Hundreds of digital camera flashes and mobile phone cameras captured the historic moment. What startled many of the onlookers and aviation experts was that the take-off and landing were so smooth and quiet. This was a quiet bird. The A380 was finally born, but it had been a long and tortuous conception.

Jürgen Thomas is uncomfortable with the moniker of 'Father of the A380' but is resigned to the fact that he's rather stuck with it. The retired German engineer is now a gregarious character, happy to chat about Bayern Munich, his garden and his love of Chopin, but for many years the minutiae of blueprints and project reports of the Airbus A380 project consumed almost all of his life. He lived near Blagnac in a leafy residential suburb near the airport, trim with trees and neat detached houses with red-tiled roofs behind large hedges.

Thomas has crisscrossed the globe dozens of times and clocked up millions of miles to sell the Airbus sizzle. The major decisions were made in the ultra-modern, low-slung office complexes that enveloped the airport. Thomas often spent fifteen hours a day at work. When he flew in from an international meeting, he would head straight into the office. He remembers flying out to see Japan Airlines in Tokyo, returning to Blagnac, flying to Zurich for a two-hour Supervisory Board meeting, then getting on the long-haul flight back to Korea for another presentation. This was the non-stop Airbus culture, and in an ironic twist the entire project was kick-started by Boeing.

'At the Farnborough Air Show in 1992, we were showing our new four-engine A340, and then Phil Condit, the new Boeing President, gave us a clue about Boeing's thinking,' he remembers, sipping a lunchtime aperitif in Le Club executive restaurant in Toulouse.

Condit told the journalists at a briefing: 'Some airlines have expressed an interest in an airplane larger that the 747-400 for entry into service around the end of the decade. Boeing is meeting with interested customers to identify requirements and define possible configuration.' Airbus's collective ears twitched.

'Well, we were naturally curious,' said Thomas. 'Jean Roeder, who headed up our pilot studies section here in Blagnac, had already told engineers that he could see a market for an aircraft larger than a 747. It was a popular lunchtime discussion in the canteen, though hugely technical. Then Jean Pierson [Airbus President] was asked if he was also considering it. At the time we were working on the UHCA – the Ultra High Capacity Aircraft – and Jean said we were looking at a plane taking six hundred passengers.'

Thomas recalls, 'There was quite a buzz. The next day Jean Pierson went along to the Boeing chalet for a private discussion and spoke to John Hayhurst, Boeing's Vice President in charge of the jumbo project. He put his cards on the table and asked if they would be interested in a joint project.'

Here was a classic case of European politics at full play. Pierson was making the offer under the instructions of Jürgen Schrempp – Managing Director of DASA, the German partners within Airbus, and a senior member of the advisory board – but there was an ulterior motive.

Schrempp was a very bright man with a very large ego. A volatile combination; outwardly ambitious for a much bigger role. He made it clear he didn't like Airbus's corporate style and, three months after the Farnborough meeting with Boeing, Schrempp announced that that DASA was already in discussions with Boeing about a superjumbo. Pierson was furious.

The New Year began with a bang. On 5 January 1993, the *Wall Street Journal* broke the exclusive story that Boeing, DASA and British Aerospace were planning a new large plane. It reported a 600-seater was being considered with an announcement expected in February 1993. The sting was in the tail: 'The companies' participation in the venture with Boeing would not require them to pull out of the Airbus consortium because they have no agreement with Airbus to produce a jet of this size.'

Boeing was certainly creating mischief and confirmed the story, while twisting the knife by describing Airbus as a marketing outfit. Undeterred, but angry, Airbus set up a joint committee, with France and Spain on board, to evaluate a Boeing-Airbus Very Large Commercial Transport, a VLCT, with Jürgen Thomas at its head.

'I remember it was very tense. We were very conscious of anti-trust legislation. After all, we were now just one single entity considering building a large plane with a large potential market. We had our lawyers. Boeing had theirs. Each company had its own law firm and we were not allowed to exchange commercial information.'

The legal costs alone were Very Large Commercial Fees. It was hardly the way to build a plane. Gradually, Thomas steered a path through the minefield and over a two-year period there was ample time to exchange ideas and information.

Thomas recalls Airbus had to find out if there was a market for a successor to Boeing's 747. But the question in the back of his mind was why would the Americans want to let go of such a lucrative position? The talks were doomed. The end came in April 1995 at the Four Seasons Hotel in Munich. The two sides gathered for a farewell dinner to mark the divorce. A few weeks later an agreement ended the project. It had cost a lot of time and wasted huge amounts of hot air ... especially for Airbus.

When the joint talks between Boeing and Airbus broke down, the French and Germans were highly suspicious. Some were furious, claiming Boeing had been deceitful. Thomas recalls that some of his colleagues certainly believed that Boeing deliberately kept the discussions going to thwart any plans. The longer the discussions went on the more time Boeing would have to develop the new jumbo.

Thomas disagrees. 'I believed that Boeing were honourable. Frank Shrontz [Boeing's then CEO and Chairman] honestly believed in making an attempt and I do think they made an honest attempt to look at this project and while we agreed on many issues, there were some fundamental disagreements about the possible market for a super jumbo.'

Thomas said he wanted to find out if Airbus could do it. There was a different type of mentality and way of working. Boeing's Randy Baseler recalls, 'We were talking to customers about our new 747 version and asking them if they were interested in this new kind of an airplane. Then the Asian financial crisis came along in 1997. And, as it is today, this was an important market. So we pulled the offering of these airplanes.'

Straight after this experience, Thomas held a pow-wow with his 24-member team and commissioned a report on what was learned. The report on the workshop – *VLCT Lesson Learnt* – on 15 September 1995 revealed that Boeing at first wanted to take the lead and this irked the junior partners.

Thomas asked the Airbus team: How did Boeing act during the study; more as a partner or a competitor? The answers were:

'More as partner, but cautious in restricting information, due to protecting the future leadership' and 'Boeing started by trying to play the lead role, but quickly recognised that team work was essential and then they were fully co-operative. Always aware that Airbus was its competitor, the Boeing people were careful not to share competitive data,' said the report.

Then Thomas asked the team a more fundamental question: what could be improved? The answer that emerged was revealing and would have far wider repercussions than purely within Airbus. It was the concept of proper European integration. The only way Airbus could challenge Boeing in building a very large aircraft was to dramatically improve the European position with a far stronger integrated approach.

It uncovered some home truths in Toulouse. There were too many cultural silos within Airbus, with the national European groups unable to work together as well as they might. This would have to change. And change dramatically. British Aerospace had learned from the meetings that Boeing's assembly processes were now significantly sharper than Airbus's. For a while, it stirred up Airbus to find new levels of efficiency.

While the European engineering and technological prowess was equal to the Americans, there was a desperate need to improve communications. This clarity and co-operation between each European partner was now imperative for a project of this magnitude. If a go-it-alone European project had the remotest chance of success then there had to be far better lines of communication and the co-operative cross-culture had to improve. This was something Europe's highly paid political representatives still had to accept. Petty national interests would have to take second place for the benefit of the wider project.

'There was a very good team spirit on our side. I think Europeans are much broader thinkers,' says Thomas. 'I had twenty-seven years of experience of working with European partners. The more ideas that you put on the table – sometimes it takes more time – but you avoid making the mistakes. It has been extremely beneficial, not just for the French, Germans and the British, but the Belgians and Dutch too who also contribute so much. And many, many others. It was on a cultural basis,' says Thomas.

The success of the longer-range 777 was focusing minds in Toulouse on two issues. Firstly on a manufacturing basis. Across

Airbus there was a determination to make improvements. More capital investment was ploughed into new production lines and better equipment at Toulouse and at Finkenwerder, outside Hamburg. Even though Boeing was still making planes more quickly and efficiently, there was the feeling that things could be significantly improved at Airbus.

The second was the A380, and its viability. It was essential that Airbus knew whether there was an appetite for a brand-new plane using more composites, and Thomas and his team set to the task with vigour. Everyone burned the midnight oil. 'If you want to overtake a dominant and leading company such as Boeing,' Thomas explains, 'then you had to put in the extra hours and make sure everything you did was better.' It wasn't what you expected from a European company based in France where so much store was placed in a regulated 38-hour week.

As an engineer, Thomas wanted to keep up to speed with all the technical aspects of developments. So Airbus's Large Aircraft Division was set up adjacent to the Airbus headquarters near Toulouse-Blagnac Airport. Thomas says that it was this attention to detail that helped Airbus.

'If Mr Phil Condit had looked at a few more details, he might not have run into so much shit. They poke at us so we poke at them. It's kind of part of the fun,' says Thomas.

After the dissolution of talks about a collaboration between Airbus and Boeing on an ultra jumbo, Boeing went back to the drawing board. Believing that the market was simply not big enough for such an endeavour, they began to look at the possibility of revamping the 747 concept. Airbus were still undecided, and while they tried to decide on the best course of action, Boeing went off and began offering two updated jumbos, the 747-500 and then the 747-600.

'These were basically new airplanes,' recalls Baseler. 'They had new 777 systems and new wings. They still had the familiar jumbo body but the 600 was a stretch version, able to carry about 530 passengers.'

While Baseler was happy with the new planes, Boeing itself was wobbling on the project. In January 1997, the Seattle company shelved its plans for a 747-500X/600X – it was simply too expensive – it was costing $3m a day. It was over. Boeing's focus for now would be on the smaller, nimbler 767-400, the 777-200X and the 777-300X.

This was a game-changer. Boeing's emphasis on smaller planes left the field open for the Airbus's A380. Mike Bair, Boeing's Vice President, product strategy and marketing at Boeing, told *Flight International* in January 1997 that the size of the market meant the amount of money the company would have to spend just didn't make sense.

Airlines weren't too enamoured with the Boeing 747 proposals anyway. Some called it 'indifference' because Boeing continued to have a conservative view of the future market. There were other more pressing reasons, however. The US board had acquired defence contractor Rockwell and it was in the process of taking over McDonnell Douglas. The termination of the MD-11 plane, a tri-jet that could accommodate between 285 and 410 passengers, was going to cost a cool £78m. Unsurprisingly, Boeing's investors didn't want to commit themselves to the 747 project, which would cost them around $7bn. The fragmentation of air routes – with the emergence of such routes as Manchester or Glasgow to Boston – meant that the domination of the 747 was over. In 1984 62 per cent of flights across the North Atlantic were by Boeing 747 jumbo jets; twenty years later, this figure was down to just 16 per cent. It was a dramatic shift in aircraft size, and one that persuaded Boeing that this was no time for another round of the Sporty Game.

Airbus stood on the threshold of a momentous decision. Should it take the plunge or save billions of pounds by halting the A380 project and plough the cash into a bigger A340?

Jürgen Thomas was bullish, although perhaps not as exuberant as Adam Brown. In March 1997, Thomas said Airbus was building a business case based on the prospect of winning 650 orders over the following twenty years. He said there was a potential for more than 1,600 aircraft larger than the Boeing 747-400. Thomas believed the A380 would create its own demand, just like the 747 had in the late 1960s.

'Then we started to evaluate which engine choice for the A380,' recalls Thomas. By 1997, this was becoming quite complicated. There were three engines on offer: the Rolls-Royce Trent 900, a derivative of the Pratt & Whitney PW4000, and a completely new beast, the GP7200, from The Engine Alliance, now a 50-50 joint venture between GE and Pratt & Whitney. Pratt was effectively competing against itself.

'We had received a precise technical definition of the Alliance's GP7200 in May and it was very similar to Pratt & Whitney's

PW4000. The PW4500 would offer us thrust of 69,000–78,000 lbs,' Thomas recalls. 'They were both very good propositions though. I was pleased.'

For General Electric, the difference was simple: it was all about cost and performance. GE, who still had to sign an official agreement with Pratt, told Airbus that if they wanted performance over cost, the consortium should pick the Alliance's new engine. Thomas recalls, 'There was a lot to clarify. We even looked at a reduced-capacity version for 480 passengers after Lufthansa approached us. But we favoured production continuity.'

At this stage only half of the 40 per cent of risk-sharing work being offered had been taken up by non-Airbus partners, although agreements were signed with Belairbus, Finnavitec and Saab. Then there was interest from Lockheed Martin who indicated a desire to move back into commercial airplanes.

Airbus still needed to keep its Far Eastern customers sweet. The worsening economic crisis in Asia in the late 1990s nearly floored both Airbus and Boeing. Passenger traffic was severely dented and the cargo sector was decimated. The impact was deeper and more prolonged than originally thought. Deliveries of 747s, Boeing's cash cow, plummeted and production dropped to one a month. Airbus felt the chill, but to ensure that there were no hitches, Thomas made substantial changes to the timetable to satisfy the launch customers.

At Filton, the research labs and wind-tunnels were still busy experimenting, but life was looking up. Iain Gray and his colleagues coined the concept of the Tiger Team. Small groups of wing and aerodynamic experts scoured Airbus looking for more breakthroughs. 'We eventually got the manufacturing, procurement and engineering working together,' Gray said. 'We met our targets and did what we said.' Airbus had wings to fly.

The A380 programme went from a concept to reality on Tuesday, 19 December 2000. The Airbus Advisory Board made the momentous decision and there was tremendous excitement in Toulouse. Its recently formed parent EADS, the European Aeronautic Defence and Space Company, heartily welcomed the decision. Airbus had fifty firm commitments from six airlines with options on a further forty aircraft. The bold pioneers were Virgin Atlantic, Emirates Airlines, Air France, Singapore Airlines, Qantas and the world's biggest leasing company, International Lease Finance Corporation. This was just enough to make it viable.

Noël Forgeard stressed the significance. 'With the launch of the A380 we are now closing the final large gap in our product spectrum. We are now able to offer aircraft in all the categories from single-aisle via wide-body to mega-liner and could therefore fulfil all the wishes our customers may have.'

A noble aim – and one Boeing shared, albeit with a different vision. As for Jürgen Thomas, his task was complete. Airbus now needed a younger man to drive forward the complex manufacturing project. The aptly named Charles Champion, a 45-year-old French engineer, took the helm in December 2000.

17. DREAMLINERS ARE MADE OF THIS

The executive suite on the 48th floor had stunning views of the lake and the city but it was singularly impersonal. It was certainly neat and clean with a few airline flags, models and dusty pictures on the wall, but it was a nondescript headquarters for a once-prestigious airline. The heavy wooden door of the Chief Executive Officer's room clicked open as two of Boeing's sales Vice Presidents were shepherded along the corridor by a secretary.

'Come on in, Scott. Nice to see you again,' boomed the airline executive with his shirtsleeves rolled up.

'Great to see you too, Brad,' replied the more senior Boeing man.

The three men chatted convivially, the Boeing VPs liberally sprinkling their bonhomie with interested questions and the odd compliment. They determined to keep the atmosphere light, but with this particular airline having teetered on the brink of bankruptcy several times any talk of the business would be somewhat downcast. Still, the CEO was positive about the future – costs has been cut, a dispute settled and passenger numbers were up – and this meant that the Boeing sales guys could launch into their pitch.

'Well,' said the Boeing VP, 'we've identified a new market that calls for a smaller aircraft, with half the passenger capacity of Airbus's A380, in the 200- to 300-seat range. It's a plane offering far greater passenger comfort. While Airbus sees the future as bigger and larger, we think differently. This will be unlike any other Boeing airplane.'

'Huh, you don't mean like the Sonic Cruiser,' the CEO joked. Scott laughed, but the Sonic Cruiser debacle was still fresh in many people's minds.

In 2001, Boeing unveiled a proposed new futuristic jet that would be transonic – just under the speed of sound – moving into the market vacated by an obsolete Concorde. The Sonic Cruiser would travel between 6,000 and 9,000 miles with a top speed of around 750 miles per hour. It was a strange time to propose such a plane, particularly as some questioned its very viability.

Jürgen Thomas said, 'I looked at it from the beginning and it was total, physical nonsense. Even some American journalists said, "How can you design an aircraft for this aerodynamic disaster area?"'

The problem with it was the drag factor. To fly effectively at such speeds you need to break through the sound barrier as soon as possible. The Sonic Cruiser would be flying at just under that speed, where the drag on the plane would be the same as if they were flying supersonic, rather than subsonic. Therefore more thrust would be needed from the engines, which would burn an incredible amount of fuel. 'It was so stupid and uneconomic,' said Thomas.

But the plans had been shelved in favour of the $12bn project Scott was about to present.

'This is the business,' Scott said. 'This plane will set the standard for everything that follows it. New technology. More carbon composites. Better reliability. We're calling it the 7E7 Dreamliner. It will be a new plane for the new century.'

Brad laughed again. 'I've had John Leahy in here describing the A380 as the "New Plane for the New Century". Anyway, let me call in some of my guys.'

Brad hit the intercom and five minutes later Scott was delivering a detailed PowerPoint presentation to five senior executives. In 20 minutes he outlined why the 7E7 would be the best fit for this cash-strapped airline.

The CEO was impressed, and could see the benefits – particularly on the environmental side – of the Dreamliner, but was reticent to give a firm answer. For the Boeing team this was typical. There were dozens of sessions like this; grabbing tired executives over dinner, snatching conversations at air shows or huddling in corners at aerospace conventions. Boeing was selling the sizzle.

The problem was that most of the six legacy American carriers – those that existed before deregulation in 1978 – were basket-cases. In September 2005, both Delta Air Lines and Northwest Airlines – America's third and fourth largest carriers – filed for Chapter 11 bankruptcy protection. Faced with pension debts they found impossible to meet, niggling labour disputes and rising oil prices, the executives appealed to President Bush's administration to help ease the burden. The situation at United Airlines and US Airways wasn't a lot better either.

'For a variety of reasons, including very intense competition, which limits any one carrier's pricing power, the airline industry has consistently failed to earn adequate profits; cumulatively, the industry has lost money since its inception,' said Robert Crandall, the former head of American Airlines.

The US executives say bankruptcy protection allows airlines to continue in sickly health without ever addressing their central problem – a basic lack of income to set against operating costs. Indeed, US carriers are so frequently in and out of Chapter 11 that it has come to be seen as good business strategy – affording some recuperation time before going back into the fray once more. Rod Eddington, the former BA boss, said such protection only served to prevent the desperately needed consolidation within America's airline industry.

Over the last decade, the major US carriers have aggressively reduced capital spending, taken on new debt and have cut annual expenses by more than $20bn – partly by eliminating more than 125,000 jobs. In 2003 Boeing showed concept drawings and computer-generated graphics of the Dreamliner to various groups of airlines. Most said, 'Well, we like the concept, but at this stage we're OK with what we have.'

However, as the Boeing team adapted the plans – and the shape and the configurations – around the world airlines' specifications, the lukewarm response began to change into a realisation that a new plane *was* required. The only question was whether Boeing was the company to build it. There was huge industry scepticism about Boeing and a general feeling that it was just too half-hearted about its new plans. After all, wasn't the Boeing 777 the aircraft for the next generation? And for many the embarrassing folly of the Sonic Cruiser wasn't too far from their minds.

Boeing may have had a genuine problem proving that it was serious about making a new plane, but the idea did begin to stick. Because of the sickly state of the domestic US market, it wasn't gaining ground at home, but it was in the emerging economies. The new 7E7 made sense and senior airline people, especially in China and Japan, were giving it an intent hearing. Japan was a nation keen to increase its involvement in aircraft building. This, many predicted, was going to be the market for both Boeing and Airbus over the next twenty years.

The Boeing board authorised further studies, and sales brochures were prepared for the airlines. Then in December 2003, Boeing's President and Chief Executive Officer, Alan Mulally, who had been the driving force behind the Boeing 777 project, announced their decision.

'Responding to the overwhelming preference of airlines around the world, Boeing Commercial Airplanes has focused its new development efforts on the Boeing 7E7 Dreamliner, a super-efficient airplane. An international team of top aerospace companies is developing the airplane, led by Boeing,' he said, hardly containing his broad smile.

There would be an even higher percentage of pre-assembly, pulling together parts from all over the world, with final assembly in the Everett facility, near Seattle. Over in Toulouse, there were some yawns about such hype. 'This was exactly what we had been doing for years, now Boeing had woken up,' said Roger Beteille, the Airbus founder.

Boeing's gamble paid off quickly. On Monday, 26 April 2004, the Boeing Company's board of directors approved the formal launch of the new 7E7 Dreamliner with a firm order for fifty airplanes from All Nippon Airways. The ANA order was the largest launch order in Boeing's history, worth $6bn at list prices. Mulally said the first planes would be delivered to the airline in 2008.

The business case for the new plane was working. It was Game On with Airbus.

Mulally was gung-ho. 'Airline interest in the 7E7 has been extraordinary. The size and speed of this order validates our view of the market and demonstrates the tremendous demand for the performance and value provided by the 7E7.'

ANA was a respected customer. Founded in 1952, it is one of the top ten airlines in the world, carrying over 52 million passengers every year to 46 destinations in Japan, and 21 overseas cities. President and CEO of ANA, Yoji Ohashi echoed Boeing's long held mantra when he announced that ANA 'will be the first airline to bring back the joy of flying to the twenty-first century'.

A return to the pleasure of flying was the key for Boeing. Unless you were paying for pampered first-class seats, the experience of long queues in immigration, lost baggage, cramped conditions and dreadful meals had killed any idea of glamour for the ordinary flier. The 7E7 would, Boeing hoped, change this forever.

Mulally got another boost a few weeks later. Air New Zealand became a launch customer, then Blue Panorama and First Choice Airways, the UK holiday company, became the first European customers. Along with 62 announced orders from four carriers, Boeing took deposits from over twenty other airlines, which alone accounted for the first two years of production at Everett. Then low-cost carrier, Primaris Airlines signed a deal for an assortment of planes, including twenty 7E7s with options for fifteen more, in a mammoth deal worth $3.8bn. Its idea was to fit the plane with 150 business-class seats.

On Friday, 28 January 2005, just days after the glitzy Reveal of the Airbus A380 in Toulouse, Boeing gave their new plane the model designation, Boeing 787 Dreamliner. Later at a signing ceremony in Washington – not long after he announced a major deal with the Peoples Republic of China for sixty aircraft delivered to six carriers: Air China, China Eastern, China Southern Airlines, Hainin Airlines, Shanghai Airlines and Xiamen Airlines – Mulally quipped that eight was indeed a lucky and prosperous number in many Asian cultures. It was an exact steal from Airbus. When Airbus decided to launch the A380, they had toyed with the idea of calling it the A388, because it was a lucky number.

What was it about the Dreamliner that so inspired airlines from around the world? Boeing's pitch was that the Boeing 787 would be the most technologically advanced plane in the sky, but most appealing was that it would use 20 per cent less fuel than today's airliners of the same size. It would also provide 60 per cent more cargo room, a great incentive for the Chinese, now the manufacturing engine of the world.

Boeing's interior design was also winning airlines over. With large windows, wider seats and aisles, there were elements of comfort that the business had not seen before. The mock-ups were impressive. Boeing started with a clean sheet for the interiors, with more space in the cabins, a different colour scheme and new lighting systems. Yet Airbus engineers were initially dismissive of the bigger windows saying Boeing has been forced to cut them into this space because of the nature of carbon-fibre composites.

Meanwhile, Walt Gillette, Boeing's Vice President of Engineering and project leader of the Boeing 787, declared: 'This is a piece of aviation history. Nothing like this is already in production. Hundreds of aerospace experts from Boeing and our partners have been working flat out to develop everything, including the tools that serve as the mould, programming for the composites and the structure of the autoclave that will bake the composite materials.'

Walt sat in his office and banged a beer-mat size of black composite on the edge of his desk. 'This is what the planes of the future will be made from,' he said, holding up the composite. 'It will allow us to create optimised structural designs and develop an efficient production process. From now on, all advanced commercial airplanes will be built with this composite.'

Gillette had already been overseeing the building process. The first barrel section of fuselage was built after several months of development work.

'The Boeing 787 Dreamliner offers breakthrough efficiency with 3,700 km (2,000 nm) more range while consuming over 20 per cent less fuel than the A330-200. It is as fast as the fastest airplanes flying today. The Dreamliner features innovations that redefine the total passenger experience like wider seats and aisles, a quieter cabin and softer lighting. In addition, the 787 is an environmental leader, with its clean, quiet engines and recyclable materials.'

Gillette was thrilled that the market had already validated the 787 Dreamliner. Twenty airlines had come in with orders and commitments for 252 airplanes – fifteen of the airlines and 170 of the orders and commitments coming after Airbus defined and offered the A350. There were some ringing endorsements too. 'The 787 Dreamliner meets ANA's requirements in safety, reliability, comfort and economics, and supports the plans to grow and strengthen our route network, with the expansion of domestic flights from Tokyo Haneda Airport and the growth of regional service within Asia,' said Yoji Ohashi of ANA.

While Doug Steenland, chief executive officer and President at the beleaguered Northwest Airlines, said, 'This plane provides

Northwest Airlines with a new-generation, long-range aircraft that will allow us to tailor our growing international route system to best address our customers' travel needs.'

Gillette thinks his plane is a magnificent beast for the future of flying. Nothing less. Using computational fluid dynamics models and supercomputers, Boeing engineers have come up with something radical. The configuration of the nacelles, fuselage, wings, empennage and materials have all been dramatically improved giving the 787 huge aerodynamic efficiency. And in the 'we-got-more' debate, the 787 is bragging that it will be 50 per cent composite material by weight – more than any other commercial aircraft. Composites are more durable, have better fatigue characteristics and don't corrode. Walt Gillette believes one important aspect of the 787 for the airlines is that the five-yearly check, when planes are stripped down and all systems tested, will be extended to ten years, which will save on the time-consuming, out-of-service structural maintenance programme. By comparison, the A350 is 37 per cent composite with an all-metal fuselage. Boeing was overtaking on the inside.

'From the moment they board, passengers will know that this is a big deal,' said Gillette. 'In the welcoming and spacious entryway, your eyes will be directed upwards toward a fixed decorative ceiling treatment. State-of-the-art light-emitting diode lighting will create a subtle but pervasive sense of having the sky overhead throughout the entire cabin.'

The windows are significantly taller and wider than those on any other commercial aircraft, with about 80 per cent more viewable area than the A300/A330/A340 airplanes. At 47 cm tall by 27 cm wide, the Dreamliner windows make it possible for passengers to view the horizon from any seat on the airplane. Electronic window shades make it possible for the flight crew to dim the amount of light coming into the cabin from the outside yet still allow passengers to see outside. Passengers can close their individual window shades completely, if they wish. Because the windows extend above seatback height, they serve the entire 787 cabin rather than just the window seats.

'We have researched what passengers want and found that they are most comfortable when the cabin altitude is maintained at 6,000 rather than 8,000 feet. The air in the cabin has higher relative humidity for increased passenger comfort and HEPA-type filtration removes particulates in the cabin air such as viruses, bacteria and fungi,' he said. The Boeing 787 will incorporate gaseous filtration to further purify the cabin air. Every seat has a nozzle to manage the immediate environment. 'This appeals to all passengers, for no two people are alike,' says the Boeing veteran.

But the plane will have a stubbier space. 'We knew we wanted passengers to be more comfortable. To accomplish this, we needed an all-new cross section significantly larger in diameter than other aircraft in its class – plus, we needed a 'double-bubble' shape instead of a true circle.'

This special shape allows almost vertical sidewalls in the cabin with a 35 cm (14-inch) width advantage over an Airbus at seated eye level, says Boeing.

The cross section offers wider seats and aisles and also gives airlines the flexibility to add an extra seat per row, making it nine-abreast, while still providing a comparable level of comfort to Airbus twin-aisle aircraft or the economy class of a 747.

On Friday, 20 May 2005, an Airbus spokesman told the *Seattle Times* that the A350 would have the same cross section as the A330. The 'lining is now thinner, so the internal cabin width is improved a bit for passengers,' the spokesman said. But even with this plan to reshape the inside walls, the addition of a few inches was unlikely to trouble Boeing's new baby.

Boeing visibly perked up. On Friday, 3 June 2005 it was reported by James Wallace, the Aerospace reporter in the *Seattle Post-Intelligencer*, that Boeing had proposals from airlines and leasing firms for 700 or more 787s. This was far more than the 429 that Mike Bair, Vice President for the 787 programme, had predicted. Scott Carson, the sales chief at Boeing, acknowledged that not all of the 700 would became firm orders; nonetheless, it would still be significantly more than anyone could have foreseen.

It was clear that Boeing had created a superstar airliner and the orders just kept rolling in. By 3 April 2007, Boeing was entitled to full bragging rights in the opening rounds against Airbus. Even before the first fully assembled plane was pushed out the giant doors at Everett, the Dreamliner had secured more than 500 orders since its first sales in April 2004. This made it the fastest-selling commercial jet in the world, hitting the mark three years earlier than the Boeing 737 Next Generation.

Mike Bair was beaming with pride when he told 3,000 employees at a celebration at Everett, 'We're clearly captivating the world's airlines with this airplane.'

An order from Japan Airlines for five more 787-8s – on top of its previous 30 planes – pushed the Dreamliner programme through the 500 mark. It was a deal worth $787 million and Boeing's stock jumped 1.2 per cent, closing at $89.90.

It was clear that the terrain was shifting – with the Dreamliner hammering Airbus's undercooked offering, the A350. Something would have to change in Toulouse to halt the rout – but no one could have predicted such a dramatic turn of events.

18. ROLLS-ROYCE RIDES HIGH ON BOTH HORSES

The impeccably turned out Corps of Commissioner officer at the door of the Rolls-Royce chalet was dressed in white gloves and peaked cap. He gave a very British salute to a stream of foreign dignitaries led across the threshold by a sales executive. Inside there was a buzz of activity, as Sir John Rose, Chief Executive, greeted a merchant banker from London and invited him to take a look at his investments at the Paris Air Show.

Mike Terrett, President of Rolls-Royce's Civil Aerospace Division, was holding court with a posse of aviation journalists in a small meeting room. He was brisk and businesslike, but happy to joke with some familiar media faces before ploughing into his presentation. On all fronts it was heartening news for Britain's engine-makers.

'At a conservative estimate, assuming our deliveries continue at current levels, the number of our engines in service will rise from 11,000 to 15,500 by 2010,' he said. But what was equally important was the support and maintenance deal for Rolls. Around 8,000 engines were covered by TotalCare, Rolls-Royce's package to look after these expensive and complex pieces of kit. While the cost of an engine is a well-kept secret, it is the after-sales that makes a tidy sum of money for the Derby-based manufacturer.

'With orders exceeding deliveries for the first time since 2001, the industry is seeing a continuing recovery, and business has picked up more quickly than anticipated,' he told the mini gathering.

His PowerPoint presentation was colourful, concise, but very telling. There were fifteen slides in all, and over the course of three consecutive slides, he outlined a compelling story. The first slide read: Trent 900 for the Airbus A380-800, the next: Trent 1000 for the Boeing 787, the third: the Trent 1700 for the Airbus A350. The message was clear: Trent engines would be on all of the competing planes.

'All commentators see a large and growing civil aerospace market,' he said later. 'Our own forecasts show over the next twenty years a requirement for 114,000 engines and £300bn worth of engine revenue with an after-market of a similar size. This civil business is actually proving to be quite resilient to the shocks, such as 9/11, and we have seen a sharp recovery.'

By the eve of the Paris Air Show of 2007, dozens of Trent 900s had been shipped to Airbus in Toulouse for the A380s slowly coming off the assembly lines. The first A380s completed hundreds of airborne and braking tests since the maiden flight in April 2005, and had accumulated thousands of engine hours. The engines, each with 70,000 lbs of thrust, were handling exceptionally well, and performance was in line with the engineers' predictions. Rolls-Royce had a lot to be pleased about.

Its civil aerospace sales were an impressive £3.7bn in 2006, with a 40 per cent share of the market for new-generation widebodied jets. The British aero-engine-maker's strength continued as sales of the Boeing 787 Dreamliner piled up throughout 2006 and into 2007. Then the recovery of Airbus, with its newly designed A350 XWBs, brought more brilliant news. At the Paris Air Show in 2007, a £1bn-plus order by Qatar Airways was confirmed with fanfare. Rolls-Royce's share price on the London Stock Exchange hit an all-time high on 15 June, finishing the day at 549.5p. Despite a weakening dollar, brokers predicted it would push much higher as the British engine-maker signed a lucrative deal with French plane maker Dassault Aviation for a brand-new engine for a new generation of Falcon 7 business jet.

It was another chapter in Rolls-Royce's incredible turnaround. Airbus and Rolls had been estranged for twenty years, since Roger Beteille found his soul mates at GE. This had been an expensive mistake for Rolls. Of the 4,274 engines supplied for Airbus planes between 1969 and 1999, only fifty had been Rolls-Royce.

Sir Ralph Robins, the distinguished chairman of Rolls who retired in March 2002 after 47 years with the company, conceded they had missed the boat. 'I regret our misjudgement of the importance of Airbus Industrie. Of course ours was a different company, with different leadership, but we had the whole Airbus programme in our pocket and we did nothing with it – not that we were in a position to do so, as it transpired,' he said in an interview with veteran aviation writer Bill Gunston.

It was true: Rolls-Royce hadn't always backed the right pony. Joined at the hip to America's plane-makers for too long, Rolls had made some strategic mistakes in the 1970s – most notably backing the Lockheed TriStar and investing in the Boeing 757, for which over almost two-and-a-half-years Boeing didn't secure a single order of significance. These decisions meant that Rolls-Royce lost significant sales to Pratt & Whitney, though at the time there were no regrets about spurning Airbus's advances. As Jim Callaghan, then Prime Minister, said, 'Rolls-Royce was the national asset we had to preserve, which meant that establishing it in the US market was the central consideration.'

In the corporate world, however, memories are short. In August 1996, GE and Pratt & Whitney joined forces to become The Engine Alliance and began to work on a power plant for the proposed Boeing 747-500X/600X, a chunkier version of the 747-400. Rolls had also been working with Boeing on the development of the Trent engine for this project, but when Boeing shelved the project, it left Rolls in an awkward situation.

Having only recently kissed-and-made-up with Airbus, Rolls had to redouble its efforts to work more closely with Airbus. The success of the Trent 700 on the A330 had seen the plane go into service with Cathay Pacific on 27 February 1995, but it was the Trent 500 engine that would cement the bond between the two companies. A budding relationship was about to bear fruit.

In 1997, the Trent 500 was selected by Airbus as the sole engine for the A340-500/600 ultra-long-range aircraft. It was launched a year later and has become a very valuable property for both Airbus and Rolls. The Trent 556 variant has 56,000 lbs of thrust, a core scaled down by about 20 per cent from the Trent 800 and has the same fan size as the Trent 700, but is significantly quieter.

The new-found love affair was profitable, though it wasn't strictly exclusive. Airbus continued to develop planes with Pratt and GE, but after the cancellation of the 747-500X/600X project, Rolls began to recognise the importance of Airbus to their business. This impetus would pave the way for the huge Trent 900s that would power the first A380s.

Jürgen Thomas at Airbus said, 'When Boeing cancelled, it gave us a brilliant opportunity. By the autumn of 1996, Airbus Industrie was working to conclude an agreement with both The Engine Alliance and Rolls-Royce. We wanted to be able to offer a choice of engines on our A380 airliner.'

By early 1999, Rolls-Royce was working harder at trying to cut the fuel consumption of its engines and introduced new compressor blade technology into two of its Trent engines to help meet the challenge. The blades – designed using three-dimensional aerodynamic analysis software – were to be used on the Trent 500 for the Airbus A340-500/600 and later on the Trent 800 for the Boeing 777.

Paul Craig, Rolls-Royce's Trent 800 chief engineer, told *Flight International* in January 1999: 'You're talking about a specific fuel consumption reduction of up to 2 per cent, so it's a big number.' He added that Rolls-Royce was satisfied that the new blades would perform reliably on production versions of the Trent 500s. 'We've done a lot of de-risking of the technology,' he said. 'We've run three Trent 800s with the 3-D aero compressors and it's all worked very well. We view this as a low-risk technology.'

The new blades were to be tested extensively to ensure that they met Extended-Range Twin-Engine Operations (ETOPS) requirements for the Trent 8104. When the Trent 8104 was put through its initial test it exceeded 110,000 lbs (490 kN) of thrust and looked a good bet for Boeing ultra-long-range 777-200ER, with two engines.

Mike Howse, Rolls-Royce's Director of Engineering, was very pleased with the progress. 'At the moment, the Trent 8104 is for the 777-200X programme that we've been committed to. But if Boeing gets to the point where they want a bigger thrust, we're pretty confident we will be in a position to do that. One of the reasons for the tests is to determine what we can get this engine to do. This is why we're excited about the swept fan and core items. The testing will give us the means of moving thrust forward and we will determine what we have to do in order to do that.'

In April 2005, Rolls-Royce announced that it had been selected by Boeing to supply the Trent 1000 engine for the

787 Dreamliner. Sir John Rose welcomed this as a highly significant decision. 'We expect this programme to provide good financial returns and to build on our successful engine portfolio which has allowed us to develop a strong market position in the civil airlines sector.' He didn't know how *good* this was going to be though. He noted the advanced technologies developed for the Trent 1000 would find applications across the company's other businesses.

Terrett was over the moon too, saying Boeing's expression of faith in Rolls-Royce reaffirms the Trent family's leading position on modern widebody airliners.

'This is a special day in the long and successful relationship between our companies,' he said.

The 747 jumbo jet experience had shown that a heavyweight titan, like the A380, required a huge power plant. And four engines. Cheap fuel has been a major factor in the huge rise in air travel since the end of the Second World War, but with oil hitting $60 a barrel in 2005, and the world's supply of fossil fuel dwindling, there was an imperative for the aircraft-makers to find better ways of flying us around the globe. Prolonged high oil prices could do untold damage to airplane business.

The A380 – and the Dreamliner 787 – will fly million of miles throughout their lifetimes. The airlines are buying this new generation of planes because of their reliability, environmental performance and lower maintenance costs. But the toughest and continuing challenge is for the engine-makers. The constant demand was for even less noise, fewer emissions yet more punching power at take-off. With Al Gore's *An Inconvenient Truth* now pricking the world's combined conscience about global warming and pointing a finger at international air travel, the engineer must find cleaner ways of taking people up into the skies.

The Trent 900 was designed for the A380 and is its fourth generation. It was unveiled along with the new Airbus A380 at the Reveal ceremony in Toulouse on 18 January 2005. It is scaled up from the Trent 500 and introduced swept fan, 3-D aerodynamics throughout the compressor and turbine sections. As Jürgen Thomas explained, the fan diameter is 116 inches to reduce the noise. He said the only way to do this is to increase the bypass ratio which meant a larger fan. The engine is very powerful, certified for 80,000 lbs of thrust, but derated for airlines to operate at 70,000 lbs for the A380-800 and 76,500 lbs for the freighter A380F, which was later postponed. But what pleased Rolls was that it beat all current and proposed environmental legislation.

The A380 is heavier than the aborted 747-500/600X by several thousand pounds, yet requires less thrust on take-off because of the advanced wing technology and high-loft devices that give it exceptional efficiency.

The early signs were encouraging. In addition to the 60-hour programme successfully completed by Trent 900 on a A340-300 flying test bed, the engine was flown on the A380 at low speed to find the stalling conditions, maximum speeds of Mach 0.88 and at the altitude ceiling of 43,000 ft. Airbus confirmed that the engines were meeting fuel-burn targets.

The Trent 900, according to Terrett, is the cleanest large engine in the world with the lowest noise emissions, though Rolls-Royce is still working to meet goals set by the Advisory Council for Aerospace in Europe, which include a halving of current noise levels, and an 80 per cent reduction in NO_2 by 2020.

The engine, however, is no longer a purely British-made product. Rolls-Royce is a global business and has strategic partners sharing the risk and revenue on the Trent 900 from Industria de Turbo Propulsores, in Italy, Hamilton Sundstrand, Avio, Marubeni, Volvo Aero, Goodrich and Honeywell. While Samsung Techwin, Kawasaki Heavy Industries and Ishikawajima-Harima Heavy Industries are all programme associates.

The Engine Alliance's GP7200 will also be used on the A380. In a similar position to Rolls-Royce after the Boeing decision, they were able to adapt the engine to the super jumbo's requirements. The agreement between GE and Pratt & Whitney keeps their engineering relationship separate, with GE producing the high-power system and Pratt, the low pressure, although the teams work together on the integration of the systems.

The first Trent 1000 for the Boeing 787 Dreamliner was tested throughout 2006 at Derby, with its maiden flight, on board an adapted Boeing 747-200 flying test aircraft, in early 2007. The Trent 1000 is due to begin commercial operations with All Nippon Airways in 2008, though it is not just Boeing shouldering the risk. Goodrich Corporation and Hamilton Sundstrand, both headquartered in the United States, became risk and revenue sharing partners on the Trent 1000 engine. Goodrich's Engine Control Systems business unit, with a UK factory in Birmingham, are designing and manufacturing the engine's control system, while Hamilton Sundstrand is responsible for the gearbox system. Similarly, Mitsubishi Heavy Industries is a risk and revenue sharing partner on the Trent 1000 engine, with a seven per cent share, supplying the combustor and low pressure turbine blades.

With both the A380 and the 787 Dreamliner featuring Rolls-Royce engines, it's clear that, win or lose between Airbus and Boeing, a Trent engine will be keeping the titans in the air.

19. A GIANT BODY FOR THE GERMANS

Hamburg is a majestic city, yet it remains solidly industrial. It's sophisticated, yet raw and earthy; artistically elitist, yet able to embrace the avant-garde; an inland European port, but with an outlook to the wider world. This northern Hanseatic city has had a pivotal part to play in Airbus's success, and the way the city and its people have embraced and encouraged manufacturing is in stark contrast to the struggles that the aerospace industry has had in parts of the UK.

Hamburg, home of so many brilliant maritime engineers, needed a new suit of clothes after their shipbuilding industry began to disappear to cheaper places such as Poland and Korea. German engineering has always been a source of immense national pride – the engineer in Germany enjoys much higher social standing than in the UK. It has also produced many aviation pioneers and was at the forefront of jet engine technology – though not always with the best intentions.

Inspired by Count Zeppelin's mammoth airships, Ernst Heinkel pursued a career as an engineer and later founded the Heinkel Aircraft Works. During the ban on German remilitarisation in the 1920s, Heinkel sold designs to Sweden to get around the sanctions, an ingenuity that was noted and appreciated by Adolf Hitler when he came to power. The Fuhrer demanded military power and Heinkel expanded his factory at Warnemunde on the

Baltic coast. He took on two talented aircraft design engineers, Siegfried and Walter Gunter, and they set about creating and designing the Heinkel He 70 and later the Heinkel He 111, which became the mainstay of the Luftwaffe.

There was frantic development of jet engines in the late 1930s as Europe careered headlong towards war. Heinkel was a veritable genius who pushed his engineers and designers to the limit. They excelled. The Heinkel He 100 was one of the fastest propeller planes, reaching 464 miles per hour (747 kilometres per hour) in 1939 and for Heinkel it was an intellectual turning point. He realised that this was as fast as a propeller plane could practically go. It was clear to him that the future demanded a new type of propulsion.

A good friend of Heinkel was the physicist Robert Wichard Pohl, director of the University of Gottingen's Physical Institute. He had an exceptional young graduate assistant called Hans von Ohain, who received his degree in 1935. As a 22-year-old from Dessau in 1933 he first posited the idea of a gas turbine engine for an airplane. While Frank Whittle – cantankerous and with a reputation for being difficult to work with – was working on the Whittle Unit in the UK, which was patented in 1930, von Ohain and his mechanic colleague, Max Hahn, were collaborating by hammering together the blades on a smaller jet engine with less power and thrust. It didn't perform well, yet the thinking was spot on. They soon ran out of development capital, but the project excited Heinkel so much he asked the pair to join his company in Rostock.

Under Heinkel's personal guidance, the company's engineers built a better factory-demonstration jet engine prototype, which was successfully tested in September 1937. The Heinkel HeS I turbojet began test flying in early 1939. It was slung beneath the fuselage of a Heinkel He118 V2 bomber and powered by a Daimler-Benz DB 600 liquid-cooled engine.

Von Ohain displayed Germany's advanced aviation technology on 24 August 1939 when Flugkapitan Erich Warsitz piloted the experimental Heinkel He178 VI, powered by Ohain's HeS 3B. Its first flight took place three days later on 27 August 1939, less than a week before the Nazi invasion of Poland, which sparked Britain's declaration of war. Within a year, Heinkel and Dornier bombers were destroying large tracts of London during the Blitz. Had Germany been able to deploy jet-powered bombers that could outpace the defending Hurricane and Spitfires, the RAF might not have been able to turn the fortunes of the Battle of Britain.

After the war Ohain emigrated to the United States under Operation Paperclip, a Cold War plan to bring leading German scientists to America. He had a distinguished scientific career and was appointed Chief Scientist of the Aerospace Research Laboratories in 1963 and later the Lindbergh Professor at the National Air and Space Museum in Washington DC.

Heinkel was also at the forefront of developing rocket technology. The Heinkel 176 tested two different rocket motors in flight: one a liquid-fuelled version built by Wernher von Braun, and the other, which used hydrogen peroxide, was built by Hellmuth Walter, an independent engine-builder. The Walter approach was better. And simpler. His rocket motor powered the Messerschmitt Me 163, which reached 624 miles per hour (1,004 km hour) in 1941, twice the speed of other operational warplanes. The technical might of the Third Reich had been able to develop an engine of ominous power and capability – and Germany would become the first nation to use jet aircraft in actual combat. It was therefore apposite that Germany should make a considerable contribution towards peaceful aviation in the post-war era.

Germany had far-reaching restrictions imposed on its aviation industry by the Allies after the war. When these restrictions were eased in 1955, the German industry was able to take on subcontracting work with Nord Aviation. From this, Germany was given a chance to break onto a major civil aircraft programme.

France and Germany had worked together on the Transall C160 project, a turbo-prop military transport plane carrying 93 soldiers, which went into service. The German work was undertaken by Hamburger Flugzeugbau (HFB), originally set up by the shipbuilders Blohm & Voss in 1933. HFB merged with Messerschmitt-Bölkow in 1969 to become the MBB and a year later became a partner in the Airbus consortium.

From all of German industry, it was Franz-Josef Strauss who became a leviathan in the Airbus story. Strauss had been a German soldier on both the Western and Russian fronts and had suffered severe frostbite. The war coloured his views on Europe and he had become a young cabinet minister in Konrad Adenauer's second CDU government from 1953 to 1955. He was minister for atomic power and in 1956 became defence minister, charged with building up the Bundeswehr. But his career hit the skids with the infamous *Der Spiegel* scandal, when the magazine accused him of receiving bribes for military contracts. A parliamentary inquiry found no evidence against Strauss but the politician was found to have lied and Adenauer's coalition government was in tatters.

Hanko Von Lachner, a former General Secretary of Airbus, insists Strauss's involvement cannot be overemphasised. 'His role went far beyond Airbus. He tackled all sorts of enterprises. He promoted the German aviation industry and, in particular, the Airbus project. He was very interested in all sorts of technology and he gained his private pilot's licence quite late in life. Without doubt, Strauss, an uncompromising right-winger, was the man in Germany who kept, at least on the government side, the programme going. Without him, we would have had some very difficult times.'

Even in the UK, there was not a political figure to compare with him for his consistent and doggedly pro-Airbus stance. 'He was a man with a strong personality and a lot of courage. He saw the overall goal, that the Airbus project was the chance for a European industry. He was an archetypal European,' says Lachner.

The Bavarian state President made a strong bid to become the German Chancellor but was beaten by Helmut Kohl in 1980. He was also chairman of the Supervisory Board of Airbus Industrie, which became something of a thankless task in the late 1980s.

Airbus's decision-making structure at the time was under huge pressure. The Supervisory Board was too unwieldy, decisions were talking too long and reform was desperately needed. Still, Strauss's untimely death in October 1988 left a temporary void in Airbus's leadership, a hole as huge as the one he left in German politics. Any reform of the structure was put on hold as attention was turned to finding a suitable successor. This was Hans Friderichs, a former federal minister of economics, and party leader of the FDP from 1974 to 1977. He gave up politics in 1977 to become chairman of Dresdner Bank and oversaw the restructuring of AEG Telfunken. But he was embroiled in a bribery scandal and was fined for tax evasion in 1987.

The new slimmed-down Supervisory Board agreed that competitive bidding among the partners was a more efficient way to do business. Airbus Industrie agreed the design for the A300-10 in 1978, but it was planned to have the new wing made by an integrated design team of French, German and Dutch designers. The project became the A310 and a national competition was started for the best wing design. The idea was to build a smaller, lighter wing with a higher performance. The German-led design was conventional, with what was known as a supercritical section and Fowler flaps. The British design was bigger and thicker but distinctively tapered from below. This was an upwardly sloping wing that produced lower drag and good clearance for the engines on the wings.

The result was a combined wing that brought the best of British and the integrated design team together, with the adoption of the Fowler flaps outboard and the vaned Fowler flaps inboard. Despite the technicalities, and after political pressure when Franz-Joseph Strauss suggested it could be made in Hamburg, Britain was eventually given the job of producing the wings. The UK would build the wings with a group of French and German engineers all helping. The supercritical wing featured a 28-degree sweep, with an area of 2,360 square feet, and a wingspan of 144 ft, compared to the A300B's 147 ft 1 in. The new wing also provided the opportunity for the Belgian consortium, Belairbus, to join Airbus.

The German government and MBB were pressing Aerospatiale for Hamburg to become the location of the final assembly line for the A321. There was some resistance from France but when the project was launched on 24 November 1989 there was intense demand. Advance sales were excellent, and so the Supervisory Board endorsed a decision to open two assembly lines, on 26 January 1990. This was a feather in the cap for Hamburg.

The Finkenwerder factory on the banks of the River Elbe has now been producing A319s, A321s and, more recently, A318s since 1992. While Hamburg is a major international port, it is now the German hub for Airbus and it has produced nearly 1000 planes since it opened. From 1976, green or unpainted aircraft began to arrive at Finkenwerder from Toulouse for interiors to be fitted, seats to be added and galleys, toilets and luggage bins to be built. It was work involving the best German organisation with 3,000 different items all fitted onto the planes.

Despite this efficiency, Airbus learned a lot from an aborted joint study with Boeing on the VCLT (Very Large Commercial

Transport). They discovered that Boeing's assembly and production was outstripping Airbus. It was clear that more investment, and new hangars, were needed in Finkenwerder, while the automation of machine tools was vital for turning out fuselage shells more quickly. Every process had to be far more precise, so advance computer technology was applied to laser-welding techniques, taken from the German car industry, to allow Airbus engineers to work faster and more accurately.

Faster though they became, expense became an issue. The dollar was falling against the German Deutschmark, which made production in Hamburg far more expensive. The management in Hamburg initiated Operation Dolores (short for dollar low rescue, and also the Spanish word for pain). The workforce was cut by a third and, through negotiated deals with the unions, Airbus staff worked on more flexible shifts. When there was demand, they could increase overtime, but when there were not enough planes to make, they would stay at home. For many Germans, it was a hard time and morale was at a debilitating low.

By 1997, Daimler-Benz Aerospace (DASA) needed to extend its narrow-body assembly line in Hamburg as production rates had tripled in three years. The German Airbus partner was doing exceptionally well and invested a further $130m in the expansion plans. New work stations were added for the A319/A321 which helped increase production from five to nine planes per month. The German partner was also trying to persuade the French to transfer all production on the A320 to Hamburg, turning the city into the narrow-body centre – and making a saving of $25 million on every plane being made.

DASA Airbus's Vice President Peter Fornell argued: 'There are essential possibilities to bring down cost by concentrating the three production lines, I think we have to find a solution within the restructuring process of Airbus Industrie.' He also said that Airbus had to look at a successor to the A320 family because Boeing would be working on a new aircraft to follow the Next Generation 737.

In 2001, the company changed its name to become Airbus Deutschland GmbH employing over 17,000 of Airbus's 46,000 people. Since then, the number at Finkenwerder has dropped to 8,700. Stadt remains a significant part of the whole Airbus business, producing carbon-fibre vertical stabilisers, spoilers, flaps and pressurised bulkheads; Nordenham manufactures fuselage shells and body panels; Laupheim, in Bavaria, produces cabin interiors and air-conditioning ducts and a variety of other factories make smaller components which arrive at Finkenwerder just in time for assembly. A new material, Glare, is being used on the A380. It is highly resistant to fatigue and used in the construction of the panels for the upper fuselage. The aluminium and fibreglass layers of Glare do not allow propagation of cracks, and it is much lighter than conventional materials and represents a weight saving of about 500 kg in the construction.

Following the launch of the A380 in 2000, a 345-acre plot of land has been reclaimed at Muhlenberger Loch, next to the current facility and with a port handy for access to the Elbe. The first building, the Major Component Assembly (MCA) is now being used for the assembly of the A380. Components for the aircraft are gathered together at one end of the assembly hangar, known as Station 41. This is where two sections of the fuselage are joined. Once this is completed, the huge tube is lifted by overhead cranes to Station 40 (or 40A as the production of the A380 cranks up) and it is joined to the wings. This is also where the engine pylons and landing gear is attached. The plane is then towed to Station 35 for avionic systems to be fitted and horizontal and vertical stabilisers. The aircraft move along the line and are then taken out by the night shift so that assembly can start again with the morning shift.

Because Finkenwerder is close to shipping channels, there are stringent rules about planes landing at the airport. This has meant that the current 8,800 ft (2,684 m) runway is not suitable for the A380. An extension of the runway by 1,650 ft (500 m) westward has met with a great deal of local protest. Environmentalists claimed it would mean more destruction of the Elbe wetlands and the Muhlenberger Loch, one of Europe's last freshwater tidal ecosystems and home to the threatened hemlock water dropwort. Nonetheless, the Hamburg government approved the extension.

Members of a local church at nearby Neuenfelde, which owns some adjacent land, and some fruit farmers have also been fighting a high-profile campaign against the runway extension, but it has become a one-sided contest. The extension was vital to allow the A380 to land. Hamburg's mayor, Ole Von Buest has been a strong supporter of Airbus. 'It could mean things move to Toulouse ... the balance between the two cities is vital,' he told the *Financial Times*.

The summer of 2004 was a significant time for the A380 builders. Two milestones were celebrated on 10 June; the topping out of the A380 equipment hall and the arrival of the special transport ship – specifically designed to carry A380 parts to Ville de Bordeaux at the new roll-on/roll-off quay on the Elbe. The massive equipment hall has been fitted out to meet the airline's specifications for all passenger cabins and service compartments of all A380s. The hall is 1,100 ft (370 m) long and 307 ft (102.5 m) wide and can hold four A380 aircraft.

It was originally planned to take twenty days to fit out the A380 passenger cabins allowing 48 aircraft per year to be delivered. But the wiring problems put paid to this. Delivery of the fully equipped and painted A380 aircraft to customers then takes place in Hamburg and Toulouse. It was intended to be an efficient and impressive system. Frankfurt Airport became the first major international hub facility to welcome an A380 as the second flight test aircraft arrived for compatibility trials in October 2005. With the help of launch customer Lufthansa, the A380 was serviced at Terminal 2, Gate E9. From here the A380 would make its maiden flight to New York JFK airport in 2007.

The A380 was originally hailed as a pan-European achievement. But the industry is now truly global. Many of the significant parts and technologies come from American suppliers. More outsourcing of Airbus's aircraft production is vital to help it achieve higher growth. Airbus's former chief Gustav Humbert was quoted as saying he planned to outsource up to 70 per cent of production and may give contracts to countries such as China, Russia and India in order to expand in new markets with potential for future orders.

For the moment though, it remains a European affair. Today's A380 undertakes a major excursion before it ever flies. The journey starts at Finkenwerder Airport. The rear fuselage and part of the forward fuselage are loaded on to the roll-on roll-off vessel, the *Ville de Bordeaux*. The ship sails to Mostyn Harbour in North Wales where a barge from Brougton plies the 22 miles down the River Dee from. Broughton, where the giant wings are assembled. The Afon Dyfrdwy (the Welsh name for the River Dee) is a compact workhorse capable of carrying 800 tonnes when fully loaded. The A380 wing complex is on the banks of the River Dee and Airbus has built a special underwater grid so the barge could fit with the transporter that takes the finished wing, encased in a pallet, from the factory. At £20 million a time, there is no room for error. Tail skins are produced by Airbus's composites plant near Madrid, using automated fibre replacement machines, while the Spaniards are also responsible for all the belly fairings and sections of rear fuselage. In all there are sixteen Airbus manufacturing sites across France, Germany, Spain and the UK, with Toulouse the final assembly plant for the A380.

On Friday, 7 May 2004, a sparkling new assembly plant was officially opened by French prime minister Jean-Pierre Raffarin. It was named the Jean-Luc Lagardère factory, in honour of the co-chairman of EADS at the time of the launch. The massive factory was expecting to turn out four A380s a month, but it too has been crippled by the wiring problem.

20. AIRBUS'S SUPER SALESMAN

John Leahy was sitting in the back of his limo gliding through LA's morning traffic on his way to a sales meeting when his mobile phone buzzed with an urgent call. He scanned the number. It was one of his Airbus guys in Manila. He listened for a few minutes, nodding occasionally as one of his lieutenants passed on some vital intelligence. The Airbus sales team in Asia had heard that Yang Ho Cho, the Chairman and Chief Executive Officer of Korean Air, was having lunch that day in Los Angeles with Alan Mulally. Cho's airline was on the cusp of a major decision: to either sign up to the Boeing 787 Dreamliner or embrace the Airbus A350.

'When's the meeting with Mulally?' he asked.

Outflanking your opponent is often the difference between winning or losing orders big enough to swing the balance of global trade. Leahy, now a joint Chief Operating Officer of Airbus, is a master of his craft and is considered to be something of a legend. A wily and tenacious customer, Leahy, Airbus's silver-tongued salesman since 1994, has a unique ability to sell airplanes. Jürgen Thomas, the father of the A380 project, said of Leahy, 'If you throw him out through the front door ten times, he comes through the window the eleventh time. You are talking about somebody who never gives up.' One airline boss described him as an 'obsessive and over-the-top perfectionist who doesn't have much else to talk about other than planes'.

While he might only talk about planes, many others only talk about him. Every Monday morning Boeing's sales meeting in Renton always includes the question: 'Where's Leahy?'

'I asked where he was every week, and I expected them to know,' said Carson's predecessor, Toby Bright, who lost his job after losing too many deals to Airbus. 'Wherever Leahy was, that was where the deals were coming down.'

The problem for Boeing was that Leahy and his team were everywhere. The Airbus chief has created one of the slickest sales organisations in the world. The endless hours spent networking with people at all levels has allowed Leahy to discover who really makes the key decisions. His schedule is punishing. Over one ten-day period, which was entirely typical, Leahy flew back and forth from the United States to attend three different sales campaigns: for Korean Air, Northwest and International Lease Finance, the giant leasing company weighing up the option of the 787 and the A350.

This resolve is why Leahy has been able to rattle Boeing so much. Brought in by Jean Pierson in 1985, Leahy was head-hunted from Piper Aircraft where he had been selling Cherokees, Aztecs and Cheyennes. At Airbus America, he quickly made his name by clinching a fistful of deals with United Airlines, Northwest Airlines, US Airways and Air Canada. Smooth, articulate and assertive, he is also punctilious about presentation.

'I remember one of the aircraft presentations to Korean Air,' said Jürgen Thomas. 'Korean Air's relationship with us was very good indeed, dating back to 1974 when they became our first customer outside of Europe. Boeing had been in a few weeks before us, but the technical presentation hadn't been right with their PowerPoint. That was fed back to us. There were some statistics that didn't add up either, so we were able to pick them up on this.'

A few days before Airbus's pitch, Leahy insisted that five people stand up and speak at the presentation. Four technicians were up all night trying to get the right balance, testing and retesting the presentation. Preparation was everything. It was Leahy's masterstroke. It was rehearsed two or three times so that everyone knew exactly how the presentation should proceed. Thomas said it was Leahy's application and attention to the airline's actual requirements that ensured Airbus and not Boeing won the big deals.

At the Airbus A380 Reveal, on 18 January 2005, in Toulouse, Korean Air announced it would be ordering five of the titans, with options for three more. Delivery would be in 2008 for the airline's high traffic routes from Seoul to Europe and the United States. Earlier, while this deal was being thrashed out, Leahy was also pressing to win Virgin Atlantic's order, knowing Sir Richard Branson was no pushover and wanted a bargain for the A380s.

'The deal was looking very good, but there was one last glitch,' said Jürgen Thomas, 'Virgin Atlantic wanted exactly the same deal as Singapore Airlines [who are the first airline to fly the A380]. If that could be agreed, we had a sale.'

The proposed deal was short of what Airbus and Leahy had expected, but as Singapore Airlines had a 49 per cent stake in Virgin Atlantic, Leahy knew that information would have been traded. It was a tough – and indeed pressurised – decision.

'Leahy told me that we had to decide by midnight because Sir Richard had gone to the opera,' says Thomas. 'We are honest people. So we came up with a suitable plan and everyone was satisfied, especially John Leahy.' Virgin Atlantic is expecting the delayed delivery of its six A380s from 2009.

The Singapore Airlines deal that predated the Virgin Atlantic order had, however, now hit a snag. The airline's business customers wanted better and later night-time departures from Heathrow, and earlier arrivals from Singapore. This was a reasonable request; however, there were complications that threatened to scupper the entire deal.

Singapore Airlines needed their new A380s to be significantly quieter in order to adhere to the Quota Count system that controls the noise caused by aircraft night operations at Heathrow and other London airports. Heathrow is one of the world's busiest airports, yet millions live under its flight path. Engine noise at take-off and landing is a major political and environmental concern. The Quota Count system, introduced by the UK government in 1995, grades aircraft on their measured noise performance – the noisier the plane, the higher the QC bands. Quotas have been set on a number of flights, especially those taking off and landing between 11.30 p.m. to 6 a.m. local time. The A380 was rated as a QC4 – the highest level – but Singapore wanted the engines to be no more than QC2. Leahy knew this was a deal breaker and quickly contacted Thomas to tell him the bad news.

Thomas, though obviously dismayed by the proposition, was well aware they had no option but to radically overhaul the engine. He and his team immediately set to work. It involved urgent sessions with engine-maker Rolls-Royce.

'It was the first Airbus aircraft where we had to sacrifice a bit of economy. The engine burns more fuel, about half a per cent more, for slightly less noise. The fan diameter was originally 110 inches but now had to go up to 116 inches. This creates more drag and more weight but the noise is less. This was the kind of pushing we got from John Leahy,' said Thomas.

The modifications saved the Singapore deal, and the tangible benefits were almost immediately obvious. The adoption of the A380 by Singapore gave a seal of approval to the project and therefore interested other airlines, most notably Qantas. 'Without this signature from Singapore,' Thomas said 'the other airlines would have waited longer, especially Qantas.' Leahy had been the driver, listening intently to the airlines and then asking the engineers to accommodate the requirements.

In the back of his limo, however, Leahy learned that Boeing had the upper hand with Korean Air, and sped through downtown LA to catch Cho, eventually meeting up with him at the Wilshire Grand Hotel. Over tea, Cho broke the news. His technical managers were leaning toward Boeing; Airbus engineers had failed to convince them why theirs was a better airplane. Leahy was not pleased.

'I guess we screwed up on this one,' Leahy concluded.

Five weeks later Korean Air announced it was ordering ten Boeing 787s, with options on ten more, investing a total of $10bn. The agreement, however, was not without controversy as allegations were made that an offsetting deal had been put into place. Korean Air has its own aerospace division, which does heavy maintenance on airliners and also builds aircraft parts for both the US Air Force and Boeing. The *Seattle Times* reported that it had internal Boeing documents that indicated that Korean Air was scheduled to make the wing tips of the 787. However, no official announcement was made.

Northwest Airlines – the world's fourth largest airline with hubs at Detroit, Minneapolis/St Paul, Memphis, Tokyo and Amsterdam, and approximately 1,400 daily departures – bought eighteen 787s to update its ageing fleet. They selected Rolls-Royce Trent 1000 engines and ordered installed and spare engines for eighteen aircraft including Rolls-Royce's total care maintenance agreement.

Life, however, was difficult for Northwest as it tried to make $2.5bn in savings and filed for Chapter 11 protection from bankruptcy in October 2005. New planes, arriving in August 2008, would be essential for survival. President and chief operating officer, Douglas Steenland, wasn't joking when he said, 'The Rolls-Royce team worked closely with us to define a solution that meets Northwest's needs.' The solution was to survive.

Leahy was clearly aggrieved that Boeing had turned things around, but he was typically bullish in response to the competition. 'Objectively, they've got the high ground right now. I wanted Korean and Northwest. They seem to be doing everything they can to stop the A350 from being an industrial launch. My job is to make sure that doesn't happen,' he said.

Since 1993, the 56-year-old Leahy has tormented his American arch-rival by leading a sales assault unsurpassed in modern business history, taking Airbus from 18 per cent of the market to 57 per cent in just over a decade. It had shaken Boeing to the foundations, but the success of the 787 suggested the Americans had turned the corner.

The $5.2bn A350 was finally given the go-ahead by EADS and Airbus shareholders in October 2005. Leahy, ever the salesman, said the biggest problem was Airbus's ability to ramp up to meet demand. 'If I could get more, I could sell more,' he told Max Kingsley-Jones at *Flight International*. He said Airbus had secured 140 commitments since the commercial launch in December 2004. He said sales would reach 210 by the end of the year; by mid-December it was 164.

'My problem is getting them out of the door. We need to do what Boeing is doing with its production ramp-up of the 787.' Leahy is right to point out the advances that Boeing has made. Increasing its speed of decision-making, while dispatching senior executives and board members into the field to drum up sales, was paying dividends. Winning back market share was a priority, and Boeing's aggression seemed to suggest they would do just that. Even Leahy admits, 'these guys could really turn it around this year'.

By 'these guys' it's clear he's referring to one in particular, his nemesis Alan Mulally. 'He has the ability to change things,' Leahy said. 'He gets an hour and a half, maybe two hours with the chairman of Korean Air, and he can reach across the table and have a handshake with the guy. That's damn near impossible for me to recover from,' he told the *Seattle Times*. Not that Leahy is despondent. By chasing deals – even when he knows he won't win them – Leahy forces Boeing to expend more capital on each account, and this financial pressure means that there is a potential for Boeing to lose a future deal.

This is a typically impudent retort from Leahy. The success of the A330, which took more than three quarters of the midsize wide-body plane market, and effectively made the Boeing 767 obsolete, proved that new planes could capture a sector of the industry incredibly quickly. Boeing's new 777 and 787 had the potential to replicate this success.

Boeing, however, was not content with simply vaunting its new product. Instead it went on a full-scale offensive against Airbus, using academic firepower to attack the Europeans. The *Sunday Times* reported that a study by US academics, including Northwestern University Professor Aaron Gellman, said the A380 would lose $8bn over its commercial life and never pay back the state aid of $3.8bn. The study was funded by Boeing, though its authors were at pains to point out that the company had not influenced their findings. Whether it had or not, Airbus were not happy. Barbara Kracht, Airbus's media spokeswoman, said in a terse phone interview, 'We deny it categorically. The A380 is going to be a very profitable programme.'

21. SEX, LIES AND BOEING'S BOARD-ROOM BOTHER

It was the *Wall Street Journal*'s website that first broke the news of Boeing's new boss. On Thursday, 30 June 2005, following a tip off, staff writers Lynn Lunsford, Joann Lublin and Michael McCarthy revealed the identity of the man charged with ending the sex, scandal and strife that had beset Boeing over the previous years. It was one of the major business exclusives of the hot summer.

In downtown Seattle, just as the *Journal*'s early editions hit the streets in New York, Boeing executives from the commercial aircraft division were entertaining airline customers and enjoying the prawns, sake and beer in a teeming Wild Ginger, on Second Street. The news clicked onto their Blackberrys: Boeing was to appoint 3M Chairman and Chief Executive W James McNerney Jr as its new CEO. The excitement surged through the room, and gossip was soon being traded over drinks and canapés. What would happen to Alan Mulally, now 59, and James Albaugh, 55, the chief of the Boeing's Integrated Defence Systems Division? Opinions were divided as to the outcome; Mulally was still a superhero to many, but doubts about his future remained.

McNerney, who himself was 55, knew about the strength and weaknesses of his new team, having been on the Boeing board since 2001. It was, however, as Chairman and Chief Executive of

3M, the yellow sticky Post-It and pharmaceuticals company, that McNerney had won his reputation as an effective, and disciplined, leader. Before he took over, 3M had been in the doldrums, their sales were poor and they hadn't introduced a blockbusting product in years. In his customary take-no-prisoners style, McNerney turned the company around by slashing costs, cutting the workforce by 10 per cent and adopting the Six Sigma strategy, a management system adopted by Jack Welch at GE that constantly measures and analyses a company's methodology. And if this wasn't enough, he'd already had first-hand experience of the aviation business, after spending three years as the successful CEO of General Electric Aircraft Engines division. To many, he was the perfect man for the job.

The *Seattle Times* splashed the story that morning as the local radio station woke up Boeing's workforce with the news. Adam Pilarski, an analyst with Avitas, told reporter Dominic Gates, 'It's a splendid choice. It's good news. He's exactly what Boeing needs, someone who knows the business but is an outsider. He's not polluted by the internal malaise.'

Richard Aboulafia, an analyst with the Teal Group, said McNerney's pedigree at the aero-engine company was a prize asset. 'Anyone from GE has a lot of prestige in this industry. He's going to be taken very seriously. In terms of satisfying investors, developing new products and gaining market share, it's tough to beat the GE legacy.'

Robert Williams, one of 200 Boeing drivers who whisks VIPs around the Seattle sites in Ford vans, was similarly upbeat. 'He must be a mighty important dude because the stock price jumped up $5 dollars,' he said. The stock price jump was indeed having a big impact. Boeing's share increase was the biggest since 24 September 2001, when US markets rebounded for the first time after 9/11. The gain pushed the shares near to the record high of $69.94 set in November 2000.

McNerney was quick to lay down some foundations. 'Our financial position is strong, and we have proven the logic of our strategy. My job is to make sure we deliver continued profitable growth by consistently meeting the requirements of our diverse customers with outstanding new products and superior service, and I look forward to meeting that challenge. As a current board member, I have come to know our leadership team and have developed an enormous respect for them and for the people of

Boeing. I look forward to working with all of them as we realise Boeing's considerable potential.'

Lew Platt, lead director of Boeing, played the diplomat. He desperately needed to keep some key players in his ball team. 'On behalf of the entire board I want to thank the leadership team and employees of Boeing for their extraordinary work during the past several months,' he said and singled out James Bell who had stepped up at a crucial time. As interim CEO, he had kept the company on track while continuing in his role as Chief Finance Officer.

'We are also very grateful for the performance delivered by Jim Albaugh and Alan Mulally, and their teams at Integrated Defence Systems and Commercial Airplanes. It's clear that we have extraordinary people in place across the company, and we are looking ahead with great confidence in Boeing's future,'

John Leahy at Airbus also praised the appointment. 'McNerney is clearly the best possible choice for Boeing. He's one of the industry stars.'

By 2005, Boeing certainly needed one. Two years before, in the wake of the Enron scandal that had shocked corporate America, Boeing themselves had had its good name dragged through the mud after a series of crises.

In the summer of 2003 it had been alleged that Boeing had stolen 25,000 pages of documents from rival Lockheed Martin to help it win military satellite launch contracts. Meanwhile, its conduct in winning a $22bn deal to lease 100 KC767A aircraft to the US Air Force as midair refuelling tankers was under close scrutiny. The Boeing board suspected its high-flying finance director Mike Sears was guilty of 'unethical conduct' by talking about a possible job at Boeing to Darleen Druyun, a Pentagon official involved in the decision on the tanker contract.

Druyun had been a key Pentagon procurement officer, supervising, directing and overseeing the management of their acquisition programme. But in August 2003, she informed Sears that she was considering retiring and Sears suggested perhaps they should have a talk about future opportunities at the appropriate time. Druyun's daughter, who had been employed by Boeing since 2000, sent an email to Sears saying Druyun was 'officially available' and was retiring from the Air Force. After several email correspondences and a private meeting with Sears at Orlando Airport, she was offered a $250,000-a-year job, with a $40k recruitment bonus on 14 November 2002. She would start in January 2005, but both she and Sears would last just ten months.

In November 2003, Druyun and Sears were sacked for breaching company recruitment policies. However, worse was to come. During the course of an investigation into the tanker deal, it was found that Druyun – while still working for the Air Force – had informed Boeing that Airbus had submitted a bid of significantly less per plane than Boeing had. This was a serious abuse of her position and she was convicted of improperly providing Boeing with proprietary pricing information of a competitor. She was sent to jail for nine months. Later, Mike Sears was found guilty of a conflict of interest and was fined $250,000 and sentenced to four months in jail.

Just a month after the dismissal of Sears and Druyun, on 1 December 2003, Phil Condit, Boeing's Chief Executive since 1996, unexpectedly resigned. He had a shining career spanning more than 35 years in almost twenty assignments, including Chairman of the board. He joined Boeing in 1965 as an aerodynamics engineer on the Supersonic Transport programme, was promoted to lead engineer for the Boeing 747 in 1968, then chief project engineer on the 757. More recently, he had been general manager of the new vision for the 777. However, despite his glittering career, Condit, to many, had become battered goods.

While Condit was personally not responsible for any wrong doing, his policies were in some respects to blame. Despite his love affair with airplane engineering, Condit's strategy had been to move away from commercial jets, leading him to begin talks with McDonnell Douglas to discuss a possible merger. These rumbled on for a few years, until Douglas suffered two major setbacks in 1996. Firstly they were forced to shelve their plans for a new 600-seater super jumbo, the MD-12, which effectively killed off their status as a first-tier commercial aircraft manufacturer. In November, a more serious setback rocked the company as they were not invited to join Lockheed and Boeing in tendering for the F-35 Joint Strike Fighter (JSF) programme. Douglas was doomed, and had little choice but to join Boeing. The Federal Trade Commission approved the $13.3bn merger in July 1997, instantly creating the biggest defence contractor in the United States.

The merger in place, and with serious competition from Airbus in the commercial market, Condit decided to concentrate on defence and space contracts. The plan had its logic, but by 2003 it was clear that it had seriously flaws, and its consequences seemed calamitous. Airbus had now overtaken Boeing with its deliveries and in 2003 Airbus's order book was $28.2bn, compared to Boeing's $11.1bn.

If the commercial airplane collapse was acutely problematic, the space business was simply disastrous. After investing $6bn in satellite technology, Condit admitted Boeing had overestimated the requirement for the technology and was forced to write off a loss of $1.1bn. This was coupled with the loss of the F-35 Joint Strike Fighter (JSF) programme to Lockheed, which was an unexpected body blow. These factors made every deal essential; it was vital to win every contract that was possible. It was no surprise therefore, that with so much high pressure on these deals, unethical risks were taken.

Condit was contrite. 'I offered my resignation as a way to put the distractions and controversies of the past year behind us, and to place the focus on our performance,' he said at the time. 'I am proud of the strategies that have transformed Boeing into the world's largest aerospace company, and I have the highest regard and respect for Lew [Platt] and Harry [Stonecipher]. They each possess the knowledge, experience and leadership to take this company to the next level.'

With all that had gone before, it was clear that the Boeing board had to regroup and put a new leadership structure into place. They opted to employ Lew Platt as non-executive chairman alongside Harry Stonecipher as President and Chief Executive Officer. Both Platt and Stonecipher were in their sixties and experienced leaders, well versed in the company's operations and strategy.

'Phil acted with characteristic dignity and selflessness in recognising that his resignation was for the good of the company,' said the new chairman, Lew Platt. 'We accepted his decision with sadness, but also with the knowledge that changes needed to be made. The board is confident that the new leadership will bring a renewed focus on execution and performance.'

Stonecipher agreed. 'Boeing has a solid foundation for the future – strong businesses, valuable assets, and thousands of hard-working, dedicated people – and we are all deeply grateful to Phil for his contributions and accomplishments. Lew and I, and the entire board, are determined that the events of the last year will no longer obscure the company's strengths or distract us from what we need to do.'

Harry Stonecipher, the former chief executive of McDonnell Douglas, and pulled out of retirement to be put back in the hot seat as Chief Executive of Boeing, became the public face of the campaign to restore Boeing's reputation and integrity. He lobbied the Pentagon, led a charm offensive with the investors on Wall Street and approved an internal code of conduct which meant even minor violations would not be tolerated. It was a policy that he would come to regret. Only fifteen months after Condit's exit, Stonecipher was also on his way through the revolving doors.

On Sunday, 27 February 2005, the Boeing board flew into Huntington Beach in Southern California for one of its six-times-a-year meetings. While they were preparing for dinner, they were told about a whole new crisis. A whistle-blowing employee had intercepted emails and correspondence between Stonecipher and a 48-year-old woman, later identified by the *Seattle Post-Intelligencer* as Debra Peabody, a divorced woman working with chief lobbyist Rudy deLeon in the government affairs office in Washington. The Boeing board – some of whom were livid – was split on how to handle this news. The next day Stonecipher, married since 1955 to his wife Joan, appeared before the board and was candid and contrite about what had happened.

Stonecipher was a charmer with an edge of toughness, and had an impressive career at GE and Sundstrand behind him, but it was by no means certain that he would be able to talk his way out of the crisis. For eight days the board pondered what to do; they knew that the story would leak. Could the company afford another setback? By Friday, the situation was still unresolved. His colleagues, especially his old friend Lew Platt, were deeply disappointed; after all, Stonecipher had only started the relationship with Debra Peabody in January, and he had approved the company's new puritan rules.

Reluctantly, they decided they had to send a strong message about Boeing's ethics and standards and asked Stonecipher to resign.

It all seemed rather harsh. But Boeing's new code of conduct expressly stated that an employee 'will not engage in conduct or activity that may raise questions as to the company's honesty, impartiality, reputation or otherwise cause embarrassment to the company.' The board ultimately had no choice.

'As we explored the circumstances surrounding the relationship,' Lew Platt said, 'we just found things that we thought reflected poorly on Harry's judgement and would impair his ability to lead the company going forward.'

The CEO, according to Platt, had to set standards for unimpeachable professional and personal behaviour, and as such Stonecipher had to go. A shocked Joan Stonecipher, who listed her occupation as a housewife and lived in the family's elegant $1.8m home on the water in St Petersburg, in Florida, filed for divorce. It was a sad outcome all round.

'It was an ignominious end for Harry Stonecipher after a long and distinguished career in the US aerospace and defence industry,' said Kevin Done, the *Financial Times*' aviation correspondent.

Now it was down to McNerney to settle the ship, and what better way than to attack Airbus? 'It's pretty clear to me that the subsidies need to stop,' he said on his first conference call on the first day of his leadership. There was an immense amount for him to do.

22. THE AVIATION WORLD AT WAR

Yash sipped his bottled water in the Mumbai nightclub. A tall, fastidiously polite Indian with well-cut dark hair, he held a long, sincere look on his face. While revellers in this sweaty nightspot slugged back shots of gin or malt whisky with Coke, Yash was firm, apologetic and strictly abstemious.

'I don't drink alcohol and besides I'm flying first thing tomorrow morning. Alcohol and flying are not good bedfellows. But please be my guest, what would you like?'

Moments later another chilled water and some bottles of Kingfisher were on the aluminium bar-top. Yash sipped his refreshment while his brother-in-law, Dr Saket Jati, perched on a bar stool, downed the beer. He and Dr Saket Jati, a consultant orthopaedic surgeon, flew in from Indore for an evening clinic and then decided to go out and relax a little.

Dr Yashraj Tongia, MBA, PhD, owns Yash Air, a pilot school 250 miles from Mumbai. A Government of India approved Chief Flight Instructor with 3,000 flying hours, Yash is one of very few people in the whole subcontinent who understands the actual requirements of the booming air business.

'Our company is an approved flying training institute having its own airport equipped with night landing and modern navigational facilities. The company has got a fleet of Cessna 152 and Cessna 172 aircraft apart from P68 multi-engine aircraft. We're rated as one of the fastest growing aviation companies in India and our shares have been valued at thirty times their original value.'

The dance floor in the basement night club was rather forlorn that evening. A few Indian women, dressed in Western jeans and tight T-shirts, swirled around on the dance floor while some Westerners who had strayed in from the hotel looked on. The European bar prices would deter most locals from even venturing past the door. Yash and Saket represent the upwardly mobile modern generation of highly educated Indians. Saket is still a visiting fellow at an orthopaedic institute in Germany, but has also set up his own hospital in Indore; Yash is rightly proud of his academic achievements; 'I'm also the only person with a PhD in Aviation in India,' he says. The title of his thesis? *Present Scenarios and Future Trends of Indian Civil Aviation Industry.*

'Yes, the A380 is an exciting proposition for aviators in India,' Yash said over the din 'but we must walk before we run. The whole nation needs to think about training our very best people in a number of new fields.' The two men talked earnestly about what needed to be done in this vast subcontinent. Their comments were largely optimistic, driven by a sense that the quality of everyone's life in India has huge potential for improvement.

While they spoke, the party continued above them; a hybrid gathering of Mumbai politicians, local worthies and Bollywood stars chatting and dancing as fire-eaters performed, fortune-tellers plied their trade, and the aroma of exotic Indian cuisine wafted over the party. Presiding over this vibrant and colourful spectacle was Sir Richard Branson, celebrating the arrival of Virgin Atlantic in Mumbai. Yash and Saket, despite both being fans of the UK entrepreneur, did not venture upstairs, preferring to continue their discussion of Indian aviation.

The Indian airline boom has taken off. While the United States has 8,000 commercial airplanes, and Europe around 5,000, India – with three times the population of America – has around 300. This is the market Boeing and Airbus wish to corner – particularly with the 787 and the A380. While many major European airlines have been vying for routes as India opens up, it is significant that it is the low-cost Indian carriers that are expanding. And they need trained pilots.

If India is to truly open up it needs to train more pilots, of which there is currently an acute shortage. This affects the current short-range regional jets, the Boeing 737 and the A319, and it's very likely that there will be few Indians able to fly the A380 when it takes to the sky. This is something that concerns Yash.

'It is very exciting for us in India. Three new airlines have started operations in the last two years, Air Deccan, SpiceJet and Kingfisher. Three more – Go Airlines, Inter Globe and Paramount – are entering the fray in 2006. They will all need cabin crews and pilots. Lots of well-trained and competent pilots.'

Yash is anxious though. He wants his country to get the high-end jobs, rather than be forced to import worn-out European captains who fancy a few years working in the sub-continent before retiring to their Spanish villas.

'The number of commercial aircraft operating in my country is expected to increase to around 400 by 2010. Consequently, we will need to increase the number of pilots by two and a quarter times in the next five years. It's not just pilots, it's maintenance engineers and technicians.'

At the Paris Air Show in 2005, Indian airlines placed 280 orders for Airbuses and 146 orders with Boeing. This was something of a surprise as Boeing had long dominated the Indian market and the pilots were initially reluctant to accept Airbus. But now, says Yash, there has been a drastic change in opinion and the new generation of pilots prefer flying Airbus. Regardless of whoever provides the planes, however, the next five years will witness another 700 aircraft in India. Yash is flabbergasted by the statistics.

'These 700 aircraft will need at least 7,000 pilots and our present output is 250 pilots per annum. Hence there is a huge supply and demand gap which cannot be met easily. The availability of pilots will become the biggest factor to impede the growth of aviation in India.'

The Indian stock market is booming, with aviation seen as one of the best investment opportunities. Consequently, raising funds from the public and financial institutions has not been a problem for new airlines. The excitement is palpable, but the current state of the airport infrastructure and the technical manpower available poses some tough questions for the future, which if not answered could lead to another dot-com-style boom and bust.

There is no shortage of capable young people wanting to become pilots in India, yet there are barriers to these ambitions. The capacity of flying institutes, with a lack of aircraft and instructors, is limiting, while wages are considerably lower for an Indian pilot than one of their western counterparts. Still, progression is being slowly made.

Yash's pilot school has grown at an exponential rate and any number of students can be enrolled. 'We have a waiting list of more than 300 students and we are in the process of executing a major expansion plan that will increase our capacity to train 200 pilots per annum.' Further to this, the local college has also started course in aircraft maintenance engineering.

Both Boeing and Airbus viewed the two giant economies of India and China as the places for the future. Indeed, India has made remarkable economic progress since opening up its economy to external business in 1991 – and aviation is a key factor in the continued economic upturn.

Middle-class Indians want to travel, and, to facilitate this, Praful Patel, India's Minister for Civil Aviation, has instigated reconstruction at a large number of airports. The Airports Authority of India, based in New Delhi, has begun an astonishing building programme of new terminals, extension to aprons and high-speed taxiways. New international airports ready to take the A380 have been approved at Devanahalli, near Bangalore, and at Shamsabad, near Hyderabad, while in Delhi the airport has been extended to handle 40 million passengers a year. Western environmentalists might balk at all this, but India wants to embrace the aviation boom as a badge of its world-leading status.

'The Indian economy over the past five decades has grown from a primarily agrarian economy into a service sector dominated economy. India is the fourth largest economy in the world in terms of purchasing power,' says Praful Patel.

Of course, it's not only to India that the aviation industry has been looking – China, in particular, has long been viewed as a market with vast potential. It had already had significant direct foreign investment – totalling 3.7 per cent of GDP, compared with 0.9 per cent in India – and its industrial muscle considerably outstrips its neighbour. The Indian financial system, and the Bombay stock market, still need major overhaul. For India, airline business was seen as a vital component of this, but it was to China that many analysts were looking.

Intra-Asian air travel growth has been accommodated by increases in frequencies and new city pairs with more non-stop flights. Nowhere is this more prevalent than in the China to Japan sector. In 1990, only eight pairs of cities had non-stop, direct services between China and Japan. At that time, there were only 59 weekly flights and 95 per cent of the passengers went through Beijing or Shanghai. By 2005, through increased air travel and competition, the number of city pairs served had increased from 8 to 45. At the same time, weekly flights have gone up nearly eight-fold, from 59 to 463. More profound is that, on average, 27 of the 45 city pairs served, or 60 per cent, have less than one flight per day. Boeing sees this statistic as evidence that there is room for significant growth on the existing city pair network.

Most of China's cities have populations of more than three million people, and twelve of these are home to over five million people. As there are only five cities in Europe and five in North America of a comparable size, it is therefore no surprise that Randy Baseler of Boeing believes the potential for future increases in non-stop service and direct flights between China and the rest of the world is 'unlimited'. He also made it clear who he thought would reap the rewards.

'Airlines in a competitive market will always increase the frequency of the flights and non-stop point-to-point services before increasing the size of airplanes,' said Baseler. 'Because that's what passengers want.'

It was hard to argue with that logic, as just a few days before the Branson jaunt to Mumbai, the biggest airplane order by an Indian carrier was announced, and it wasn't good news for Airbus.

Air-India, the country's national flag-carrier, has enjoyed a monopoly since it began operating its first flight to London in June 1948. However, its reputation within the industry has taken something of a dip. Some aviation experts have attacked the airline, suggesting it has become bloated and expensive with poor service compared to the rising stars of Emirates, Singapore and Cathay. However, with the government desperate to breathe life into the sleeping giant, Air-India was forced to improve – and forced to invest in either Boeing or Airbus planes. Their order would be worth somewhere in the region of $6.5bn, and both Boeing and Airbus were desperate to land it. Would Air-India go for the Airbus hub-and-spoke approach, or the new direct Boeing strategy?

On the chess board the moves were between Boeing's 777-200LR and the Airbus A340-500; the 777-300ER versus the

A340-600, and the 787 versus the A330-200. In the end, the Boeings stole the show. Air-India announced a mouth-watering order for eight 777-200LRs, fifteen 777-300ERs, and twenty-seven 787 Dreamliners. It was a significant and crushing Boeing victory, and one that Airbus called into question immediately.

Dr Dinesh Keskar, Vice President Sales at Boeing, said, 'We won it fair and square. Objective calculations of finances revealed that with a Boeing fleet of fifty airplanes, Air-India could have a cumulative operating profit per year of $185m.' Keskar hammered home his point by saying that 'This operating profit will be higher if the price of crude oil continues to increase because the national carrier will realise savings of more than two million gallons per airline per year with the 777-300ER. John Leahy of Airbus didn't quite see it the same way, believing that preferential rates helped Boeing win the deal. His was not the only sceptical voice about the motivation behind the deal.

Two weeks before the mega deal with Boeing, the Indian transport minister Praful Patel and Norman Mineta, the US's Transportation Secretary, signed an open skies agreement. This agreement abolished all restrictions that a previous agreement from 1956 had put in place, and ensured that only US and Indian carriers could operate direct routes between the two countries. It was an advantageous agreement for both parties, allowing increased passenger and cargo services, and one that showed India's commitment to forging better relations with the United States – though not with Airbus.

'We are not disappointed, but astonished,' said Vice President of Airbus, Nigel Harwood, 'Only Airbus could have delivered all the aircraft in the timeframe demanded by the state-run carrier in its own tender.' Harwood argued that Airbus had not been given an opportunity to present the A380, a fact denied by Air-India. Many analysts agreed that there appeared to be a political game afoot. Brahma Chellaney from the Centre for Policy Research in New Delhi was quoted as saying 'Such huge contracts are decided at the political level and that's what has happened this time too.'

Whether the decision was political or not, the conclusion was much the same: India – along with other emerging countries – is a principal battleground where the flight of the titans will be won and lost. But there were now pressing issues over subsidies and the ethics of winning business.

On 25 May 2005, a political battle was beginning in Washington. Room 2167 of the Raeburn Office Building – a warren of committee rooms and politicians' offices located on Independence Avenue, a few blocks from the Smithsonian's National Air and Space Museum, and two minutes' walk from the United States Capitol – was buzzing with anticipation. John Mica, the Republican Congressman from Florida, banged his gavel on the block promptly at 10 a.m. to start a session that would reverberate all the way back to Toulouse and to the European governments. The House of Representatives Transportation and Infrastructure Subcommittee on Aviation was about to send out a clear message to the Europeans.

The 62-year-old congressman looked stern and businesslike and spoke firmly: 'More than 600,000 men and women in the United States dedicate themselves every day to advancing the science and economics of flight by designing, producing and delivering sophisticated aircraft to customers around the globe,' he told the gathering.

'Let me state clearly: this administration and the US Congress cannot and will not tolerate the unfair subsidisation of manufacturing, promoting, financing or development of commercial aircraft. Where else can any other business secure a loan at deeply discounted rates of interest where the repayment of the loan is based on whether or not the business is considered an economic success?'

He continued: 'I think most people in the United States would love to be in a position to borrow money to buy a business or buy a house, where they need not repay the loan if the person or company happens to be short of cash that year, or the owner loses his or her job. Those terms have been available to Airbus since its creation in 1969.'

This wasn't Boeing speaking. This was a senior American politician.

'The United States must draw a line in the sand and take every possible measure to stop the unfair subsidisation of the development, manufacture, promotion and financing of all commercial aircraft,' he declared.

It wasn't as if Mica was an anti-European redneck. His grandfather was born in the Slovak village of Kopcany and the family moved to the US in December 1907. Mica, proud of his Slovak roots, had even led the effort in Congress to support

Slovakia's entry for NATO membership. But the tone this morning was of remarkable unity. With both Republican and Democrat clear on one issue: Airbus's subsidies must stop.

The Americans were riled. The congress committee was told that, over its 35-year history, Airbus has benefited from massive EU subsidies that have enabled the company to create a full product line of aircraft and gain more than a 50 per cent share of large civil aircraft sales. Every major Airbus aircraft model was financed, in whole or in part, with government subsidies taking the form of 'launch aid'.

It was the subsidy for the A350 that was reigniting the trade war. American and European officials had been in deep conversation since May 2004 when a previous agreement ran out. President Bush instructed United States Trade Representatives to pursue all options to end the Airbus subsidy, including the filing of a World Trade Organisation case, if need be. But Airbus argued that the A350 needed the subsidy.

Mike Turner, head of BAE Systems, said in September 2005, 'When the Airbus board needs investment they come to the shareholders, EADS and BAE Systems. We and EADS now are considering the case for the launch of the A350. But a lot of that will depend on the support that we get from the governments, because we cannot compete on fair terms with the Boeing 787 Dreamliner. I think the A350 and the 787 are comparable in terms of the capabilities and the performance that they give the airlines. The differential will be the huge amount of support that Boeing has received, if we didn't get the same support from the European governments, which I think we'll get.'

Europe, unsurprisingly, was not initially willing to agree to the goal of ending new subsidies, so, on 6 October 2004, the United States started the first stage of dispute settlement proceedings at the WTO by requesting consultations with the EU. The EU responded by requesting consultations on alleged US subsidies to Boeing. This manoeuvring suggested that deadlock was inevitable. However, it soon seemed that a detente might not be too far away. On 11 January 2005, an agreement was reached between the EU and the US on a framework for negotiating an end to subsidies. A ninety-day period was set for the negotiations. By March, however, this framework was in jeopardy.

It was clear that not everyone was following the common objectives, and the EU's sudden volte face was forced by some member nations' refusal to withdraw launch aid – particularly for the Airbus A350. In a circular argument typical of the dispute, the European Union argued that the funds are necessary to offset the subsidies that Boeing receives from NASA and the Department of Defense.

Joel Johnston is a supporter of American aviation. From his neat and tidy office with its book-lined shelves, and photographs of America's most exportable planes, he looks out towards the seat of the world's most powerful nation. There is a glorious panorama over the Capitol in Washington, and the Lincoln Memorial.

This is the former headquarters of the Gannett newspaper group, publishers of the *USA Today* newspaper, and every 45 seconds a Boeing or an Airbus swoops in low over the Potomac river as it makes a low-level approach to National Ronald Reagan Airport. This is now the headquarters of the American Aerospace Industries Association, a trade body that defends American interests.

John Douglass, its president and chief executive, said, 'We are trying to avoid an over-emotional reaction to the World Trade Organisation action. A long dispute is in no one's interest and we hope they will continue a parallel negotiating track. But the bottom line is launch aid must end.'

But the AIA has to steer a hyper-diplomatic path because many of America's leading aviation companies are also major suppliers to Airbus. American aviation, in general, has been cautious about criticising Airbus too much. There are now thousands of jobs in the United States dependent on Airbus. Many of the components and much of the new technology is sold by American-owned companies.

For example, the landing gear of the A380 is manufactured by Goodrich, arguably the best in the world. Goodrich, head-quartered in Charlotte, North Carolina, also makes the LED exterior lighting system, flight control systems, engine sensors and power generators. Then, the A380's alternative choice of engine, the GP7000, is a creation of The Engine Alliance, part of the avionic systems were made by Honeywell, while other integrated systems were made by Curtiss-Wright Controls, both companies based in New Jersey.

'We've got to differentiate between Boeing and the companies that don't want a ruckus because they supply both sides,' says

Johnston. 'The Goodrichs and Honeywells just wish it would go away. I think the reason Boeing for years marched the US Congress up to the cliff and then yanked them back at the last minute was because Boeing got too much flak from the airlines, so they caved.'

Johnston said, as soon as Airbus was committed to the A380, and had started talking to customers, then Boeing suddenly launched the 7E7 with a different philosophy. 'Boeing's assumption was that Airbus would be tied down for a few years. Then Airbus turns around and says, "We're going to try the A350" because the airlines have basically told them the A330 wouldn't compete against the 787. The American position is that we are willing to draw the line, and here is the difference: we are saying we won't call you on the A380 if you don't call us on the 787 Dreamliner.'

Obviously there is much debate as to what even constitutes a subsidy. To many American politicians, the Airbus case against Boeing is utterly unfounded.

'We don't agree that NASA and Defense contracts provide subsidies to Boeing,' said Congressman Peter F Allgeier. 'But, in any event, Airbus and its parents, EADS and BAE Systems, have space and defence businesses that rival Boeing's. Therefore, even under the EU's unfounded approach, Airbus benefits as much if not more than Boeing.'

BAE Systems was being dragged into the wider debate. It was named as one of the US Defense Department's top-ten contractors and involved in billions of dollars' worth of Pentagon contracts, including the Joint Strike Fighter. And EADS was seeking incentives from four US states to locate a new aerial refuelling tanker facility in the United States. It plans to manufacture the tankers by converting Airbus large civil aircraft, the development of which, of course, has been subsidised.

The European Investment Bank also underwrites Airbus's programmes, including a €700m loan to EADS to help underwrite the costs of developing the A380. Allgeier said, 'The European Commission Sixth Framework programme alone granted €1.1bn to aerospace projects. The research programmes at the EC level are also supplemented by research and development programmes at the national level that provide even more funds to Airbus. Launch aid is a particularly distortive type of subsidy because it shifts the enormous up-front expense and commercial risk of developing new aircraft from Airbus to the European taxpayer.'

Launch aid also frees up funds that Airbus would normally need to invest in developing its new aircraft programme. For example, in March, as Airbus was asking for $1.7bn for developing the A350, its parent company BAE Systems spent $4bn to purchase the US manufacturer of the Bradley Fighting Vehicle.

The issue hit the fan. On Monday, 30 May 2005, while the UK was enjoying a bank holiday and the rest of Europe was navel-gazing after France's bombshell decision to vote no in the European Union's referendum on a proposed constitution, the US Trade Department hit back.

'In light of the European Commission's unwillingness to halt new subsidies for large civil aircraft, and with EU member states preparing to commit $1.7 billion in new risk-free launch aid subsidies for Airbus, the United States announced that it will file a request for the establishment of a World Trade Organisation dispute settlement panel to resolve the dispute.'

The WTO is a more viable forum in which to litigate trade tensions than its predecessor, the General Agreement on Tariffs and Trade (GATT). The WTO has a stronger arm on subsidies, and provides an improved dispute settlement mechanism to adjudicate these disciplines. The request was filed the following morning, as the UK newspapers reported that an anonymous European Union official was offering to cut the loans by 30 per cent. This move was intended to placate the Americans. The official, quoted in the *Scotsman* newspaper, said, 'Peter Mandelson has proposed to suggest to our member states that they reduce by around 30 per cent the amount of launch investment that would be made available for the A350.'

This sparked derision from the Americans. The US Trade Representative Rob Portman said, 'We continue to prefer a negotiated solution, and we would rather not have to go back to the WTO. But the EU's insistence on moving forward with new launch aid is forcing our hand.'

The two players, and indeed the governments that are trying to defend their interests, have begun a trade war that is likely to rumble on for years. The politically sensitive nature of the dispute, coupled with the amount of jobs at risk, means that neither the US nor the EU is likely to want to back down first. How this will affect Boeing and Airbus is difficult to predict. The only thing that is certain is that they will continue to duke it out both in the air and on the ground.

Nowhere was this better exemplified than in the week when the 777-200R Worldliner broke the record for non-stop distance flying, while the A380 was on its Asian tour. It was a perfect exposition of the two companies' differing ideologies and confidence in their strategies. But these victories rather masked the problems the two companies have faced. The month-long Boeing strike affected production, meaning that approximately twenty deliveries were unfulfilled, while at Airbus the scale of delays on the A380 was only just emerging.

It was not just the difference between point-to-point and hub-based aviation that would ensure whether the companies would be successful – it depended on strong management, effective infrastructure and some good old-fashioned luck. Trade battle or not, Airbus would soon find out that it had run out of all of these assets.

23. A TEMPORARY TRUCE IN PARIS

The traffic snarled to a snail's crawl on the way to Le Bourget. It held up everyone desperate to get to the Paris Air Show. Everyone except for the French President Jacques Chirac. His motorcade, with police motorbike outriders and black Renault security limos, sped through from his official home at the Elysees Palace.

The Paris Air Show is a celebration of the technologically advanced, of people pushing the aviation industry into the future; however, in June 2005, it had an atmosphere more like the Wild West: everyone knew a showdown was about to begin.

On 13 June 2005, as the crowds swarmed in for the opening day of the first international show since 9/11, there was an expectation of a week of grand theatre – principally provided by Boeing and Airbus. The observers and pundits were not let down. Both Boeing and Airbus, and many of the supporting cast, would make this a week to savour.

Boeing was up smart and early. At 8.30 a.m. Randy Baseler stood on the first-floor deck of the press enclosure waiting to be interviewed. It was a cloudless morning with stunning blue skies, and behind the Boeing marketing chief an array of the newest planes were laid out. Baseler was smiling and upbeat. While a kneeling television assistant pulled the trouser leg of tousled Bloomberg Television presenter Rishaad Salamat to get him in camera view, Baseler was unphased by the unconventional interviewing style.

'Boeing is back,' he said clearly in his soft West Coast drawl, before predicting it would be a winning week for Boeing. Even though Boeing was still without a new Chief Executive, the previous few weeks had given them a lift with the Air-India and the Air Canada decisions. There was a palpable sense that they just about had the edge over their rivals.

Down on the runway, just 400 metres from Baseler, was an object of much attention: the Airbus A380. Gleaming and buffed to perfection, her four Rolls-Royce engines turned in their shells in anticipation of its maiden air show flight. A flurry of nervous security men in suits and sporting discreet AICS lapel badges scoured the faces of the air show visitors coming up to the barrier to gawp. Nearby a group of Gendarmerie in black bloussons, dark-blue trousers and heavy ankle boots looked menacing and prepared for trouble. If not start it.

The curious came to pay homage. Some laughing and joking Boeing guys, in neat dark suits and Boeing ties, walked over from their nearby pavilion to have their pictures taken with the rival beast in the background. A fleet of electric golf buggies brought people up to the temporary perimeter to take a peek at the big bird. Then at 10 a.m. a whirlwind of activity began with the arrival of President Chirac, accompanied by Noel Forgeard and Tom Enders, the new joint chief executives of European Aero-nautic Defence and Space Company (EADS). The VIP entourage scaled the steps of the A380, though behind the smiles there still remained a certain amount of tension. The proposed appointment of Enders, formerly of DASA, and in particular Noel Forgeard, had caused a bitter disagreement between management, share-holders and even countries about how much power they should wield. Germany was particularly against Forgeard's intention to increase the group's control over other divisions. The in-fighting was temporarily resolved, but it took some of the lustre from the sight of the shining new plane's performance.

The Airbus A380 did not disappoint the crowds. Each day it gave a series of controlled, smooth and balletic aerial performan-ces, swooping past the crowds effortlessly and almost silently. On board, the pilots performed a series of surprisingly tight orbits at angles that appeared to be at the edge of the full protection loop of the fly-by-wire control system. Given that the A380's maiden flight was only on 27 April, and that the plane had only completed 21 flights before its arrival at Le Bourget, it was a *tour de force*. There were ten other planes making their debuts, but the buzz was all about the A380.

There was more to the display, however, than simply pleasing the aerophiles.

By the end of the air show, the A380 had amassed more than 100 hours of test flights. Most extremes of the A380s flight had been tested, including the maximum operating Mach number of 0.89, cruising at 43,000 ft and the operation at the maximum take-off weight of 1,220,000 lbs (553,880 kg). Furthermore, the aircraft had carried out thirteen automatic landings, emergency gravity-fall wheel extension, flight at full altitude limit, operation of the flight controls with the envelope protection system disabled and deployment of the emergency air turbine.

'I think that in the run-up to the show the context was more strained than usual with our competitor openly questioning whether Airbus would remain the leader,' Forgeard said later. 'I am very pleased that our performance during the week answered that question with a resounding yes.'

Alan Mulally, however, was not going to allow the Paris Air Show to be remembered as the year of the A380, particularly after the good start they'd had. If the A380's large shadow had cast itself over Boeing, then Mulally would have to do something a little bit out of the ordinary. While preparing his slideshow presentation with his aide Tom Downey, Vice President, Communications, and Lisa Weldon, the former security executive, the answer came to the Boeing chief.

'Why don't we invite Forgeard to see the 777?'

His two aides looked at him in astonishment, wondering if he was serious.

'I mean it,' he added. The showdown had begun in earnest.

The sky-blue Boeing 777-200LR plane was parked right bang up in front of the Airbus media salon balcony, just metres away from the translucent-white A380. So Mulally and his colleagues walked out into the milling crowds, passed the electric cars lined up in the road and wandered along to the EADS chalet. There was some commotion at the door as the French official immediately recognised the Boeing chief.

'Can we talk to Monsieur Forgeard please,' enquired Mulally. For a few moments the Boeing entourage were left waiting, until an obviously harassed EADS official appeared and explained that Forgeard was not around

'Isn't he the CEO of EADS?' asked Mulally impishly.

'Oui, but he is at the Airbus chalet.'

Mulally pulled out a pen and scrawled a note. 'Hi Noel, would you like to come and have a look around our 777? Alan.' He signed off the missive with one of his trademark squiggles and handed it to the EADS official. The note would not long remain a secret, and a response would not come until the following day.

It was Lynn Lunsford, the respected aviation writer on the *Wall Street Journal*, who raised the issue at the following morning's Airbus conference.

'We hear that you have been invited to go and see the 777? Are you going to accept this invitation?' she asked

Forgeard smiled: 'Mais oui, we will go and visit the 777.'

The acceptance was greeted with interest and intense curiosity. In what had become a raging and fervid rivalry, which had so often threatened to combust into open hostility, Forgeard's calm reaction to Mulally's invitation was nothing short of extraordinary. For the first time in a long while, a temporary truce was called.

Only a couple of reporters were around at about 9 a.m. on the Wednesday when Mulally and Forgeard met for the guided tour. Forgeard was joined by John Leahy, Gerard Blanc – Airbus executive vice president of operations – and Allan McArtor, chairman of Airbus North America. On Mulally's side, were Lars Andersen, vice president of the 777 programme, and Frank Santoni, chief test pilot and the man who'd taken the first 777 on its maiden flight eleven years earlier. The Boeing guys could not have had more history with the plane, and were ready now to show their rivals just how far it had come.

The Airbus delegation positively bounded across the tarmac towards the new 777 and were soon greeted by the Boeing contingent. Inside, Forgeard, Leahy and Blanc tried out the seats in the sumptuous first class while Boeing's Lars Andersen gave them an informal welcome. Two 777-200LR Worldliner jets were in flight tests, but the interior of the Paris model had been sumptuously kitted out to make potential customers drool. The front cabin didn't have many seats, and the overhead and side baggage storage bins had been removed to create a great deal of space. The lighting was subdued and the ceiling curved, like a mini-cathedral arch, to emphasise the possibilities of the 777's first-class interior.

The tour soon passed into the rear of the plane, through into the economy section. Towards its rear, however, it began to significantly narrow, while the overhead baggage bins seemed to be more prominent. The seat space also seemed tighter, while the general ambience was not quite as pleasant. There was a reason for this, and John Leahy noticed it immediately. As an innovative marketing tool, Boeing had decided to mock up an A340 cross section inside the 777 to show off its more impressive space. It didn't impress Leahy, however.

'Is that an A340 cross section?' he enquired with a quizzical look.

'Errr, yes, that's right,' said Andersen.

'Gee,' replied Leahy, 'you'd better get your measurements sorted because it looks too small to me.'

Moments later the party re-emerged into the bright Paris morning. Forgeard then led his new-found Boeing friends down and over onto the double-decker A380. The *Seattle Times*' aerospace reporter Dominic Gates grabbed Alan Mulally on his way out for a comment. 'Man, it's big,' he replied. 'It's a really big plane. And we know big airplanes. It's stubby. It looks like it should be stretched to have smoother aerodynamic lines. The wing is really big. It's a big airplane for a small market,' replied Mulally, with a grin.

Gates dropped in another question: 'Any worries about delivering the 787 on its tight schedule, and with this whole new manufacturing process?'

'It's what we do. Is it a big job? Yes. We're really focused on it. I'm really pleased with the progress. I review it every week.'

Gates pressed him further on some of the issues that had come out of the airshow. Airbus had questioned the quality of some Boeing customers – for example Primaris, an American budget airline, which was due to launch in late 2006, was still trying to raise the money for their twenty 787s and Leahy alleged that the Indonesian airline Lion Air, who had placed an order for sixty 737s, didn't have the money.

Mulally seemed unfazed. 'We have a lot of start-up airlines. Will some of them fail? Sure. But we'll still sell the airplanes. They'll go somewhere. We are not delivering more airplanes than are needed.'

Mulally added that Boeing had been distracted in recent years by the need to revamp its production lines to make them as efficient as the ones Airbus has in Europe. It also had been busy developing the 787. As a consequence, relations with some of the major carriers had stalled somewhat, but Mulally wasn't going to allow that to happen in the future. The efficiencies Boeing had put into place gave them the ability to price its airplanes more aggressively, and Mulally had instructed his team to turn up the heat on Airbus.

Less than an hour later, the friendly airplane visits over, it was business as usual, with Airbus announcing another 138 orders – dwarfing Boeing's announced orders at the air show. Ever the showman, Leahy revealed he might have another forty or more orders to announce that day, including more A320s and another A350 order. Leahy clearly wanted to rub Boeing's nose in it after they had earlier predicted they would end 2005 with more orders than Airbus – something Boeing has failed to do since Leahy had arrived.

But not everything had been going Leahy's way – nor would it in 2005. June had started badly for Airbus, when it had been forced to acknowledge that the first deliveries of the A380 would be delayed from mid-2006 until early 2007. This was due to unspecified production difficulties, which were later revealed as weight problems. Then Emirates airlines, which had been expected to announce a big order for the A350, said it was not ready to make a decision. They weren't the only ones to be causing Airbus problems either.

In September 2005, LOT Polish Airlines announced a controversial order for up to fourteen Boeing 787s to replace its ageing 767s. The political pressure had been intense as Poland was a new member of the European Union and was expected to select Airbus. President Chirac, Chancellor Schroeder and Prime Minister Tony Blair had all been part of the Airbus lobbying campaign. Earlier in the year, after a meeting with Chirac, Polish President Aleksander Kwasniewski said he would seriously consider the arguments made by France, Germany and Britain for buying Airbus planes. But Poland had recently been a strong political ally of the United States.

In January 2003, Poland, along with other former communist countries, signed what was known as the 'Letter of Eight', which supported President Bush's plans against Iraq. It upset the French and Germans who were vehemently opposed to the war against Saddam Hussein's regime. Not only did Poland send thousands of troops to Iraq, but in January 2003, the Polish government announced it would buy nearly fifty F-16s from Lockheed Martin. The deal, worth about $3.5 billion, was a blow to France, which was offering its Dassault-built Mirage.

On Thursday, 29 May 2003, before Poland joined the EU, President Bush made an unexpected trip to Krakow to thank the Poles for their support. In an interview in the White House library, he said: 'I think it's unfortunate that some of the countries in Europe will try to bully Poland for standing up for what you think – what they think is right . . . Poland needs to be in the EU and Poland can be a friend of the United States and the two are not in conflict.'

But there was more to the Lockheed deal than pro-American sympathies. To win the fighter competition, Lockheed Martin had promised offsets – investments in Polish industry – that were worth several billion dollars to the country's struggling economy. Similarly, Airbus was prepared to increase its purchases of goods from Polish aviation companies – from about $12 million to $20 million per year. The Polish government owns 68 per cent of LOT, but promised that the deal to replace LOT's aging 767s would be based on an independent evaluation of which planes are best for them. When the deal was eventually announced, however, few industry observers believed that politics had not been a major factor.

Was Airbus losing its mojo? asked *Business Week*. Boeing, after trailing Airbus on orders for the past three years, broke their record for sales – with 800 orders in 2005, 132 more than the 1996 record.

Discounts of over 30 per cent offered to early customers on the A380, which lists for about $250 million, meant that margins were already going to be narrow, said Ben Fidler, a London-based analyst for Deutsche Bank.

The late-delivery penalties were likely to be paid via non-cash arrangements, such as discounts on spare-parts purchases and crew training, that could be spread over several years. The result? If A380 deliveries begin in 2007, as Airbus now predicted, the delays would cost them, according to Fidler from $150 million to $200 million. Profits would pick up as research-and-development spending on the A380 winds down. That, and Airbus's backlog of orders, would give its parent, EADS, which posted first-quarter profits of $403 million in 2005, a fivefold rise over the same period in 2004, with sales up 16 per cent, to $8.6 billion.

Despite this Airbus had begun to struggle. It was just bad luck. Leahy was sidelined by illness in the spring just as Airbus was hoping to score A350 launch orders from Air Canada and Northwest Airlines Corp. In his absence, Boeing not only lured those customers away with its 787 but also racked up a $7 billion order from Air-India for fifty long-range jets.

Business Week claimed Airbus had damaged its credibility by staging its glitzy Reveal ceremony on Tuesday, 18 January 2005. This was an all-singing, all-dancing Airbus extravaganza with front row seats for Jose Luis Zapatero, the Spanish Prime Minister; Gerhard Schroder, the German Chancellor; and Tony Blair, the UK Prime Minister and Jacques Chirac, the French President, sitting next to each other. Airbus's confident assertion that the A380 was on schedule was not echoed by industry insiders, who had predicted that delays were likely. Forgeard and Leahy said that while they were aware of potential delays earlier, the magnitude of the problems wasn't evident at the time.

A savvy chief executive might have avoided such embarrass-ments, but Airbus didn't have even an average CEO as the Franco-German power struggle continued to rage. This prolonged leadership uncertainty put Airbus at a disadvantage. After all, it had raised to a new level the concept that the executives signed the deal with the customers. 'With no CEO and no John Leahy, there was nobody to fight at the same weight as Boeing,' says Doug McVitie, a Scottish aerospace consultant who formerly worked at Airbus.

With the success of the 787, it was clear that Airbus needed orders for the A350. While Airbus had a backlog of 1,535 orders for other planes against 1,225 for Boeing, the 787 could enable Boeing to open a wide sales lead.

In marketing the A350, Airbus had been hampered by uncer-tainty over its design and financing. But as airlines began showing interest in the 787, Airbus had to match this and become more ambitious. 'By not having the right airplane soon enough, we lost some orders,' conceded Leahy.

In Paris, at a hastily called news conference to celebrate Airbus's win of a sixty-plane order for the proposed A350, Forgeard said his company could launch the plane without European government aid if necessary.

'Which does not mean that we will spit on any form of support that would be jointly agreed,' he added. 'We shall do the A350 anyway, since we have the orders.' Forgeard said after joining Leahy. Coming straight from a meeting with President Chirac, Forgeard bustled in with his trademark wide-eyed, impish grin at the assembled reporters. He listened while Leahy gave a confident assessment of the A350's prospects.

'We're sitting at ninety [A350 orders] right now and it's only the first day of the show,' said Leahy. 'Having a hundred by the end of the week is in the bag.' Leahy was later shown to be exaggerating. Airbus had nothing like this number in the bag. To Boeing, this meant that they were – despite the sales and the successes – still number two. It was something they were going to have to deal with.

Charlie Miller, a Boeing communications vice president, surprisingly admitted being second had been rather good for the Americans. He explained that Senator Tom Pickering – a seasoned American diplomat, an envoy with a deep well of experience and political wisdom, and a Boeing vice president – had coined a new company motto: Boeing must continue to have the mentality of being second and the fiscal discipline of being first.

At a drinks reception on Wednesday at the Paris Air Show with people sipping Scotch and bottles of beer, Lew Platt mingled, dispensing his business card to a group of Japanese journalists. All accepted the greetings in a reverential manner as the affable Boeing president towered over the aerospace correspondents. Some of the more gnarled and seasoned US correspondents were pressing Platt about potential chief executives for Boeing. 'Yes, we have five or six potential new chief executives, including two internal candidates. But there's been no job offer yet and nobody has been turned down.' But he dismissed suggestion that John Leahy was on the short list. 'He wasn't even on the long list,' said Platt.

Platt also took the time to pay tribute to interim Chief Executive Officer James Bell, who was formerly the chief financial officer. 'He's not actively being considered as a candidate today, but I've had discussions with several board members about the quality of the job James has been doing. He's been doing an excellent job.'

Outside, overlooking the veranda, a massive advert for Boeing was taxiing on cue. A beast of a military transport plane roared into the open space in front of the party. 'We sold a hundred and thirty-eight of these to the US defence forces and four to the RAF,' said one Boeing salesman. It was an impressive statistic, but the biggest deal for Boeing would not be a military plane.

Steven Udvar-Hazy is the most important person in world aviation. A self-made billionaire, originally from Hungary but now an American, his opinion matters more than anyone else on the planet. He is the chief executive of the world's largest leasing company, International Lease Finance Corp, and his endorsement would change the fortunes of Airbus and Boeing. At the airshow he revealed he was close to a major agreement to buy Boeing's 787 Dreamliner. This seal of approval was significant. He already had a handful of A380s.

'We're making definitive progress with Boeing, and we're very hopeful that before the end of the year we can announce a transaction on a purchase of 787s,' he told a group of reporters. An agreement on price and other terms had been negotiated and he was in discussions with General Electric and Rolls-Royce, the two engine manufacturers for the new airplane. ILFC planned to take delivery of an unspecified number of the 787s within a year or eighteen months of All Nippon Airways receiving their first 787 in 2008. His positive pro-Boeing comments came as Airbus announced that ALAFCO, the Kuwait-based leasing company, had agreed to buy twelve Airbus A350s and had an option to buy six more.

Airbus executives believed this was proof that the new airplane would be a hit with airlines. Leasing companies take a long-term view since the survival of their business depends on owning airplanes that airlines will want to lease. ILFC is a favourite customer for Boeing and Airbus because the firm buys airplanes, then immediately leases them to airlines.

Leahy unveiled that the ALAFCO deal took his A350 order book over the symbolically important tally of 100 sales – or so it was claimed. But Mulally was equally ecstatic about ILFC's support.

'The biggest fundamental difference is that the 787 is an airplane that came from a clean sheet of paper,' said Udvar-Hazy. The plane's design benefited from years of sending out different schemes – even ones like the Sonic Cruiser, which were almost ludicrous. Boeing was ridiculed at the time for throwing out so many ideas but Udvar-Hazy said it was probably money well spent in testing the water. The 787 was attractive because of its low maintenance costs and because Boeing had designed the plane so an owner can easily switch between Rolls-Royce or General Electric engines 'What matters to us is that airlines can make money with our airplanes,' said the leasing company leader.

The A380 also broadened its customer line-up with the Paris Air Show announcement that India's Kingfisher Airlines had ordered five of the double-decker aircraft, along with five A350-800s and a similar number of A330-200s. Airbus was definitely benefiting from its continued dominance in the emerging nations.

But, on Tuesday, 14 June 2005, there were two contrasting announcements by Jet Airways. Naresh Goyal, the chairman of Jet Airways and a respected veteran of the Indian aviation business, announced an agreement with Boeing for twenty airplanes, including six B777-220LR Worldliners, four B777-300ERs and ten Next Generation B737-800s. These would be used on the Indian and US routes. Goyal said: 'Boeing has been a partner since our inception in 1993 and we are proud of our close association with them. I personally value the sustained support and co-operation that Jet Airways has always received from them and look forward to further strengthening and expanding our mutually rewarding association.'

While journalists were picking up this announcement from the Boeing office pigeonhole, something strange was happening less than fifty yards away in the Airbus pavilion. The selfsame Naresh Goyal, chairman of Jet Airways, was sitting down next to a beaming Forgeard and Leahy.

Leahy opened the session: 'It is a great pleasure to announce today that Jet Airways will purchase ten A330-200 with options for ten more.' He explained: 'Jet Airways is India's leading private airline and in twelve years they have become the leading private Indian airline in the market right now. And some would say the whole region.'

It was quite obvious what was going on. Like Qatar Airlines, Jet Airways were hedging their bets. So much for commonality. Leahy, however, looked delighted. 'Still today, more people ride on trains in India in one day than fly in an entire year. Think about opening that market to air travel. At the next air show, perhaps I'll be announcing an even bigger aircraft,' he half-joked. But Goyal would later bounce back to Boeing. In December 2006, Boeing and Jet Airways announced a $1.5 billion order for ten

787s with delivery scheduled to begin in 2011. 'This order reflects our desire to be the leader in offering the highest quality of service that is reliable, comfortable and efficient for our customers with the most modern aircraft,' said the Indian airline leader. 'These 787 Dreamliners, which will be used in conjunction with our 777s ordered in September 2005, will bring a new level of world-class service as we expand our international operations with routes to Europe, Asia and the US.'

The Indian interest carried over into the following day. Dr Vijay Mallya, the flamboyant chairman of the United Breweries Group, announced that Kingfisher Airlines would be ordering the A380. The UB Group had become the second largest drinks company in India and created its beer brand as a lifestyle brand for modern India. There is Kingfisher fashion, food and music – which drew comparisons with Sir Richard Branson – and now there was the airline to match.

'I remember in 1990 when I started UB Air I was struggling to buy two Dornier turboprops aircraft,' he said. 'Today, in 2005, as an Indian company, I think it is a matter of great national pride that we are able to firmly order the A380 and become the first Indian operator to fly the super jumbo. The world is waiting with baited breath,' said the bearded Indian, dripping with gold bracelets and watches, and a diamond stud in his earring.

He burst into a big smile once more and said: 'We are a private company, we are 100 per cent owned by United Breweries Holdings Limited, so we are not here spending government or public funds. This is a significant transaction in excess of $3 billion. We have the conviction to do it and do it with a great deal of confidence. It will be a great step forward for Indian aviation for Kingfisher to fly the Airbus A380.' It was a grand piece of theatre from Airbus.

The curtains closed on the 2005 Paris Air Show with Airbus retaining its leadership position – just. Airbus had revealed new orders and commitments for 280 aircraft with a combined value of $33.5 billion. This included 125 commitments for the newest Airbus – the A350 – from international leasing companies and carriers in India, the Middle East and South America. But some of these orders soon evaporated as the Dreamliner gained ground. The popular A320 Family also logged orders from low-cost carriers and mainline operators, while new and repeat customers booked orders for the A330.

The game was turning full circle and again Sheikh Ahmed bin Saeed Al Maktoum played a dramatic part. On Sunday, 20 November 2005 – four years after his historic announcement to buy the A380 – his airline agreed to spend another $9.7bn. This time it was Boeing's turn to throw a jubilant party.

Emirates had agreed to purchase 42 777s from Boeing with rights for a further twenty. The planes will have General Electric power plants in a $2bn contract to provide engines and twelve years' maintenance for the 42 twin-engined fleet. The massive order included ten 777-200LRs, twenty-four 777-300ERs and eight of the 777 freighter version. It was an early Thanksgiving present for the Americans, though the Sheikh still had one keenly awaited decision to make – whether to back the 787 or the A350. 'We haven't decided yet which way we will go,' was all he would say on the matter. Both Airbus and Boeing would remain on tenterhooks.

The Emirates chairman had other things on his mind at the Dubai airshow, not least the appearance of a very special guest. The A380 sparkled in the sunshine, dazzling its new-found friends. The global interest in the super jumbo was huge and, the previous week, thousands of spectators had turned out to watch it touch down in Australia for the first time at Brisbane Airport after an overnight flight from Singapore, where it arrived on its inaugural Asian tour.

There was – despite the excitement down under – no hiding the fact that Airbus now faced major issues on delivery. Airbus's new President and Chief Executive Officer Gustav Humbert – who had taken over from Forgeard – said a weight-saving effort had required structural redesign. Or, more brutally, the plane was too heavy and needed to shed weight. Rumours began to emerge of problems with picky airline customers and their elaborate cabin designs which were taxing the Airbus engineers. And there was talk of hefty compensation payments for late delivery.

As early as June, just after the A380's first official public performance at the 46th Paris Air Show, Noel Forgeard, now the chief at EADS, was full of praise for the plane and its response to the tests. But, amid all the gloss and sheen, there was a serious point to be made.

'As everybody knows,' he said, 'there is a moderate shift in the programme. The fact is that we've deliberately set ourselves a very tight schedule, knowing full well that this would be hard to match. But there's still no better incentive than setting stringent objectives to get the highest productivity and efficiency. But I have to admit that we also have some industrial issues and delays, especially on the electrical wiring front, which we are in the process of recovering throughout the organisation,' he said. This now ranks as amongst the understatements of the century.

'All this leads to a shift of a few to up to six months depending on the individual situation of each of our customers, who are currently being informed. In any case, our objective is to deliver the first aircraft to the first operator, Singapore Airlines, in the latter part of 2006.' And this was wishful thinking, rather than the reality.

The technical progress meant that test systems planned for MSN004 – the second A380 to fly – were conducted on MSN001. MSN004 began its test flying in October and this plane would be much closer to the A380 used by Singapore Airlines. The first Airbus A380 was purely for test purposes and was not intended for sale to airlines.

The public profile was terrific. The A380 became the showstopper at the 85th birthday celebrations for Qantas. It was a fantastic public relations coup. But Qantas now wanted an even longer-range jet. Would it be following Emirates with an order for the 777-200ER? Boeing was wooing Qantas with a modified version with six auxiliary fuel tanks and fewer seats that could make London to Sydney non-stop in both directions. Qantas Chief Executive Geoff Dixon was impressed and described the airplane as a 'hub-buster'. And if Qantas bought the longer-range 777, what about Singapore Airlines too?

Airbus had now begun to formally pitch the A350. An announcement of the formal industrial launch of the programme was made by the board of EADS on 6 October 2005. Gustav Humbert – accompanied by Charles Champion, Chief Operating Officer and head of the A380 programme, John Leahy, Chief Operating Officer Customers and Tom Williams, Executive Vice President Programmes – presented the plans in Paris. Humbert underlined the interest that customers were showing for the new programme and spoke confidently of Airbus's ability to manage this alongside the ongoing A380, the A400M and the planned industrial ramp-up to achieve 400 deliveries next year. John Leahy made his usual flourishes saying the A350 takes the best of the A330/A340 Family, the best of the A380 Family and the new technologies that will be available in the next four years.

'The A350 is the right long-range twin-engine aircraft for that very important 250–300-seat market. It is the right size, the right range, has the right comfort, with a double-digit cost reduction over today's standards, an all-new cabin, true Airbus commonality, with a fly-by-wire cockpit that is part of a real family. This is something no other manufacturer can offer – and a true sister ship for the twenty-first century for that very impressive A380,' Humbert concluded.

By the end of the Dubai Airshow, Airbus had firm commitments for the $160–$165m plane from ten customers, including several leasing companies. It was offering two versions – the A350-800 carrying 253 passengers in three classes with a range of 8,800 nautical miles, and the A350-900, a 300-seat version with a range of 8,000 nautical miles. But the growing success of Boeing's 787 Dreamliner was an ominous signal for John Leahy and Airbus.

Meanwhile, after 37 years with Boeing, Alan Mulally, at 61, who had done so much for Boeing as the Chief Executive Officer of the commercial airplanes division, decided to take up one last challenge before heading off to golf course heaven. He had been unsuccessful in landing the top job when Jim McNerney pipped him for the post, but had the good grace to stick around for over a year to help the new boss. Now, on 5 September 2006, his appointment as president and chief executive officer of the Ford Motor Company was announced. Here was another iconic American manufacturing business with a global reach in need of some fresh thinking.

Bill Ford, the automobile-maker's executive chairman, paid handsome tribute to Mulally's time at Boeing, calling him 'an outstanding leader and a man of great character'. It was a sentiment echoed all around Boeing, where there was genuine sadness at his departure. It was good news, though, for Scott Carson who had patiently awaited his turn. After 34 years with Boeing, and now in his early sixties, he was anointed President and Chief Executive Officer of Boeing Commercial Airplanes. It would be an enjoyable tenure for the former vice president.

And before the industry congregated once again later at the Paris Air Show in 2007 – without Mulally and many others – there would be a calamitous fall from grace by the European planemaker. It would be touch-and-go whether Airbus could ever survive the trauma.

24. AN ELECTRICAL SHOCK FOR AIRBUS

It ranks as one of the greatest industrial blunders of the modern age – the Airbus A380 wiring cock-up. With sophisticated systems and some of the finest engineering brains in Europe, an international project such as the A380 should have been idiot proof. But it wasn't. One of the biggest technological projects of the 21st century was nearly derailed by a huge misunderstanding over two versions of the same computer software.

The whole fiasco – beyond belief for tens of thousands of people with experience and long careers in the aviation industry – will go down as one of the costliest messes in commercial history, wiping billions of euros off the value of Airbus's parent EADS.

The problem was the 348 miles of bundled electrical wiring which wends it way around every A380, all of it hidden from view of the air traveller. Airbus mechanics spent weeks routing all the colour-coded cables through the walls, floors and bulkheads, but, when it came to the point of connecting them, they simply didn't fit. The problems only emerged when the electrical cable harnesses were due for installation in the A380's actual fuselage. The planned cable routes didn't agree with those on the real prototype aircraft. It was a whopper of an error.

One Airbus insider said, 'It should never have happened. But there were national egos at play and people who should have known better just presumed it would all get fixed. But it didn't – and nobody took control until it was too late.'

The problem arose because the Hamburg engineers were drawing on a two-dimensional computer program, while their counterparts in Toulouse were working on a newer three-dimensional version. The Airbus engineers were frantic when they found out. They were racing to sort out the wiring problems which had sparked the delay. Then they realised the full extent of the disaster.

The engineers used the same CATIA – Computer-graphics Aided Three-dimensional Interactive Applications – that were successfully applied on the Boeing 777. They were well known at Airbus too and powerful computer tools capable of showing the whole aircraft in minute cross-section. The celebrated architect Frank Gehry, who designed the Guggenheim museum in Bilbao, uses the software to define his award-winning buildings which look impossible to build, while all the major motor manufacturers use CATIA to design modern cars.

But Airbus began upgrading the software – from Version 4 to Version 5. Boeing's 777 team used Version 3. A software upgrade on a PC or Mac is now a fairly simple affair, but for engineers using CATIA it required huge amounts of extra training.

Airbus found that migrating experienced CATIA engineers from Version 4 to Version 5 was taking between six months and a year of training before they regained their full ability. Yet this kind of upgrade is well known in the car industry, and different CATIA versions are regularly used in parallel during a transitional period from one car to another. But Airbus didn't have time to spare, so, to enable the smooth transfer of data, Airbus developed its own translation software, Airbus Concurrent Engineering (ACE). The Hamburg team was in the lead role – but something wasn't right. The A380 programme manager, Charles Champion, expressed disappointed that the transfer of data from Germany to Toulouse was still not working well enough. The German side – still working with the tried-and-tested Version 4 – were not able to feed their design plans for the cable harnesses into the standard and continuously updated database of the A380 Digital Mock-up, the main blueprint for the giant jumbo.

So there were separate fuselage sections of the plane being built in Hamburg and Toulouse, and both parties were oblivious to the impending disaster. The German development work for the electric cables on the A380's sections 13 to 18 went on in isolation, while the design plans for the adjacent sections 11 to 12 and 15 to 21 in Toulouse – struggling with the newer Version 5 – underwent continuous further development. It got worse. As the prototype testing continued, changes and improvements were made which were not carried through to the future production process.

Airbus knew it had a calamitous situation on its hands when the sections of fuselage were brought together to join them up in Toulouse. They simply didn't fit – and no amount of stretching could change the situation. An emergency meeting of production managers gathered to find a solution – but there were no quick fixes and Noel Forgeard's executive office at EADS in Paris needed to be told.

Forgeard blew a gasket when he was informed. This pet project, which he had steered personally, and on which he had staked his reputation, was now on the line. Airbus insiders say that, at first, he shook his head and didn't want to hear.

'Get it fixed. Wiring? You're telling me that the electrical wiring doesn't fit? With all the technical hurdles we've overcome and you're telling me it's simple wiring. Sort it out,' he told Airbus executives at an EADS management meeting.

Another unnamed Airbus engineer told *Newsweek*, 'It was a very aggressive environment. There was a saying you'd hear all the time: "If you don't do it, I'm going to smack you." '

Someone was going to get a large smack for this mess. While the Frenchman ranted at his German colleagues and shocked many of them by blaming the Hamburg factory for the delays, he also did something which undermined his own credibility – he dumped his shares.

Then an internal memo gave a rare insight into how John Leahy truly felt about his own products. A disgruntled Hamburg manager revealed to *Der Spiegel* that Leahy had written to colleagues on 10 November demanding improvements in the jets – which he claimed were inferior to Boeings. The letter was specifically critical of the A350 and its comparison with the Boeing 787. But the tone angered Airbus managers, who sensed the whole missive was a backside-covering tactic to deflect attention from his own mistakes. What it revealed was that senior employees at both EADS and Airbus knew of the problems much sooner than they previously admitted.

Tom Williams, an affable and approachable Airbus executive, was given the task of explaining the problems. He revealed that the CATIA tools were not sufficiently accurate when it came to designing electrical systems. It was made worse by Airbus's switch to aluminium wiring when the model was designed for copper wiring, which has very different physical properties. As ever, Boeing would be watching and benefiting from Airbus's bad experience.

Williams said, 'We've slowed everything down. In some areas, it's stopped. Our production problems are not due to any radical redesign we are having to do.' But he agreed the complexities caused in A380 production by the demands of airlines – which required extensive customised interiors and computer systems – can affect the wiring, some of which goes into the seats.

Forgeard, now running the parent company EADS, was fighting like a rat in a pipe to hold onto his job. But Jacques Chirac's power and prestige was waning as his tenure came to an end. Forgeard was quite clear on who to blame for the A380's latest delay: Humbert and Hamburg. 'When I worked for Airbus, we never missed our own targets.'

Meanwhile, BAE Systems wanted out. They had had enough of EADS's in-fighting and Airbus's mounting calamities. They now had a perfect excuse for an exit. In April, EADS confirmed to the stock market that early-stage discussions were going on for the potential disposal of BAE Systems' 20 per cent stake. It had been agreed back in 2001 that Airbus would have a Put Option Intention Notice to sell their stake. EADS said it would be happy to take over this stake, and private discussions began about the valuation and actual price.

The A380 made its British debut flight into Heathrow Airport on 18 May 2006, to carry out airport compatibility checks in conjunction with airport operator British Airports Authority. The Heathrow visit went well as the jumbo parked at new Pier 6 in Terminal 3. The 280-metre-long three-storey-high pier has aircraft stands to accommodate up to four A380s at a time.

The summer was getting hotter and hotter for Airbus and for EADS. The parent company was forced to make a public statement from Amsterdam on Tuesday, 13 June 2006. Only one A380 aircraft would be delivered in 2006, and only nine the following year. Compared to the initial delivery target, there would be shortfalls of five to nine aircraft deliveries in 2008 and of around five aircraft in 2009. The annual shortfalls would cost around €500 million a year from the original plan. This was all blamed on the late delivery and costs attached to a recovery plan

– it didn't include the termination of contracts under the new timetable.

The following day was Black Wednesday for EADS and its shareholders. At last, the market was responding savagely to the full gravity of the dreadful situation. EADS's shares plunged by 26 per cent to close at €18.73, after dipping by as much as 34 per cent. Across Europe, brokers were jettisoning EADS shares like a troubled aircraft throwing off excess fuel before landing. The news from Airbus was that the A380 would be delayed by another six months. The stock lost some €7 billion ($8.8 billion) in market value by midday, which, according to Reuters, was equal to half a per cent of the entire French economy.

Airbus President Gustav Humbert tried to steady the ship. After a day of phone calls to airlines he ordered the immediate setting up and implementation of his action plan. 'Airbus is fully aware of the burden this industrial issue represents for the airlines who are anxious to begin operating the A380. Airbus is working with its customers to facilitate their operations, while ensuring a successful entry into service,' he said.

But pressure mounted on Forgeard, as disgust spread about his controversial decision to exercise the right to sell his shares. The French financial regulator, AMF, carried out an on-the-spot investigation in Toulouse as part of an inquiry into insider trading.

Forgeard vehemently denied using insider information, but he pocketed €2.5 million ($3.2m) for himself and his four children each made €1.4 million after exercising his share options in March. He said he was 'shocked by presumptions of his guilt' and that his dealings were wholly transparent. Tom Enders was forced to admit it was 'inopportune' of Forgeard to exercise his options at such as sensitive time.

EADS tried to clarify the matter by saying its company insider trading rules stipulated that directors may only exercise their stock options within certain specific periods (four opening periods of three weeks each year), and provided they do not have any privileged information. One of these periods opened from 8 to 28 March 2006, when Forgeard and five other directors, including Fabrice Bregier, head of the successful Eurocopter division, duly exercised their options not long after Lagardère and Daimler-Chrysler said they would cut back their stakes in EADS.

On Tuesday, 27 June 2006, the *Financial Times* reported that Forgeard's reign was almost over. EADS was still looking for a compromise as its two major shareholders – Lagardère with 7.5 per cent, and DaimlerChrysler, with 22.5 per cent – tried to formulate a solution to what was now the biggest crisis since Airbus was created. Even the French government, still holding 15 per cent of EADS, was tightening the noose around Forgeard's neck – although the French Finance Minister Thierry Breton said he would leave the decision for Lagardère and DaimlerChrysler to resolve. The weekend board meeting would be crucial.

Even Forgeard's old friend and supporter, the French President Jacques Chirac, was lining up against the business, questioning the whole logic of the company's structure. 'There are management problems at EADS with two presidents and two chairmen,' he admitted in a television interview on France 2. 'We're now discussing fixes to the management of EADS . . . It is probable that we have to do something and something will be done.'

When asked if Forgeard should quit, Chirac shrugged and said he did not want to prejudge anything. But privately he wasn't too keen to see Gallois, a French socialist, as the boss. The troubles at EADS spilled out into open warfare, with both German and French factions squabbling over the top jobs.

The time had come. On Sunday, 2 July 2006, Forgeard and Gustav Humbert resigned after pressure from EADS's major shareholders – Lagardère, DaimlerChrysler and the French government. At the Farnborough Air Show, it was also rumoured that the A380 programme director, Charles Champion, was facing the bullet. The joint EADS chairmen, Manfred Bischoff and Arnaud Lagardère, announced that the board had accepted the resignation of Forgeard and Humbert. Forgeard was replaced by a railway-man who knew about prestige projects – he was responsible for the TGVs in France. Louis Gallois, 62, president of the French railway company SNCF, took over as EADS's Chief Executive Officer, working alongside Anders, while Humbert was succeeded by Christian Streiff, 51, the deputy chief executive of French building-materials group Saint-Gobain, and a spare-time novelist. Streiff, Airbus's Chief Executive Officer, was about to discover plenty of potential material for a scary thriller.

Humbert showed a modicum of remorse for what happened. 'As president and CEO of Airbus, I must take responsibility for this setback and feel the right course of action is to offer my resignation to our shareholders.'

Forgeard, on the other hand, appeared unrepentant, insisting his resignation was voluntary and that he wasn't sacked. He said that neither the stock sale nor Airbus's operational problems were the reason for his departure, and pointed out that he had left the jetmaker a year ago. 'I did it solely for the company's interest, to end a situation that could have compromised the resolution of Airbus's current problems and EADS's development,' he said.

Jean Claude Noel, a professor at INSEAD's Global Leadership Centre in New York, wrote in *The Economist* in October 2006, 'Noel Forgeard personified the arrogance and sense of entitlement of the French "elite". Graduating from the *grandes ecoles* can signal a superior cognitive intelligence and obviously helps foster high-level relationships, but it is no substitute for practical leadership. The severity of the plight that EADS and Airbus are in today should be enough warning that the cosy French model has reached its limitations.'

Arnaud Lagardère, the co-chairman of EADS, was forced to eat humble pie too. 'I have the choice between being considered someone dishonest or someone incompetent who doesn't know what is going on his factories. I prefer the second version.'

He wasn't the only one who appeared clueless about what was happening at Airbus.

No one was able to give a definitive reason for the mess. It left thousands of workers asking the same question: 'How and why did this happen?' Streiff's very first official duty on taking up his appointment as Airbus boss in July was to order a new investigation into the alarming A380 production delays. Throughout the summer, he demanded daily reports on every aspect of production. Gradually he was able to concoct his own horror story. It was the industrial equivalent of *The Texas Chainsaw Massacre*. Then, on 3 October, he announced the results of this investigation alongside Enders and Gallois, with EADS's Chief Financial Officer Hans-Peter Ring assisting. Streiff, who had worked in the manufacturing sector for 26 years with the multinational Saint-Gobain Group, knew about fixing things. But this was an astonishing admission.

'The production process, not the aircraft itself, has a critical error. This is the weakest link in the entire production chain and has been preventing us up to now from ramping up to the full production rate. The problem is to do with the design of the electrical cable harnesses for the fore and aft fuselage. This comprises 530 kilometres of wires which are connected to 100,000 individual cable sections with 40,300 connectors and 350 kilometres of length per aircraft. The A380's wiring is twice as complex as the A340-600's,' he explained.

'The analysis we have performed in recent weeks suggests that the situation is much worse than we had feared. There were incompatibilities in the electronic design program with which we developed the cable harnesses and their layout. The cable harness installation kits for the front and rear fuselage could not therefore keep up with the rest of the aircraft and did not fit when they came to be installed. Moreover, we did not have enough time to change the cables during the development phase. Now we face the task of having to harmonise the design software and the database. But this will take some time,' he added.

Streiff appointed cabin expert Rüdiger Fuchs solely responsible for all A380 activities in Hamburg. He was given the support of an extended team of experienced Airbus staff – ordered to check the programme progress twice a day. Fuchs was to report directly to the new A380 programme manager, Mario Heinen of Luxembourg, who had built an excellent reputation as the manager of the A320 programme.

But how would it be fixed? The first task involved was the laborious job of ripping out by hand all the wiring from the existing planes – months and months of arduous, painstaking work. Airbus's Tom Williams now used a fashion analogy to describe what was happening. He called it *haute couture* and the aim was to replace this with *prêt-a-porter*. But, while catwalk styles are replicated from the London, Paris and Milan fashion shows and out into the retail shops within days, this was no garment-industry solution. It was a highly intensive manual process. Not really what the silky smooth Airbus commercial plane production ethos was all about. Commentators were now calling the A380 the Toulouse Goose – a sarcastic reference to Howard Hughes's ill-fated Spruce Goose.

Airbus had to throw everything they could at this problem. A hit squad from across the company was set up to complete the electrical cabling of the first fifteen A380s. Specialists from Broughton and St Nazaire were flown in to assist their colleagues in Hamburg and Toulouse. But, while Airbus was recouping its organisational procedures, the computer software remained a problem. A complicated mixture of CATIA Versions 4 and 5 remained in operation. MSN003 – the first A380 prototype to be fitted with the revised cable sets – became a 'teaching model', while the other test aircraft were upgraded for the standard, final cable sets.

New cable harnesses had to be developed by the multinational hit squad using Version 5 of the CATIA software. This would give Airbus a fighting chance, so that from the sixteenth aircraft a single CATIA 5 dataset would be available to speed up production and win back lost time. Deliveries promised for 2007 would not be made until 2010.

On 4 September, the inevitable happened. Charles Champion, a charming Frenchman and head of the A380 project since 2001, fell on his sword – it was a kind of industrial hari-kari. It was a sad ending for the 51-year-old Champion who was well liked and a highly respected engineer. But the flaws were made on his watch, so he was formally replaced by Mario Heinen. To save face, Champion was given an advisory role with Streiff.

There was a certain irony in this, because the test programme was progressing well. Champion's exit took place on the same day that an A380, carrying 474 passengers, made its first seven-hour 'Early Long Flight' to check the cabin systems and passenger comfort, including the air conditioning, the kitchens and galleys and, an essential item, the toilets. A series of flights from Toulouse, captained by Frank Chapman, Airbus's Experimental Test Pilot, flying with Jacques Rosay and Jacques Drappier, the Chief Instructor Pilot, carried over 2,000 Airbus volunteers who had been clamouring to experience the new giant in the sky. By now, five A380 aircraft had been involved in the flight test programme, four powered by Rolls-Royce Trent 900 engines. The programme had totted up nearly 2,000 hours in 600 flights. The verdict: the new jumbo was fantastic.

In the meantime, speculation was increasing about BAE Systems' stake. Mike Turner and his board, increasingly exasperated by the mess, wanted out of the relationship. BAE Systems denied an *Observer* newspaper report that the directors were about to sell their holding. Spokesman John Neilson said it was premature to suggest what the board would recommend. But it wouldn't be long before the board made its position crystal clear.

On 3 October 2006, Airbus told its A380 customers about a further delay in the delivery schedule. According to this revised plan, the first A380 for Singapore Airlines would not be delivered until October 2007. Thirteen more would be delivered in 2008 and 25 in 2009. The industrial ramp-up would be completed in 2010, when 45 A380s would be delivered, including the first freighters, if there were still buyers!

Streiff said that, in addition to management changes and the hit squads, training was being organised to bring the employees using those CATIA tools to the optimum level. 'With the right tools, the right people, the right training and the right oversight and management being put in place, the issue is now addressed at its root, although it will take time until these measures bear fruit,' he said.

To regain its competitive edge and to counter the financial impact of the delay, as well as the weakening dollar, Streiff launched the Power8 programme, which had been developed by 100 internal experts over the previous three months. He also asked for a review of all the Airbus locations to be conducted, and administrative costs were to be reduced by 30 per cent. The objective was to reduce costs, save cash and develop new products faster with leaner production. The programme aimed for annual cost savings of at least €2 billion from 2010 onwards, which could deliver €5 billion in savings by 2010.

The question of whether to move parts of the A380 production and delivery from Hamburg to Toulouse was also debated, the idea being that A320 final assembly would then be relocated from Toulouse to Hamburg. But it was questionable whether Airbus would save any time and money if the custom-built A380 halls in Finkenwerder had to be rebuilt in Toulouse.

But Streiff's bold action was causing friction with EADS. He wasn't paying enough heed to the parent company's wishes. He wanted the power to make changes, but EADS wanted more control to avoid further mishaps. It ignited yet another management dispute. In October 2006, he was forced out after just three months in the post.

A detailed study of the European aerospace industry by investment bank Goldman Sachs suggested that the number of Airbus sites should be halved to save money. This caused panic among German politicians – from regional and national level all the way to the office of Chancellor Angela Merkel. At the summit meeting of the French and German heads of government, a topic for discussion included a possible purchase of EADS shares by the German government, to maintain the balance.

DaimlerChrysler chief executive Dieter Zetsche and Tom Enders were reluctant for more German state involvement; what they wanted was more private investors to come on board and share the burden.

The crisis dominated the headlines for days. There was no respite until Louis Gallois took over at the helm of Airbus on 10 October. Gallois promised a fair distribution of workloads only in general terms – but he was in the classic French mould of the *grandes ecoles*.

A graduate of the Ecole des Hautes Etudes Commerciales, as well as the Ecole Nationale de l'Administration, Gallois began his career on the staff of the French Department of the Treasury in 1972. In 1981, he became Head of the Cabinet Office of the Ministry of Research and Industry, becoming Director General a year later. In 1988, he was nominated to the position of Head of the Civil and Military Cabinet office of the French Ministry of Defence. In 1989, Gallois moved into industry when he was appointed Chairman and CEO of the aero engine makers SNECMA, now part of Safran. In 1992, he became Chairman and CEO of Aerospatiale, which is now part of EADS. In that role he was a member of the Airbus Industrie Groupement d'Intérêt Economique (GIE) supervisory board.

Gallois, who was Streiff's former boss as well as his successor, announced that he would continue with Streiff's recovery strategy. The plan was painful for thousands of loyal Airbus people. Several Airbus factories were to be sold off to risk-sharing partners, who would then contribute their products on more favourable terms as independent suppliers. The model for this was the hived-off Boeing factory in Wichita, Kansas, which has become Spirit AeroSystems and supplies fuselages and wings for the Boeing 737. In June 2007, it was tipped, along with GKN, the UK engineering group, to take over large tracts of Airbus UK's manufacturing work in Filton, where 6,500 people were employed.

Then a most significant European link was broken on 13 October 2006, which ended the UK's major stake in the whole European Airbus project. EADS bought BAE Systems' 20 per cent stake in Airbus for €2.75 billion. The value was determined by an independent expert during the put option process which was launched by BAE Systems in June 2006. EADS paid in cash and became the sole owner of Airbus. It was the end of an era for

British influence in the whole Airbus project. But, with aviation now a global industry, there was little room for nationalistic sentiment. It was an amicable divorce allowing BAE Systems, the world's fourth largest defence company, to make bigger inroads into America.

The jobs cull would also begin. In France and Germany, workers who had given their careers to Airbus were selected for redundancy. Airbus Deutschland announced a package of measures: 'SiduFlex' (the German acronym for 'security through flexibility'), which would run for two years. More than 1,000 out of 7,300 German contract staff would lose their jobs. And work currently in the hands of outside contractors would be returned to the company. Permanent staff would no longer receive overtime payments, but bank their extra hours as flexitime. Other working hours would be reduced to up to 28 hours, but with full pay retained.

There was some better news. On 4 December 2006, Gallois announced the kick start of the development of the new extra-wide-bodied A350 AWB. He actually sounded as if he believed the latest iteration of the A350 could now take on the Boeing 787 Dreamliner. He said that the development of the plane would cost about €10 billion ($13 billion), a vast sum for a business which had wiped out nearly half of this sum (€4.8 billion) because of the delays to the A380. One person that would need convincing was Steven Udvar-Hazy, the chief of ILFC, the world's biggest aviation leasing company, who had increasingly expressed strong reservations about the A350.

Gallois said that the company would have to pay for the new plane out of existing cash flow and cost savings. A huge amount of money would be needed from 2010 until 2013 when the first A350s would be delivered. But Gallois was also being hampered by another matter out of his control. Most of the costs were in euros, while the sales to airlines are in US dollars. As the euro and the pound gained in strength against the dollar, Boeing gained a 20 per cent price advantage. The only solution was to outsource more work from Europe to risk-sharing partners around the world.

As China's economy boomed, Airbus signed a framework agreement with a Chinese consortium, comprising Tianjin Free Trade Zone, China Aviation Industry Corporation I and China Aviation Industry Corporation II in Beijing, for the establishment of an A320 final Assembly Line in China. Chinese consortium representative Feng Zhijiang and Gallois shook hands in the Great Hall of People in the presence of the Chinese President Hu Jintao and French President Jacques Chirac. Under the agreement, Airbus would set up an assembly line in Tianjin, and a joint venture between the Chinese consortium and Airbus would make planes. The agreement, to begin in early 2009, aims to ramp up production to reach four aircraft per month by 2011.

This would not go down well in the heartlands of France and Germany. Gallois's plan was to push through the painful restructuring plan, the sale and closure of factories and bring in more partners to outsource more of Airbus's planes. But this demanded political willpower to make it happen. And France was heading for a presidential election in the following spring.

The cull of workers across the business began, anathema to the French workforce and trade unions unused to the American way of dealing with boom and bust. It was the first time in history that Airbus had been involved in mass lay-offs and job cuts.

As the French headed into a presidential election campaign, Nicolas Sarkozy, the French centre-right candidate, made Airbus and the protection of French jobs one of his election calling cards. His opponent, Segolene Royal, the socialist candidate, also made Airbus an election issue. In Toulouse's grand square, more than 15,000 protesters, waving banners and chanting, began a march for the Airbus HQ. The indignation of the workforce was summed up in the banner saying: 'Is there a pilot on the plane?' It was a good question.

Airbus was struggling to keep hold of its existing customers. Federal Express was part of what could have been a stampede in November 2006 when it cancelled a $3 billion order for its ten planes. It swapped over to Boeing and ordered ten new 777s instead. In the end, the Memphis-based carrier decided to throw in the towel, with the corporate lawyers rubbing their hands as compensation packages of around $100 million were discussed. The future of the A380 freighter was now in the balance.

Only UPS, the 100-year-old American parcel-delivery business, was still interested. 'We think it's a great plane. But we're concerned about their [Airbus's] ability to make the proposed delivery schedule,' said its spokesman.

In February 2007, UPS finally received a proposed delivery schedule. At the same time, however, UPS announced it had also ordered 27 new Boeing 767-300ER freighters to be delivered between 2009 and 2012. UPS said the order was not related to its review of its order for ten Airbus A380 freighters. But it had a bearing.

Eventually, Airbus signed an agreement setting out a timetable for the freighter version. Deliveries of UPS's A380s were originally scheduled to begin in 2009 and run through to 2012. But pressure was mounting back in Hamburg as the rewiring work was taking up extra time. Then Airbus dropped another bombshell, which didn't go down well at UPS. Airbus decided to suspend work on the cargo version to focus on the passenger model, but customer services forgot to tell its only freight customer.

The world's largest package-delivery company, which operates as the eighth largest airline in the world, found out when reporters called for its reaction to Airbus's decision. UPS spokesman Norm Black tried to be diplomatic, but there was a frosty tone in his voice. 'It certainly was not a very courteous handling of a large customer.'

UPS held an emergency board meeting, where they made a cool decision. They cancelled the order of the ten planes originally earmarked for 2009 to 2012. It was the instability of the delivery date, not the communications failure, that caused the cancellation, said Black. Still, as a general rule, it is good business practice to keep customers in the loop regarding failing production schedules.

'Customers ought to hear something from us, not from the media,' said spokesman Clay McConnell. But he said that the diversion of resources would not impact on the 2012 delivery date.

It was all too late. 'Based on our previous discussions, we had felt that 2012 was a reasonable estimate of when Airbus could supply this plane,' UPS's Chief Operating Officer David Abney said. 'We no longer are confident that Airbus can adhere to that schedule.'

This was a costly blow for the A380's freighter project. Across the pond there were signs that the giant American airlines were at last emerging from their restraints. On 15 November, US Airways launched a hostile takeover bid for Delta, after an initial friendly offer of a merger was spurned. With Delta just emerging from Chapter 11 bankruptcy it would be easier to cut jobs and slash the costs. And then take a look at buying some new planes. The combined American commercial airline operators had lost an astonishing $35 billion over the previous five years. The blood letting would have shocked even Hannibal Lector, with 40 per cent of the workforce losing their jobs, nearly 170,000 people all told. But 2006 ended with a small glimmer as the airlines pushed over the line into profit, after losses of $2.4 billion in 2004. This would allow them to start thinking seriously about new planes. Would it be Boeing or Airbus?

25. A FLIGHT INTO AMERICA

I t had all been a very bad dream. The American airline market was awakening from its Chapter 11 nightmares. The great passenger carriers of America had been slumbering as the world began buying up the next generation of commercial jetliners. Now this combined marketplace would become the next battleground. And, for Airbus, this was a challenge reminscent of the early days of the A300. They had not managed to sell a single A380 in the United States.

On a clear blue Sunday, 25 March 2007, an Airbus A380, Flight LH 8948 from Frankfurt to Washington Dulles airport, took off on another sector of its 'proving flight', which was grabbing the headlines. It was the kind of pick-me-up that battered Airbus desperately needed. The A380 was going to the American capital. At Gate E5 at Frankfurt airport, invited passengers, journalists and officials prepared to board the Lufthansa A380. This was a simulation flight across the Atlantic with a full load of passengers.

The gate was the only one equipped to handle the double-decker Airbus with its three passenger piers in place. The delays in production were pushing Airbus to complete the certification process before it could be handed over to Singapore Airlines. This giant had already been approved by Europe's EASA and the FAA in the US, but it needed one more badge to prove its long-haul credentials.

More than 450 people were ready for the trip of a lifetime as they awaited the A380 flying in from Hong Kong – carrying a full load of passengers so that the ground and flight crew could simulate an actual airport landing, embarcation and then a trip to the US. The whole flight movement had begun on 19 March with the first flight from Frankfurt to New York's John F Kennedy airport. This was the first time the A380 had touched down on US soil. That day the aircraft carried 458 passengers, mostly Lufthansa staff who had won their seats in an internal prize draw. The complement included 23 Lufthansa cabin crew and four pilots – two from Airbus and two from the German carrier. The American press were out in force, with television stations beaming live pictures across the nation as the plane landed just before noon. There was meant to be a simultaneous landing with a Qantas A380 at Los Angeles airport. But it was fifteen minutes late, didn't have any passengers on board and LAX didn't yet have the gates to handle the new jumbo. Despite the massive interest, the American airlines were playing hard to get.

On board the New York flight, John Leahy was engaged in a back-to-the-wall mission: to stop any more Airbus customers defecting to Boeing. After arriving at JFK, Airbus took a planeload of airline executives and about forty journalists for a ninety-minute spin out over the New York skyline and the Atlantic coast. 'We look forward to talking to United and Northwest,' said Leahy. 'We have a bit of a game-changing airplane, but it's up to you to decide,' he said over the plane's PA system moments before take-off from New York.

Leahy did not get any new orders but his plane, which has about 50 per cent more floor area than a 747-400, impressed. 'It's a remarkable airplane and engineering feat,' said Rakesh Gangwal, the former chief executive of US Airways. Since leaving US Airways, Gangwal has set up Indigo, a low-cost airline in India which operates the single-aisle Airbus A319. Indigo would never need a plane as big as the A380, but Gangwal said critics who believe the plane is too big or the market is too small will be proved wrong.

Speaking over the PA system before take-off, Leahy said passengers would notice how much quieter the A380 is than other jets. It has half the cabin noise of a 747, he said. The noise level did make an impression with many passengers. After the big jet landed back at JFK, Leahy again got on the PA system. 'Thanks for coming,' he said. 'We hope at least a few of you will buy an A380.'

The stress on Leahy must have been huge. His health had suffered throughout the previous few years and he had checked into the Mayo clinic for emergency heart surgery. But you had to admire his chirpy ability and resilience to keep bouncing back. A few days later, the Frankfurt flight into Washington rekindled the US critics of the European subsidies handed out to build the jumbo. So, instead of sparking sales, it reignited the row over who would be paying for the A350's development.

Boeing, by comparison, had been on cruise control. Throughout 2006, Boeing stuck to its knitting. Like a glorious ocean liner, the company glided serenely as Airbus struggled to get into the lifeboat. As 2007 began, Boeing announced net sales of 1,044 commercial aeroplanes during the previous twelve months. Another bumper year – indeed, a record. The 2006 total surpassed the previous Boeing record of 1,002 net orders in 2005.

A roll-call of airlines, some well known and others more obscure, had turned up in Seattle with their chequebooks. The airline sales people arrived in Seattle were given the five-star VIP tour and the sales pitch. Each time it was more ka-ching on the imaginary cash register.

If not the Americans, then who were buying planes? It was a global A–Z of airlines: in June 2006, Singapore Airlines announced its intention to purchase twenty Boeing 787-9 Dreamliners, with first delivery anticipated in 2011. This became a firm order in October with the option to purchase twenty more. Singapore Airlines will have its 787-9s delivered from 2011 through to 2013, providing growth as well as fleet renewal.

Icelandair exercised purchase rights for two additional 787-8s. The planes will be delivered in 2012, two years after Icelandair takes delivery of its first two Dreamliners, ordered in February 2005. Air Pacific, the flag carrier of the South Pacific island republic of Fiji, announced an order for five Boeing 787-9s, with three additional purchase rights. The first will be delivered in 2011 and will fly routes from Nadi, in Fiji, to Australia, New Zealand, North America and Japan. Air New Zealand also announced its planes, powered by Rolls-Royce engines, would be delivered in December 2010. 'Being the first airline to introduce the 787-9 aircraft will enable Air New Zealand to provide a superior, first-to-market experience for our customers and is a most desirable position for us to be in given the unprecedented sales success of the Boeing 787 model,' said Air New Zealand Chief Executive Officer Rob Fyfe.

Avianca Airlines, Colombia's flagship air carrier, announced an order for ten 787s, making it the first South American carrier to take the jet. Then Aeromexico, supported by the International Lease Finance Corporation, signed a deal for three. In Britain, Virgin Atlantic announced it was buying fifteen 787-9 Dreamliners, marking the largest 787 order from Europe at that time. The order was worth $2.8 billion at list price, while Monarch Airlines, a low-cost leisure flier based at Luton, announced an ordered for six 787-8s, with purchase rights for four more. It was a deal worth $916 million. Almost weekly, smaller orders were trickling through too, like the Royal Jordanian order for two planes and a double for Arkia Israeli Airlines, based in Tel Aviv, while PrivatAir, an international business aviation group headquartered in Geneva, bagged a single 787-8 for around $153 million.

'2006 was another outstanding year for our customers and for Boeing,' said Scott Carson. 'Beyond the order totals, we are very excited about the breadth and depth of our 2006 order book. We have secured significant orders from customers around the globe and across our product line as we continue to build a strong, well-balanced backlog.'

The Dreamliner was taking shape too. In the past 24 months, the 787 team had demonstrated the strength and power of composite manufacturing technology. Nine composite fuselage sections were manufactured at facilities in Seattle and Wichita, Kansas. A demonstration wing box was also built in Seattle. Extensive testing on systems components was under way at sites around the world.

'Our technology development effort is proceeding as planned,' said Mike Bair. 'We understand the technologies needed for the airplane and the team of professionals from Boeing and our partners are working tirelessly to develop and prove them. We know what our programme challenges are and we're working through them together,' said Bair in a Boeing press statement.

In June 2006, Fuji Heavy Industries and Boeing celebrated the start of major assembly for the first 787. Fuji began to assemble the centre wing section at its factory in Handa, Japan, near Nagoya. 'When I look at this piece of structure coming together I know that we are seeing the future of our industry,' said Bair. 'We have introduced new materials, new processes, new tools and a new way of working together that is ushering in a new era in commercial aviation.'

When it was completed, it was flown from Japan to Charleston, South Carolina, where Global Aeronautica integrated it with other 787 structures before sending it on to Everett. Meanwhile, structural testing on the composite wing box began in Japan. The test piece measures approximately seventeen feet front spar to rear spar and fifty feet from aeroplane centreline to the tip of the composite structure. It is four feet deep at the thickest section. It will weigh 55,000 lbs.

Six months later, the roll-out of another specially modified freighter helped with the successful pickup of parts from Japan. The load consisted of a forward fuselage section made by Kawasaki Heavy Industries, the central wheel well and centre wing tank, made by KHI and Fuji Heavy Industries and joined up at Fuji. These were then loaded onto the 747-400 Large Cargo Freighter – dubbed the Dreamlifter – at Centrair Airport in Nagoya.

Then came a red letter day at Everett, as the gigantic composite wings for the 787 were delivered on 15 May 2007. The Boeing is the first commercial aircraft to use composite materials as its primary structure and the first to feature an all-composite wing. Manufactured by Mitsubishi Heavy Industries in Nagoya, each wing is 98 feet long. Standing on edge in custom-made tooling, the wings were delivered together to Boeing using the Dreamlifter.

For Boeing, all factories had begun production, major systems laboratories were up and running, aircraft assembly had begun and flight testing was under way. More composite work was also surging ahead nearer home. The fabrication of the first composite stringers for the vertical fin began at the Composite Manufacturing Centre at Boeing Frederickson in Pierce County, Washington. The vertical fin is the largest major Dreamliner assembly built by an internal Boeing supplier. CMC delivered its first vertical fin to Everett in the spring of 2007. There were now 135 sites around the world where the 787 design was hooked up using the CATIA digital design tools provided by Dassault Systems.

A company such as Goodrich was a major beneficiary. The Colodrado-based firm won an order to supply the flight-deck lighting system and cabin attendant. Goodrich's Aircraft Interior Products' speciality seating systems team in Colorado Springs developed and manufactured the floor-mounted, standard cabin attendant seats as well as high-comfort cabin attendant seats. The flight-deck lighting system was being assembled by Goodrich's Lighting Systems team in Lippstadt, Germany, and Tampa, Florida, were producing the all-LED-based system. Boeing awarded eleven contracts to Goodrich including the cargo system, wheels and electric braking system, exterior lighting, nacelles and thrust reversers, proximity sensing system, fuel-quantity-indicating system and fuel-management software.

The larger passenger windows have captured the imagination as a vital part of the new flying experience and PPG Aerospace were chosen to provide electrochromic windows. The 787 will feature new technology allowing passengers to electronically shade their windows, replacing the basic plastic screens found on current aeroplanes. The new electronic shades, known as variable trans-mittance, are like sunglasses for the aeroplane. Passengers will be able to see out of the big Dreamliner windows even when they choose to shade them. This will change the whole experience of flying at night.

Meanwhile, Boeing's boss Jim McNerney promised a new broom on the ethical front. He went before the US's Senate Armed Services Committee on the Boeing US Government Global Settle-ment to talk about his company's ethics.

'It is my privilege to represent the 155,000 men and women of Boeing. And, while I regret the circumstances that bring me here before you, I appreciate all the same the opportunity to testify . . . Companies doing business with the US government are expected to adhere to the highest legal and ethical standards. I acknowledge that Boeing did not live up to those expectations in the cases addressed by the settlement we're discussing here today. We take full responsibility for the wrongful acts of the former employees who brought dishonour on a great company and caused harm to the US government and its taxpayers.'

This settlement was tough but fair. It was one of the largest settlements of its kind – $615 million. 'We recognise that the mistakes were ours and ours alone,' he said. 'Ultimately, our goal is to make ethics and compliance a clear competitive advantage for Boeing.' And he promised to strengthen Boeing's culture which personally recommits every employee to ethical and compliant behaviour, including re-signing the Boeing Code of Conduct. It all sounded sweetness and apple pie.

Mike Bair, speaking about the programme's progress at the Paris Air Show 2007, said that the team was working hard to prepare for the premiere. 'This is a magical time in the programme. When you are building the first airplane of an all-new type, the pressure is incredible and the hours are long but accomplishments are immediately visible and the challenge brings out the best in our people.'

Bair also stressed that subsequent aeroplanes are also coming together nicely. 'It's easy to focus on the first airplane but it's important to remember that we are building hundreds of these airplanes. Each airplane is just as important as the first and must be built as thoughtfully as the first and come through on time,' said Bair. 'Our international team of partners is well aware of this and focused on meeting our commitment to our customers – all of them.'

Boeing was also looking into the future. Future all-composite planes will include the 787-3, a model for shorter routes. ANA and Japan Airlines have ordered 43 787-3s for domestic operations in Japan. Deliveries of this model will start in early 2010. Later in 2010, the company will start delivery of the 787-9, a longer version of the aeroplane that will carry more people on longer-range flights. Air New Zealand, Singapore Airlines, Continental and Qantas are among the eleven customers with orders for 115 787-9s. Boeing is also working with interested customers to define the 787-10, which has yet to be launched.

'It's not a matter of if for the 787-10; it's a matter of when. We continue to see good interest in this airplane and are working to define what the best offering will be. We have time. In fact, we've moved out the anticipated entry into service for the -10 because there is such high demand for the initial versions of the airplane. We see the 787-10 being introduced sometime around 2013,' said Bair.

Everywhere there was immense application and activity at Boeing Commercial Planes. With more than three million square feet of new factory space around the world to support the manufacturing of the Dreamliner, the project was the world's largest joint effort in industrial globalisation. With this kind of momentum, winning Boeing's American heartland would be a tough one for Airbus to crack.

26. THE FUTURE BATTLE

The world is now clamouring for the emerging generation of jet planes. The Airbus A380 has been crowned the new 'gentle giant' of the sky, while Boeing's 787 Dreamliner is currently being put through its paces before it too becomes a commercial passenger phenomenon.

By the autumn of 2007, Airbus had shown it was on the path to recovery. The new French President, Nicolas Sarkozy, and his German counterpart, Chancellor Angela Merkel, met in Toulouse for a summit to thrash out new inter-governmental arrangements for the European planemaker. Both DaimlerChrysler and Lagardere were invited, and Tom Enders, the new unitary head of Airbus, was optimistic. After 37 years, Airbus was moving towards a more efficient business structure. Looking on with interest from Lausanne, Airbus founder, Roger Beteille would certainly approve. Enders, in an interview with the *Financial Times* aerospace correspondent Kevin Done, conceded that many of the past problems were created by a 'high-level paradox'. On the one hand, the business was hugely successful; yet the A380 crisis had cost vast sums of money. And, if lessons could be learned, it was very similar to Boeing's audacious bet to build the Boeing 747 back in the 1960s. Keep tight control of the project at all costs. Enders said he now wanted Airbus's parent, EADS, to have a single chief executive and board. 'EADS must become a normal business,' he said.

And, after the final separation from BAE Systems, the business would be free to pursue more defence contract work. After all, Airbus was only a part of the larger EADS business; it wasn't the complete picture. Enders said that the defence, space and helicopter business had delivered 40 per cent of the profits. 'It's only thanks to this that there is not a lot of red ink on the balance sheet,' he admitted. And Airbus wanted to compete in America too, using its aircraft platform for an American tanker deal, working with Northrop Grumman and GE.

What was endearing was that Boeing and Airbus were both able to retain their different styles and approaches. At the Paris Air Show in 2007, the A380 undertook a spectacular display every afternoon to the delight of the adoring French crowds. The double-decker sped silently along the runway then suddenly lifted off the ground, climbing at a steep angle of about 40 degrees. It was incredible to watch such a massive plane making such tight turns around the airfield as it banked, virtually standing in mid-air on its wingtip.

The flight was stunning visual theatre – but one where Airbus and Boeing disagree. Boeing doesn't conduct flying displays of its commercial jets at air shows. Perhaps it all goes back to the Boeing history of Tex Johnston's test flying of the Dash 80 back in 1955. 'There's no particular value to doing that,' said Scott Carson. He believes it is dangerous. 'One of the reasons we don't fly commercial product at air shows is that people crash airplanes at air shows,' he said bluntly. 'Flying a big heavy airplane at low altitude in an air-show environment, with all the testosterone that goes along with being a hotshot, you put unnecessary risk into your business, into your programme, into the crowd surrounding the show.'

Airbus's super salesman John Leahy was far more relaxed. 'It's going to compete with the Mirage [a French fighter jet],' he joked. Then, responding to Carson's comments, Leahy turned more serious. He explained the A380's aerial acrobatics are only possible because of the 'flight envelope protection' technology. Airbus controls are restrained by the computer within certain bounds so that it is impossible for the pilot to bring the wings up enough to stall the aeroplane. By contrast, Boeing systems are set up to avoid wild movements of the flight controls that could put excessive loads on the aeroplane structure. But Boeing designs it so that the pilot has the final say. A captain on a Boeing plane can override the system in an emergency. It's a major difference in approach.

Airbus thinks its approach is safer, because it allows a pilot in an emergency to take stronger counter measures without fear of stalling. Boeing thinks the pilot needs to have the ultimate control. Leahy said the Airbus A380 pilots at the show were 'going right up to the edge of a stall', confident that they cannot go over the edge. 'You are within a few knots of the airplane just falling out of the sky,' he explained.

The 2007 show drew some 300,000 visitors. It was another vintage year at a time when the air travel industry is booming. 'It's the best show ever recorded by a plane maker,' said Leahy. But would this be the end of the road for such environmentally challenging displays?

A United Nations report singled out transport as a black spot in the fight against global warming. It said surging usage of cars and planes will push up greenhouse gas emissions in coming decades. The report said 2 per cent of carbon dioxide emissions comes from aviation, but emissions were likely to rise by 3 to 4 per cent a year because traffic growth of 5 per cent will outpace efficiency gains of 1 to 2 per cent.

Airbus says the A380 burns 17 per cent less fuel per seat than rival large aircraft and produces only 75g of CO_2 per passenger/ kilometre, which it says is almost half of the target set by the European Union for cars manufactured in 2008. But EADS head Louis Gallois agrees environmental issues will be 'one of the biggest challenges for the eventual A320 successor'.

Neither Boeing nor Airbus can afford to be wrong. With that aircraft, 'you really are betting the company,' says Gallois's colleague Tom Williams.

The air-transport sector has been on the defensive. It says studies show that it contributes a mere 2 to 3 per cent of global carbon dioxide emissions and, even with growth, will not top 5 per cent for the next few decades. But this will not wash and the industry now realises that more needs to be done. Boeing's Scott Carson acknowledges that 'as our fleets double, we cannot allow our emissions to double'.

And the pitch is changing quickly. A year ago, if you complied with regulations, that was sufficient, but not any more. The airlines and the passengers are beginning to demand more efficient planes. Efforts are being driven by the Advisory Council for

Aeronautical Research in Europe, which called for a reduction, by 2020, of carbon dioxide (CO_2) emissions by 50 per cent, noise by 50 per cent and nitrogen oxides (NO_x) by 80 per cent.

Both Airbus and Boeing say they are spending heavily on green technologies. Boeing puts the figure at 75 per cent of its research while engine-makers must now deliver environmental solutions.

'We estimate that an aircraft equipped with a geared turbo-fan engine would reduce emissions of CO_2 by around 3,250 metric tons per aircraft per year. So on a typical mission length, if all the world's aircraft flying those routes were GTF powered, it would be like adding a mature forest of seven million acres – or a forest roughly the size of Belgium,' says Pratt & Whitney President Steve Finger.

Bench testing with a mix of biofuels made from agricultural feedstocks has started. The tests, using a mix containing 30 per cent methyl ester vegetable oil, are aimed at demonstrating the engines can emit 20 per cent less CO_2 without changes to the engine or performance losses. Boeing and Airbus say their newest products will have a per passenger fuel burn of less than 2.9 litres per 100 km, while the current fleet average is 5 litres.

But it is not simply the builders – new ways of flying will also save fuel. Airlines, aeroplane-makers and engine-makers are urging governments to do their bit by improving air-traffic management. Recent tests in Sydney and Amsterdam showed that a reduction of as much as 400–800 lbs of carbon emissions per flight was possible with properly managed take-offs and landings and better approaches. Stacking planes over London, awaiting a landing slot at Heathrow, Gatwick, Stansted or Luton, only increases the carbon emissions, and fewer delayed planes will mean energy savings.

So the industry understands the environmental challenges. But the passenger experience matters too. Boeing and Airbus have both promised the passenger something extra special for the up-and-coming generation of fliers. The Flight of the Titans will go on for some time. The A380 and the 787 are here to stay – both Airbus and Boeing will see to that.

BIBLIOGRAPHY

A series of original interviews at both Airbus and Boeing were conducted for this book. But a score of excellent secondary sources was also used. The aviation publication *Flight International* is a remarkable repository of world-class information. It would have been difficult to write this book without the accumulated wisdom of such a wonderful publication of record. Boeing's own newspaper, *Boeing News*, was also an excellent source of material. The Aviation History Collection in the Seattle Public Library, 1000 Fourth Ave, Seattle, was an invaluable source of background reading. I must single out two books in particular: the seminal work of the battle between Airbus and Boeing, *The Sporty Game*, by John Newhouse, Alfred A Knopf, 1982, and the erudite volume, *Close to the Sun*, by Stephen Aris, Agate, 2002. Both excellent books.

Other books used were: *21st Century Jet – The Making of the Boeing 777*, by Karl Sabbagh, Pan Books, 1995; *Boeing 707 Pioneer Jetliner*, by Rene J Francillon, MBI Publishing, 1978; *Boeing – The First Century*, by Eugene E Bauer, TABA Publishing Inc, Washington, 2000; *Air-frame*, by Michael Crichton, Arrow, 1997; *Boeing 747: The First Twenty Years*, by Jim Lucas, Browncom, 1988; *Airbus Industrie: Conflict and Co-operation in US–EC Trade Relations*, by Steven McGuire, Macmillan Press, 1997; *Airbus Industrie: The Politics of An International*

Collaboration, by David Weldon Thornton, Macmillan, 1995; *Dogfight: The Transatlantic Battle over Airbus*, by Ian McIntyre, West Port Connecticut Praeger, 1992; *Airbus*, by Guy Norris and Mark Wagner, MBI Publishing, 1999; *Yeager*, by Chuck Yeager and Leo Janos, Arrow, 1986.

Other publications and periodicals used in this book were: *Financial Times, Sunday Times, The Times, Herald, Wall Street Journal, Fortune Magazine, The Economist, Le Monde, L'Express, Der Spiegel, Seattle Post-Intelligencer, Seattle Times, Times of India, Airline World, Aviation News, Airfinance Journal, Aircraft Illustrated, Asian Aviation, Aviation Week and Space Technology, Wingspan, Planet Aerospace.*

INDEX

Braniff 114
Branson, Sir Richard 200, 212, 215, 234
Bregier, Fabrice 242
Breguet and Nord (HBN) 47, 48, 50, 72, 83
Breton, Thierry 243
Bright, Tony 199
Bristol Brabazon 30
Bristol Britannia 31
Britain:
    and Airbus project 50, 51, 52, 65, 75, 77–80, 95–7, 99–100, 112, 113, 147–8, 158–9, 160, 168, 197
    aviation industry 64–7, 70–1, 78, 97
    and Concorde 46–7, 50, 78
    leads way in civil aviation 29, 30–2, 35
    wartime aviation industry 27
Britannia Airways 71
British Action Committee for Aerospace 79, 95
British Aerospace (BAe) 17, 28, 36, 95, 98, 99, 100, 113, 117, 120, 147, 148, 149, 150, 151, 15, 155, 156, 157, 158–9, 160, 166, 218, 220, 221, 241, 246, 249, 260–1
British Aircraft Corporation (BAC) 46, 47, 50, 66, 75, 97
    One-Eleven 54, 65, 67, 68, 71, 72, 96
    Two-Eleven 54, 67
    Three-Eleven 54, 80
British Airport Authority (BAA) 241
British Airways (BA) 14–15, 17, 24, 25, 78, 80, 91, 94, 100, 101, 103, 112, 114, 119, 128
British Caledonian 16, 119

British European Airways (BEA) 16, 36, 44, 47, 50, 64, 65–7, 69, 70, 74, 80
British Overseas Aircraft Corporation (BOAC) 16, 33, 34, 44, 45, 58, 80
Brizendine, John 97
Broadhurst, Sir Harry 74–5, 85
Broughton, Martin 15–16
Brown, Adam 37, 83, 88–9, 91, 115, 118, 170
Buck, Les 97
Buffenbarger, Thomas 141
Bugge, Peter 36
Bush, George W 175, 218, 228
Byers, Stephen 158

Callaghan, James 111, 112, 113, 184
Camus, Philippe 158, 159
Canadian Pacific Airlines 33, 34
Caravelle 36, 37, 38, 39, 47, 50, 64
Cargolux 109
cargo market 24, 26, 104–5, 108, 177
Carson, Scott 136, 180, 199, 237, 256, 261, 262
Carter, Jimmy 111, 114
CASA (Construcciones Aeronáuticas S.A.) 84, 85, 113, 117 159
Cashman, John 130
Cathay Pacific 16, 104, 120, 128, 184, 215
CATIA (Computer-graphics Aided Three-dimensional Interactive Application) 126, 239– 40, 245–6, 247, 257
Cavaillé, Marcel 95–6, 97
Chamant, Jean 79
Champion, Charles 172, 236, 239, 243, 246
Chapman, Frank 246